Jig Cook
and the
Provincetown
Players

Jig Cook
and the
Provincetown Players

THEATRE IN FERMENT

Robert Károly Sarlós

The University of Massachusetts Press

Designed by Mary Mendell

Parts of chapters two, four, seven, and most of chapter three appeared in earlier versions in *Theatre Research/Recherches Théâtrales* (1969, 1970) and its successor, *Theatre Research International* (1977).
Acknowledgment is made for permission to reprint the following copyrighted material: Hutchins Hapgood, "The Instinct to Conform," *New Republic,* November 29, 1933. Reprinted by permission of the New Republic © 1933. Helen Deutsch and Stella Bloch Hanau, *The Provincetown: A Story of the Theatre* (New York: Russell and Russell, 1931; 1972). Copyright © 1931 by Helen Deutsch and Stella Bloch Hanau; copyright renewed.

*To the memory of
my father, Miklós, for languages and
my mother, Böske, for beauty*

Contents

Acknowledgments

I am indebted to many:

—to A. M. Nagler for discipline and "the limits of scholarly surmisal";

—to Omar Paxson for making me act; to Basil Busacca for making me read O'Neill;

—to Provincetown Players and their families for sharing documents, memories, and insights: Nilla Cram Cook foremost; Susan Jenkins Brown, Kathleen Cannell, Dorothy Commins, Jasper Deeter, Floyd Dell, Samuel A. Eliot, Charles Ellis, Alice Hall, Charles Hapgood, James Light, Norma Millay, Emily Nordfeldt, Margaret Nordfeldt, Jean Paul Slusser, Julia Ward Stickley, Cleon Throckmorton, Pauline Turkel, Lawrence Vail, Marguerite and William Zorach;

—to libraries and archives, librarians and archivists, fellow scholars for guiding me to documents and sources: Yale Collection of American Literature (Ann Whelpley and Donald Gallup); Yale University Library (Mary LaFogg); Harvard Theatre Collection (Helen Willard and Jeanne Newlin); Fales Collection, New York University (Theodore Grieder); New York Public Library (John Gordan and Lola Szladits); Lincoln Center (George Freedley, Paul Myers, Dorothy Swerdlove, Rod Bladel); Museum of the City of New York (Sam Pearson); Princeton University Library (Mary Ann Jensen); Newberry Library (Diana Haskell); Alderman Library, University of Virginia (Helen Troy); Stanford University Library (Celeste Ashley); University of California, Los Angeles (Hilda Bohem); University of California, Bancroft

Library (Leslie Clark); University of California, Davis (Ted Gould, Sherry Smith, Marion Whalon);

—to friends, colleagues and students for reading, researching, typing, criticizing and nurturing parts of this manuscript: W. Beeson, A. Bunting-Hill, G. Chesley, C. Closson, R. Cohn, B. Early, R. Fahrner, R. Fier, E. Gorenzel, J. Grider, A. Gulick, S. Halpert, J. Holden, K. Holoman, S. Howard, L. Jencks, C. Jorgensen, W. Kleb, P. Krueger, S. Langsner, L. Matteson, D. McDermott, N. Medovoy, T. Natsoulas, D. Ogden, L. Owings, N. Peattie, D. Ranstrom, W. Salkind, R. Scott, G. Silva, R. Solomon, C. Taylor, J. and R. Viargues, S. Vohs, A. and A. Woods;

—to the Research Committee of the Academic Senate at the University of California, Davis, for its steady financial support of this project;

—to Richard Martin, Mary Mendell, and Pam Campbell at the University of Massachusetts Press, for advice, assistance, encouragement, and patience with manuscript and author;

—to Charlotte, Lilian, and Tibor Sarlos, who received the Provincetown Players into the family.

Preface

      This book began fifteen years ago as my dissertation—a chronological account of the Provincetown Players. It served as my Americanization as well, in the best sense of that word. Some intimations of significance were cautiously inserted, others slipped in without my awareness.

      Those unexpected insights were my first justification for reworking materials and ideas used in the thesis. Among others were the perceptions and sensibilities I gained in the intervening years. These were not always results of research, teaching, directing, or the contemplation that went with them, but frequently the result of personalities and events that have altered the state of American theatre and modified my understanding of current practice as well as history.

      Naturally, too, I was encouraged to write this book by questions I was asked, and by plays, manuscripts, and documents that surfaced after the pressures of the academic deadline were removed. Even though acknowledged in their proper place, personal reminiscences lovingly shared have a special place here as well.

      A familiar disease of scholarship is infatuation with one's subject and, to the detriment of perspective, blindness to all negative features of the beloved. It is true that I still see the Provincetown Players as an epoch-making phenomenon, but my love has grown more mature over the years. Strengths and weaknesses, admirable and infuriating characteristics made up the community beloved by me—and I ask Dionysos and Apollo that I may give it afterlife as it has given me life.

Vella, Switzerland, June 6, 1978

Note on vocabulary Where I crossed boundaries of disciplines I clarified the few technical terms as best I could in the context. I feel obliged, however, to define my use of some words which ought not to require explanation.

"Amateur" is used to indicate an attitude (or person assuming it) toward an activity distinct from "professional" because it is seen not as part of, or secondary to, earning a living wage, but on the contrary as transcending it and embracing every aspect of life.

"Anarchy" refers to a condition in which action and impulse are self-regulated, not institutionally dominated. An "anarchist," consequently, is one who believes that order derived from free choice is both desirable and possible.

"Theatre," when not referring to a building, always denotes performance in toto, never standing pro partibus such as text or picture.

"Theatrical," consequently means relating to, or in the nature of performance in four dimensions.

R.K.S.
Davis, California, June 6, 1981

Introduction:

Renascence and Innocence

 ". . . anarchism and art are in the world
for exactly the same kind of reason."
Margaret Anderson,
"Art and Anarchism," LITTLE REVIEW

"Groups like ours are about to inherit the whole duty of dramatic man," George Cram Cook wrote in the Provincetown Players circular in the fall of 1920. It was a far cry indeed from the comment made a hundred years before by a cultivated European: "In the four quarters of the globe, who reads an American book? or goes to an American play? or looks at an American picture or statue?" [1] One can almost hear the sneer at "American." When the theatrical experiment engendered by Cook began, cultivated Europeans were still sneering at the idea of American theatre and drama. Not that there were no theatre buildings, dramatic publications, and theatrical entrepreneurs in the United States, but American playwrights and actors, designers and directors were still virtually unheard of in Europe. The Provincetown Players, however, made their own theatrical declaration of independence, and Eugene O'Neill brought that accomplishment's news to the old world.

Although the Provincetown Players is a distinctly American phenomenon and very much a product of its time, this study does not treat it as isolated in time and space. As a group, it has questioned the premises upon which American show business rested, as well as the division of labor practiced in European theatre for over twenty-five hundred years, and it has actively challenged universal assumptions still made about the social role and function of artistic creativity, imagination, and ideas. Therefore I chose to view it not only as inseparable from the American and international fabric of ideas prevalent in its time, but also against the broadly understood theatrical traditions that give its radical initiatives meaning and historic significance.

The contention that American cultural and artistic trends depended upon and were imitative of European examples, that the United States was a cultural wasteland except for oases created by immigrants is nearer the truth in theatre than in many another field. American theatre began with visits of English actors who, commencing with George Frederick Cooke's 1810 tour, gave rise to the star system that glorified some performers, humiliated others, enslaving them all. Following the British example during the nineteenth century, American theatre grew into an industry rather than an artistic profession. Increasingly it demanded plays that were of value only as vehicles for stars. Robert Montgomery Bird's *The Gladiator* (1831) and *The Broker of Bogotá* (1834), written for competitions sponsored by Edwin Forrest (1806–1872), the first native star, are cases in point.

Indigenous talent was thwarted by rampant commercialism. The careers of Steele Mackaye (1842–1894) and James A. Herne (1840–1901) serve as examples: both began as actors, turned to playwriting, and failed for lack of sufficient business acumen. A daring innovator in visual aspects of theatre, Mackaye understood the revolutionary potential of electric light; the first American dramatist to emulate Ibsen, Herne pioneered in the use of intimate theatres. At the onset of the twentieth century the recognized authority in American theatre was David Belasco, who stood in sharp contrast to these daring innovators. Playwright, director, designer, and manager, Belasco was revered as a priest of the profession; in clerical garb topped by ethereal white hair, he applied photographic naturalism to the production of escapist melodramas.

After 1910, however, art theatres began to make inroads into show business. Immediately preceding the First World War, theatrical groundbreaking fit well into a broad cultural context. A refreshing wind of intellectual and artistic renascence swept the country: a reaction against isolationism, a productive alternative to self-exile. Native creative impulse was determined to come into its own.

Against the background of Marconi's practical use of the wireless (1901), the Wright brothers' successful experiments (1903), Einstein's theory of relativity (1905), Ford's introduction of the Model T (1909), and Dr. A. A. Brill's transplanting of Freudian theory and practice to America (1909-1911), a profound cultural upheaval was taking place. First Chicago, then Manhattan's Greenwich Village became a haven where provocative personalities confronted young men and women with radical artistic and social ideas. Their eager response touched off a spiritual revolution.

Nineteen twelve was an election year: Woodrow Wilson became president, but the Socialist Eugene V. Debs received over a million votes. Harriet Monroe initiated *Poetry: A Magazine of Verse;* Max Reinhardt brought the oriental pantomime, *Sumurun,* to New York; and Max Eastman became editor of *The Masses,* an irreverent magazine of protest. Poets competed for inclusion in *The Lyric Year,* an anthology of the year's best verse; Edna St. Vincent Millay's "Renascence" was included, and, although not one of the winners, became the most memorable poem of the year.

Nineteen thirteen ushered in the first public exhibition of radically modern artists to America, the Armory Show; the dramatic representation of the Paterson silk strike by John Reed and Robert Edmond Jones in Madison Square Garden; and the second American tour of the Irish Players. To emulate these visitors, Maurice Browne and Ellen Van Volkenburg assembled an amateur theatre group. They called themselves the Chicago Little Theatre. Margaret Anderson started a periodical in the building used by the ensemble, and honored them by naming the publication the *Little Review.*

The visions and works of Edward Gordon Craig, Frank Lloyd Wright, Alfred Stieglitz, and the American dadaists furthered cultural awakening. But the impact of outstanding women was perhaps greater. Gertrude Stein's poetry was arriving from Paris; in a lower Fifth Avenue apartment decorated exclusively in white, Mabel Dodge gathered both old insurgents and young rebels—"movers and shakers"—at her celebrated Evenings. Emma Goldman's powerful lectures on anarchy, as well as her very publicly known private life, set many young people against accepted tradition. Following her lead, Margaret Sanger championed birth control. The high priestess of unfettered dance, Isadora Duncan aroused emotions to a comparable degree: she symbolized freedom in artistic as well as in social intercourse.

The period between 1912 and 1917 brought forth the last bloom of American innocence.[2] A new ferment created an atmosphere in which dissent and experiment became respectable. A growing influx of eastern and southern European immigrants, an outpouring of midwestern talent (especially from the Chicago Renaissance) and a steady flow of Ivy League intellect (Harvard liberals in particular) resulted in a momentous confluence: the Greenwich Village vortex. Older insurgents—Outsiders of labor, Questioners such as

William James and John Dewey, Scoffers of the type of Veblen, Darrow, and Steffens, Amoralists best exemplified by Mencken and Huneker—engendered an innocent rebellion, a new irrationalism, carried on by the typically cheerful, younger rebels—Liberators, Poets, Intellectuals, and Radicals. When the twenties arrived, these pathfinders came to be regarded as "has-beens" by a new generation of "would-bes" who were attempting to build careers on the breakthroughs of their predecessors.[3]

One phase of this general dissent and experimentation was the little theatre movement. André Antoine's Théâtre Libre, Otto Brahm's Freie Bühne, and J. T. Grein's Independent Theatre exercised a profound influence, but Americans devoted to theatre insisted on finding singularly American ways to reform American theatre. Art theatres mushroomed across the country between 1910 and 1916. Like their European counterparts, they fervently desired to do away with petrified traditions, were eager to give new plays a chance on the stage, and actively supported artistic and social radicalism. More important, the little theatre movement was dedicated to seeking "a better system of values; a more dependable and enlightened audience; and an impulse coming from the artists rather than from the investors."[4]

The two important crops of little theatres (one in 1911-12, another in 1915-16) produced the Drama Players and the Little Theatre in Chicago, the Wisconsin Dramatic Society in Madison and Milwaukee, the Toy Theatre in Boston, the Neighborhood Playhouse and the Washington Square Players in New York. Surveying little theatres—including some in Philadelphia, St. Louis, Kansas City, Lake Forest, Illinois, and Fargo, North Dakota—in 1917, Thomas H. Dickinson found common characteristics. Invariably they were located in "a small building for plays given in an intimate way," operated "upon the theory of absolute economy of management," were propelled by "a guild of artists," and gained moral and financial support from "a system of alliance with the audience."[5] Dickinson found that these groups united theatre workers with their audience in replacing commercial traditions with new, artistic ones.

Few of these groups, however, took up an essential function of theatre and produced native drama, which from the outset was the avowed purpose of the Provincetown Players, who opened a new chapter in American theatre history.[6] This gathering of rebellious, bohemian artists and intellectuals decided to make theatre collectively and in a consistently amateur fashion, first on Cape Cod, then in Greenwich Village. In the summer of 1915, they yielded as a group to a spontaneous urge to dramatize issues directly affecting their own lives. Some of these issues were of such narrow interest as the love affairs of Jack Reed and Mabel Dodge; others as momentous as Frank Tannenbaum's church occupations on behalf of the International Workers of the World. By September 1916, however, this creative collective became enthralled with a sense of mission: to engage in the production of American plays reflecting the cultural upheaval—with the writer only one member of the organic producing group.

Most significant movements in theatre history are attempts at rebellion, reform, or innovation, and most individuals who initiate such attempts do so on grounds of their expertise in the field. The group that forms the subject of this book based its own rebellious efforts on a proud confession of ignorance and consequent defiance of theatrical tradition.

The collaborative nature of creative activity in the theatre has rarely been explicitly denied,[7] yet both in theory and in practice the relative dominance of one among the cooperating artists has generally been recognized. Throughout most of theatrical history this dominant artist has been the playwright. In some periods (as in fourth-century Greece, late Renaissance Italy, and eighteenth-century England) the position of command was assumed by the actor. Since the emergence of the director, hegemony has usually been claimed for or fallen to the person with that title whether actor, designer, organizer, or playwright. Even directors like the Duke of Sachs-Meiningen, who championed ensemble playing, have retained control over the production. In the current century designers have often dominated collaborative processes.

The Provincetown Players was a most unusual organization in that it stood for theatre as collective creativity in which the person temporarily functioning as playwright served as a first among equals. This group of dedicated amateurs expected and required its active members to be by turns playwrights, actors, designers, stagehands, playreaders and business managers; and proposed to have the member whose script was about to be staged in charge of production. Most plays were one-acts, three or four of which were customarily organized into "bills," thus the rotation of functions in this cooperative process was, in theory, constant. After two summers the Provincetown Players moved from Cape Cod to New York City, where in six seasons they produced ninety-seven plays by forty-seven American authors, foremost of whom were Eugene O'Neill and Susan Glaspell. Most of these plays would never have reached the stage had not artistic considerations rather than commercial ones been paramount.

The Provincetown Players grew into the most daring, and the most characteristically American undertaking in United States theatrical history.[8] Even if the group had not served as a proving ground for Eugene O'Neill, it would still be the most influential Off-Broadway theatre. The Provincetown Players provided a stage and a group process for American playwrights; helped publish many of the plays they produced; started careers for actors, directors, and designers; boldly experimented with a wide range of theatrical styles and production methods; pioneered in introducing the Negro into legitimate theatre; based all activity on artistic rather than commercial considerations; enabled spectators to participate in the creative process; and reflected, as well as influenced, the current intellectual renascence in the United States.

As the group grew in size and experience, its amateur spirit gradually gave way to a more businesslike attitude. After the Players' production of *The Emperor Jones* became a "hit" in 1920, they presented several plays on Broadway. Unable to cope with the artistic and organizational expansion demanded by such undertakings, and torn by internal strife, the group ended its career in the spring of 1922 by declaring a year of rest.

The collective was founded by George Cram ("Jig") Cook: it was his infectious enthusiasm and dedication to spontaneous group creativity that brought about and continued to sustain the experiment. He received vital philosophical reinforcement from Hutchins Hapgood, and powerful organizational assistance from John Reed. As new personalities and ideas entered the group, ideals and operations underwent subtle but crucial change, eventually culminating in the crisis that ended the Players' existence. That ending was also due in part to Cook's keen sense of personal and collective failure, and to O'Neill's development past the group's usefulness to him. But by that time the Provincetown Players' impact had altered American theatre.

This book is an attempt to relate the contribution of Jig Cook and the Provincetown Players primarily to American theatre and culture; secondarily to wider artistic and intellectual crosscurrents. It will consider aspects of operation that were dignified and formal, as well as those that were not. The bohemian atmosphere in which the Players operated has made an indelible impression upon this study, as has the varied nature of the evidence upon which it had to be built. Facts, opinions, and hypotheses derive not only from printed sources and unpublished manuscripts but also from theatrical ephemera, personal correspondence and interviews with Provincetown Players and with those who knew them. The creative process is best understood in its own peculiar atmosphere; therefore, the amateurish, rebellious, and informal spirit of the Players' collective will be evident in these pages.

The Provincetown Players was intricately knit into the web of young creative America of the teens and twenties of this century. Besides being gifted and enthusiastic writers, artists, or thinkers, members of the group were also passionate drinkers and lovers, and proudly so. The initial collective of married as well as unmarried couples virtually lived in each other's summer homes in Provincetown, raised their children Montessori style, and participated in one another's creative work. In New York, beyond their theatrical function the Players also served as a club where one might drink and talk with Waldo Frank, William Carlos Williams, Max Weber, the Millay sisters, Bobby Edwards, Sherwood Anderson, Hyppolite Havel, Inez Millholland, Norman Hapgood, Alexander Berkman, Henrietta Rodman, Theodore Dreiser, or Charlie Chaplin. To characterize the generation that saw the height of the Provincetowners' career, the image of the Harvard Class of 1910 is often invoked. That class included Edward Eyre Hunt (founder of the Harvard Dramatic Club), John Reed and Robert Edmond Jones (founders of the Provincetown Players), the eminent journalist and drama critic Heywood Broun, the poets Alan Seeger and T. S. Eliot, and the later pundit Walter Lippmann.

As the foregoing list suggests, characters who participated in events described in this book did not belong to, and thus cannot be treated as, a homogeneous subspecies: not all were literati, visual artists, or political animals. Hence, names that might need no explanation in a more narrowly focused work, carry no magic aura here. Yet, beyond a brief phrase or clause, the kind of gloss required seemed disruptive of the flow of ideas. Therefore a series of short biographies, gathered in Appendix B, intends to relieve readers of the frustration experienced when names that do not signify anything are used as milestones of an intellectual landscape.

The peculiar spirit of the Provincetown Players is an indispensable key to understanding the capricious beginnings, the chaotic operations, the rhapsodic quality of plays and production—and the sudden halt with which the Players ended. Only such a collective of dedicated amateurs could conclude eight seasons' activity by announcing a one-year interim, a period of recuperation, freshening of faith, and reevaluation. This cessation of activity grew out of the Provincetowners' feeling that they had failed to adhere to their own artistic credo, a failure they believed was caused by theatrical success. In part it reflected the Greenwich Village generation gap, described by Malcolm Cowley as having separated those who had lived there before 1917 and "had revolted and tried to break new trails"—and those who were arriving from France or from college and "had followed the high road." [9] It pitted true believers in the amateur group process against those advocating a more professional approach to theatre. Before the interim had run its course, Oliver Sayler perceptively analysed the Players' plight:

> Through the laxity and irresponsibility dangerously inherent in group organization, there was only a helter-skelter effort to recruit new blood, no adequate playreading, no intelligent, insistent and persuasive invitation to gifted writers in other fields to try their hand at the theatre. In such an impasse, the logical end of an epoch was at hand, and with it, an opportunity for survey, reminiscence, appraisal of a group which for seven years . . . roused and filled more expectations for native American drama than all the other forces in our theatre put together. [10]

This study deals with that period beginning with the first demonstrable activities in 1915 of the people who later called themselves the Provincetown Players up until the interim declared by this group in 1922. Despite certain personal and organizational links that will be touched upon, the Experimental Theatre, Inc., which resumed operations of the Macdougal Street Playhouse in 1923 under the Provincetown name, and was governed by the triumvirate of Eugene O'Neill, Robert Edmond Jones, and Kenneth Macgowan, was a separate and essentially different venture that still awaits study.

The Wharf

*". . . that remarkable and never repeated summer
at Provincetown . . . was really huge in import, and huge
in various satisfaction."*
Marsden Hartley,
"Farewell, Charles," in THE NEW CARAVAN

1   The formation of the Provincetown Players was "an organic thing like a plant growing." [1] Consequently the group's first stirrings remain a mystery, about which many myths but few facts survive. Accounts, even by participants, are contradictory.

Members of the amorphous collective that first wrote and staged plays in the summer of 1915 arrived at that activity spontaneously, although they did not gather by mere chance. Provincetown, on the tip of Cape Cod, was a habitual summer residence for artists and writers disillusioned with prevailing social and artistic norms.

Chief initiator of the ferment that later crystallized into the Provincetown Players was George Cram Cook (everybody called him Jig), who had a love for everything Greek and dreamed of a Platonic community. His third wife, Susan Glaspell, who had published a series of novels, became a partner in the venture. John Reed, the flamboyant poet and reporter who later helped shape the Communist Party of America, was also an originator of the group; he was living on the dunes with Mabel Dodge. Another founding member was Mary Heaton Vorse, a successful author of popular novels and a labor organizer who had, according to legend, "discovered" Provincetown in 1907; her second husband, Joe O'Brien, had been a newspaperman. The anarchist Hutchins Hapgood, Mabel Dodge's "confidant," also had strong ties with labor, had written sociological studies, and shared Cook's desire to create the "beloved community of life givers"; his wife, Neith Boyce, was a writer of short stories and novels. Brör Nordfeldt was known for bold post-Impressionist paintings; Wilbur Daniel Steele for eminent short stories. William Zorach was a pioneering cubist painter (later a sculptor); his wife, Marguerite, a tapestry maker. Ida Rauh, who painted, sculpted, and wrote poetry but had really yearned to act, was there with Max Eastman—their marriage was kept secret from friends—who had given up teaching philosophy at Columbia in order to edit the revolutionary *The Masses.*

John Reed played host to the painters Charles Demuth and Marsden Hartley, as well as to his Harvard roommate, Robert Edmond Jones. Reed and Jones had been prominent members of the Harvard Dramatic Club, and had combined theatricals with politics in 1913, when they staged the famous Paterson Pageant in Madison Square Garden.[2] Jones was the only one in the group with professional theatre experience, but all had found creative expression in other fields and were irritated by Broadway's stupor:

> We went to the theatre and for the most part we came away wishing we had gone somewhere else. . . . Plays, like magazine stories, were patterned. They might be pretty good within themselves, seldom did they open out to—where it surprised or thrilled your spirit to follow. They didn't ask much of *you,* those plays. Having paid for your seat, the thing was all done for you, and your mind came out where it went in, only tireder.[3]

Aware of alternatives offered by Edward Gordon Craig, Isadora Duncan, the Irish Players, and especially Maurice Browne's Chicago Little Theatre, these people longed for a theatre that challenged its audience's imagination and creative participation.

A major direct influence upon many who came to make up the Players was that of Maurice Browne and his Chicago Little Theatre. Brör Nordfeldt had designed that avant-garde amateur company's first production of *The Trojan Women,* Elaine Hyman (later known as Kirah Markham) was in the cast, Floyd Dell wrote an "enraptured" review.[4] Lucian Cary and Jig Cook, both of whom belonged to the circle of Browne's friends, were presumably in the audience, along with other future participants or supporters of the Provincetown. In fact, such long-term profitable relationships as Cook had with Emma Goldman, Francis Buzzell, Florence Kiper Frank, Theodore Dreiser, and Cloyd Head were made largely by way of the Chicago Little Theatre. And although Browne's theory and authoritarian practice was mostly aligned with Gordon Craig's individualistic ideas, he attached religious significance to work in the theatre (he thought of it as a way to St. Augustine's "City of God"), and was fascinated by parallels he perceived between the Irish Players and the spirit of ancient Greek theatre festivals. Moreover, the Little Theatre provided at least one "striking example of 'collective creation.' " [5] Their *Passion Play*'s episodes were suggested by the actors who also "did their own casting" [6] and helped devise the action.[7] In his autobiography, Browne, although disclaiming paternity (bestowed on him by press and public) for the American little theatre movement in general, allowed that "there were at least two American Little Theatres in which it flatters me to think that dramatic blood of mine may have flowed." These two were the Washington Square Players and the Provincetown Players, with the latter of which (in Browne's opinion) "autochthonous American Theatre had come to birth." [8]

Floyd Dell, the "textbook case" bohemian[9] had first brought seeds of midwestern rebellion to New York theatre when in 1913 he left the editorship of the *Chicago Evening Post*'s *Friday Literary Review* to his close friend, Jig Cook. Asked by Henrietta Rodman, a high-school teacher who broke the dress code and whose love life apparently split up the Liberal Club, for a contribution to the housewarming of the Club's new radical wing in Macdougal Street, Dell responded willingly:

> I found that there was no stage, no curtain, no costumes, and no money. So, gathering a group of people who wanted to act, I proposed to present a play "in the Chinese manner," without scenery and with much make-believe, and I proceeded to tell them a fable, which Arthur Davison Ficke and I had invented over a luncheon-table [in Chicago], of St. George in Greenwich Village—a satire upon the earnest Bohemianism of our little world. St. George was to be one of those young men who go about urging young women to free themselves from the bonds of conventionality; the rock on which the poor damsel was immured was a parlor chair, and the Dragon was her very correct and respectable aunt. Having freed the girl, St. George found that she wanted him to marry her; he did, and they settled down, and presently a baby appeared, brought in by a stork propelled by the Property Man in the best Chinese manner. Not knowing what to do with the baby, Priscilla—that was the name we gave her—took advice of a neighbor, Mrs. Flub, who urged the Montessori System upon her. "What! You've never heard of the

Montessori System? Why, my dear, it's simply a lot of things. And you put the baby down among the things—and you never have to bother about it again!" Thus relieved of the burdens of parenthood, Priscilla turned practical, and started a tea-shop! Helen Westley was the Dragon, and Sherwood Anderson, visiting Greenwich Village at the outset of his literary career, adorned one of the minor parts. *Everyone invented his own lines and forgot them, and made up new and better ones on the spur of the moment; and the play, because it made fun of our own earnest "modernity," was tremendously successful,* and was thus the first of a series of little plays that were given over a period of several years, during which we acquired a movable stage, a curtain, footlights, scenery, and costumes galore, but lost, inevitably, that first fine careless rapture.

In my exuberance I designed and executed most of the scenery, and, against the protests of all my friends, acted in most of the plays myself, as well as writing them. But where these productions fell short of dramatic art, they did succeed in being *gay communal ritual.* In them the village laughed at itself and relished the mockery.[10]

Among the amateurs whose support Dell enjoyed were Kirah Markham (Elaine Hyman), Edward Goodman, Ida Rauh, Justus Sheffield, and Pendleton King.

In the Boni brothers' Washington Square Bookshop, one floor above the Liberal Club, someone asked Robert Edmond Jones if a theatre building was essential for play production. Jones's reply was to stage Lord Dunsany's *The Glittering Gate* amidst the bookshelves. Allegedly that impulse gave life to the Washington Square Players in the winter of 1914, although Lawrence Langner, who recounts both events, denies the legendary connection.[11] Max Eastman relates that Ida Rauh, his wife at that time,

> had long talked of founding a theatre to be sustained by subscriptions instead of ticket sales, one which could ignore the box office and adhere to pure standards of art. . . . the conception of the Washington Square Players was Ida's and the organization was born at a meeting in our house attended by Lawrence Langner, Eddie Goodman, and others who subsequently put it across. Ida was absorbed in its beginnings and had the leading role in one of the three plays put on at its first performance at the Bandbox Theatre.[12]

She was not the only future Provincetown Player involved in the birth of the Washington Square Players: George Cram Cook, Susan Glaspell, and John Reed were others.[13] In contrast to the majority, these four rebels insisted on producing American dramatists, in order to give vent to, perhaps even resolve, indigenous frustrations. Therefore Harry Kemp is correct in saying: "it was not until George Cram Cook conceived the idea of the Provincetown Players that the distinctively American Little Theatre began." [14]

2   In 1915, "that remarkable and never repeated summer at Provincetown" did not begin with the promise that it would be "really huge in import, and huge in various satisfaction." [15] At the homes of the Cooks, the O'Briens, the Hapgoods, the Steeles, and of Reed, disenchantment dominated the atmosphere. Passionate discussions, which were coupled with imbibing, touched on the war, theatre, love and marriage, experiments in art and psychology. A desire for something unexpected and refreshingly new became the basis of a communal life that gradually led to the writing and staging of plays. Hutchins Hapgood later gave this sensitive analysis of the mood and the impulses:

> When the War broke out at Provincetown we had, in spite of our reckless excitement, *a remnant of faith.* We had, most of us, believed in something—a cause, a method of art, or some enduring civilization. When the explosion came we hoped to see the fruition of our faith. The social revolutionists for the moment felt, that this civilization would prevail over the old ideas. But as the year passed their spiritual disappointment became even greater. It was before the Russian Revolution came to bring spiritual meaning again. . . .
>
> Mabel Dodge was in Provincetown the summer of 1915. She had had a violent reaction to her broad social interests of the previous years; her life was then full of vivid broadening impulses.
>
> Surrounded by her new "faithful" at Provincetown, she made it her business to keep them together in a little group, and also almost unconsciously to impregnate them and all others she could reach with the suspicion and dislike for all those outside the group. In that sense, it was quite barbaric. . . .
>
> [But] Mabel was a symbol rather than a cause. She was far from

being the only poison-distributing center. We were all of us so, in some degree—to a far greater degree than we had ever been before.

The *positive response* to these negative forces was also present within the group; it *found expression in an inchoate creative urge*. . . .

It seemed to them that, if a simple beginning of an answer to these questions was made, a step might be taken in the solution of our bigger social problems, in our deeper self-consciousness; that without self-knowledge and honest reconsideration our political and economic effort is useless. In other words, without *a truthful effort for a deeper culture*, all our large social purposes are impossible. . . .

So they wrote, staged, and acted their own plays. At first *in each little piece there was something fresh and personal*—as if something was springing again sweetly from the earth. They were of course not "great" things. Their very modesty was promising. It was a delightful change from the preoccupation of the War and the poison of 1915. It was an escape from that dry poison and also from the meaningless theatricalism of the Broadway theatres. It meant much to us all; *at once we were expressing something sweetly personal and sweetly social*. And all Provincetown was interested.[16]

Three factors in the group's birth are beyond dispute: the plays were first thought of as a profoundly therapeutic party-game for a small, close-knit group; the idea no sooner emerged than it materialized in the form of scripts; Jig Cook was *spiritus rector* before it all began.[17]

The first "bill" of the Provincetown Players-to-be consisted of two brief comedies, each rooted in vital experiences of the collective. They were half improvised during the latter part of summer in a seaside house the Hapgoods rented at 621 Commercial Street.[18] *Constancy,* by Neith Boyce Hapgood, treated the stormy loves of Mabel Dodge and John Reed; *Suppressed Desires,* by Susan Glaspell and George Cram Cook, the excesses of amateur psycho-analysis.

In its most complete surviving version *Constancy* (titled *The Faithful Lover*),[19] is a somewhat clumsy but amusing dialogue between Moira and Rex whom the audience, familiar enough with the adventures of Jack and Mabel, easily recognized. Reed, hardly back from the Mexican Revolution, was taking off to cover the war in Europe; how he and Mabel reacted to the performance is not recorded. The playlet's background, in the words of Mary Vorse, follows:

The summer before, Mabel Dodge had a large house to the Eastward with lots of company and her young son John Evans. Come evening, Kendrick and his canopy top drove up. Mabel said "adieu" to her guests, and she and Jack Reed were conveyed to Race Point, where they spent the night in a silken tent. They went early, for they liked to see the sunset. Presently, Jack went to the wars, in which Mabel was completely disinterested. After a while Jack cabled Hutch Hapgood, "Bobby et mois nous aimons. Console Mabel." Hutch replied, "Mabel consolée. Amusez vous bien." When Jack returned, he was outraged that Mabel wouldn't resume the affair with him. He accused her of inconstancy. He had been casually inconstant in a physical way (the Bobby affairs had turned out to amount to nothing), while Mabel was spiritually inconstant.[20]

The script's chief weakness is Moira's unequivocal strength because it prevents dramatic conflict. She has loved Rex, but has sobered under the influence of his repeated inconstancy—and tells him so. Surprised and outraged, he sees his return despite promises made to another woman as constancy, and her rejection as inconstancy. The author and Joe O'Brien played the parts.[21]

Suppressed Desires, by Susan Glaspell and George Cram Cook, is a spoof on home-brewed psychoanalysis, a new fashion then among sophisticates. Written for and rejected by the Washington Square Players a year before as "too experimental," [22] its action is rooted in a family situation. Stephen Brewster is plagued by his wife's constant search for manifestations of "subconscious" desires in his dreams, words, gestures, and facial expressions. His antagonism peaks when Henrietta applies the method to her younger sister, Mabel, a guest in their home for two weeks. Stephen manages to plant the idea with Mabel that she has a subconscious desire for *him*—causing Henrietta to reject psychoanalysis forever. The script retains much of its flavor (it is still regularly performed by amateurs); although the dialogue is repetitious and awkward in places, the puns supporting the comedy are lively and the theme is still timely. The authors took the parts of the couple; it is not known who first acted Mabel.

The first play was done on the balcony; for the second, the audience moved out onto the former "stage" and looked into the living room—in an unconscious experiment with interchangeable performer-spectator space. Little information regarding the staging of *Constancy* is gained from a letter Cook wrote his wife a year later.[23] Having taken a picture supposed to represent

1 Lewis Wharf, 1915; one of the two smaller buildings burned in 1916. (*Metropolitan Magazine*)

Enemies, he confesses, "I got Neith to arrange the set more like *Constancy.*" But the surviving photograph was not taken on the balcony; neither does it bear out the legend that "Bobby Jones made scenery from sofa cushions." [24]

As the evening became the talk of Provincetown's artist colony, repeat performances were demanded by many who missed the first one, and the demand was satisfied. Then, before summer was over, the two new plays were presented to larger audiences. Significantly, each of these new plays "had something to say" about more than the intimate affairs of the group that put them on, and they were staged not in a private home, but in a theatre. This theatre, improvised in the fishhouse on Lewis Wharf, became the core of the Provincetown legend.

3   The Bangs A. Lewis Wharf was built sometime between 1830 and 1880. It was purchased in 1915 by Joe and Mary (Heaton Vorse) O'Brien, and stood at 571 Commercial Street, just across the road from where the Cooks were then living.[25] Three gray and weathered buildings enlivened by touches of faded red paint were situated along the nearly 100-foot

2   Rear view of Courtney Allen's model of the wharf after the fire, showing the roll-away door in the back. Provincetown Museum of the Cape Cod Pilgrim Memorial Association. (R. K. Sarlós)

length of the wharf:[26] a fishhouse approximately 24–26 feet wide, about 34–36 feet long, and about 24–26 feet in height; and two smaller structures, one of which burned in 1916. In the fishhouse, which featured two large doors set on rollers, the Players installed their theatre. It included a stage 10 by 12 feet built in four separate sections.[27] One of the two movable doors was located behind the stage. It could be rolled open, thus allowing the sea to serve as a backdrop.[28]

Although both unpublished and published accounts differ on the question of overall dimensions, it is possible to conclude that the total area of the fishhouse encompassed nearly nine hundred square feet. If one hundred and twenty square feet were used for the stage, and some area allowed for aisles, the remaining space would have easily accommodated over one hundred spectators.[29]

The stage was now set, its four sections allowing the use of different levels and a variety of combinations. The lighting equipment consisted of lanterns with tin reflectors in footlight position, and of assorted lamps held backstage by four people. Four other crew members stood ready with shovels and sand in case of fire.[30]

To satisfy those who had only heard of the original performance, the first production in the fishhouse (sometime in August) revived the two plays presented at the Hapgoods'. Two new plays, written expressly for performance in Lewis Wharf, were given on September 9.[31] One of these, *Change Your Style,* by George Cram Cook, satirizes the feud between objective and non-objective art. It revolves around Marmaduke Marvin, Jr., a banker's young son and a would-be painter who, ignoring his father's instructions to paint in the "sane" academic style, endangers his allowance by choosing bold and "outrageous" post-Impressionist styles. He takes lessons from Bordfeldt ("Head of a Post-Impressionist Art School") rather than from Crabtree ("Head of an Academic Art School") as ordered by Marvin, Sr., and cannot sell his abstract, cubist paintings. Marvin, Jr., is gently pressed for at least a promise of payment toward his overdue rent by Mr. Josephs, "the beneficent landlord who . . . was easily recognized as the beloved John Francis, the friend of writers and artists." [32] Marmaduke tries to pay in paintings which, he promises, will appreciate with time. As the landlord contemplates accepting one that is hastily dubbed "the eye of God," Myrtle Dart ("Lover of the Buddhistic") appears. A wealthy lady who wants to rent a room "to meditate in," Dart sees in the painting "the spiritual form of the navel," and is impelled by it "to pronounce the holy syllable OM". She pays a hundred dollars for the painting, more than the three months' rent Marvin owes. Now Marvin, Sr., arrives, to learn that his son is studying with the wrong teacher, but also that the right teacher's paintings do not sell. When Marmaduke announces *his* sale, his father is impressed: "The tide is turning. You mustn't change your style now, my boy. . . ." But the painting is returned, because Mrs. Dart has heard that it was "the eye of God" prior to becoming "the spiritual form of the navel." She demands her money back and Marmaduke's fears of being commercial evaporate. Though the sale has gone sour, the landlord believes the picture will be talked about and therefore valuable. As the banker resigns himself to supporting Marmaduke "as a defective," the dialogue ends with a gleeful toast to "defective artists."

Despite its heavy-handed humor, the play is interesting because issues have hardly changed, and the clichés (e.g., the artist corrects a painting that was hung upside down) were presumably still fresh. Charles Demuth headed the cast as the young artist; Nordfeldt took the part of Bordfeldt, and the author played the banker. The names of Max Eastman, Louis Ell, and Ida Rauh were typed in for the remaining roles—Kenyon Crabtree, Head of an Academic Art-School, Mr. Josephs, and Myrtle Dart—but each name was crossed out, and those of Edward Ballantine, Frederic Burt, and Stella Ballantine penciled in. This probably means that three cast members were replaced at the play's revival next summer, when Burt and the Ballantines are known to have joined.

The other new work, Wilbur Daniel Steele's *Contemporaries,* was timely and daring both theatrically and politically. Long believed to have been lost, this play in fact survives in manuscript.[33] Its dialogue recalled to spectators the previous winter, one of great depression and extreme cold, during which a young I.W.W. organizer, Frank Tannenbaum, "had won a·day of front-page glory and six months in jail by leading a band of homeless men into a church."[34] The action unfolds on a stage dark but for the indirect glimmer of a candle, apparently rendered by the ocean's reflected light through the open roll-away door of the fishhouse. The focal character is young Sam, whose late-night return his anxious parents are awaiting at a lodging for transients "In a congested quarter of the city." Sam enters stealthily; he believes the authorities are after him for having joined a crowd near the church, to hear a speaker who "Comes right straight out about the churches and the priests and all, and they's scared to touch him on account of the mob, and the mob's with 'im." An officer and a priest soon arrive, pursuing a fugitive. Mother gives up Sam with a heavy heart; but to her great relief he is not the wanted one. After a sermon against those who cry "We will throw off all restraint: our conscience shall be our law," Priest asks Sam to turn informer and leaves. Old John, who sneaked in unnoticed behind Sam, speaks up to defend the rabble-rouser, whom he describes as a prophet of universal brotherhood, the savior of the world. As Old John is expelled, the sun rises; the characters are wearing Roman dress, their city is Jerusalem. The cast included Cook as Father, Rauh as Mother, Eastman as a grumbling Lodger, Robert Emmons Rogers as Priest, and Vorse's son Heaton as Sam.[35]

With this second program given at the Wharf, the first season of the Provincetown Players, "who closed without knowing they were the Provincetown Players," was over.[36] The venture might have ended if it had not been for Jig Cook. Through the winter of 1915–16 he continued to build his dream city which, of course, had a theatre: "why not write our own plays and put them on ourselves giving writer, actor, designer, a chance to work together without the commercial thing imposed from without? *A whole community working together, developing unsuspected talents.* The city ought to furnish the kind of audience that will cause new plays to be written."[37]

Cook did not stop at dreaming; he prepared for action. He set about establishing the yet unorganized collective in New York City. On February 15, 1916, he wrote his wife Susan (who had gone back to Iowa): "I am at the Masses waiting for Floyd and Max to go to lunch. Just wrote Jack Reed about the theatre places—including his apartment. Max tells me Jack was furious when my telegram proposing 43 Washington Square for theatre arrived. He thought I only meant the floor above his. I meant his. Did it half-jokingly." [38]

Three weeks later *Suppressed Desires* was presented at the Liberal Club; a performance at Ira Remsen's Macdougal Street studio followed shortly.[39] According to Edna Kenton, these events sparked some "talk of a New York home for the Provincetowners," but a "seceding committee" composed of Cook, Dell, Rauh, Reed, and Lucian Cary quickly abandoned all plans.[40]

4 Productions during the summer of 1916 in the old Wharf—the second season of the yet amorphous group—brought profound changes. By mid-September, the Provincetown Players had become more audience oriented and more organized, had attracted two experienced actors and a playwright for whom theatre was a vocation.

Although the amateurs had altered Lewis Wharf a little in 1915, the thorough clearing of the fishhouse, the returning of boats and gear to the owners, and the installation of electricity did not take place until 1916. A notice in the *Provincetown Advocate,* to the effect that the Wharf was in the expert "hands of carpenters, who are making sundry interior changes," dispels the fond myth of a community work project creating the theatre.[41] The alterations were quite limited, as a continued lack of dressing rooms indicated. By the end of June the entire collective had reassembled, and on July 13 the first bill of three plays was given in the renovated fishhouse. The Players distributed printed announcements, and at fifty cents a ticket the Wharf Theatre was sold out.[42] Two days before the scheduled opening the Wharf caught on fire, and only the combined effort of Players and firemen saved the fishhouse, although one of the little shacks perished: "Two walls were badly charred, so they stained the other two black to make charred and uncharred look alike. The curtain had burned, but they bought another. The new curtain went up on scheduled time, and the Provincetown Players made their first appearance before a packed house." [43]

On the opening bill *Suppressed Desires,* which was revived from the previous summer by popular demand, was followed by Neith Boyce's new work, *Winter's Night.* Woven more skillfully than *Constancy,* its dialogue employs three characters and succeeds in creating occasional suspense.[44] The action follows Daniel Wescott's funeral and involves his widow and brother in a conflict of love and honor. Jacob tells Rachel that he has always loved her and that her marriage to Daniel kept him a bachelor—and therefore a member of the household—all these years. Now he feels free to claim Rachel's love and, loading his gun for a fox hunt, offers to marry her. She rejects Jacob in consternation; he insists as she protests. Sarah, a distant neighbor, arrives for an overnight visit—in time to interrupt the confrontation. Jacob ambles out, saying nothing more; a shot is heard and as Sarah follows to see what happened, her shriek of horror ends the play. The actors were Nancy Schoonmaker, Jig Cook, and Mary Heaton Vorse; the latter once recalled that her shriek as Sarah caused quite a stir.[45] The Gelbs pass over this play as one so poor "that its plot has been forgotten by all concerned," but the story has influenced several writers. To hear Floyd Dell tell it, *Winter's Night* was based on an episode oft recalled by Jig Cook: sitting up at a family wake, Jig's second wife, Mollie, was nearly seduced by a brother-in-law.[46] Dell claims that both he and Sherwood Anderson used the incident for a short story. Even more germane is O'Neill's first full-length play, *Beyond the Horizon.* Written in Provincetown after years of intimate contact with the Players, it revolves around a man who—like Jacob Wescott—gives up his beloved to a younger brother.

Reed's *Freedom,* not a "stirring, bitter prison play" as Deutsch and Hanau imagined, but a hilarious farce, completed the program.[47] As Guard in Sweetwater Penitentiary locks Trusty's cell, "a large block of stone heaves out of the wall, falling silently on the bed." It is followed by three would-be escapees. Romancer assumes command in Tom Sawyer style: escape to him is not worth the trouble unless it is accomplished according to literary tradition. Poet cares more about singing than achieving sweet Freedom; Smith alone appears in earnest. The team cannot persuade Trusty to join them because he is too reluctant to lose his hard-earned status of trusty and return to bumming. As Poet is absorbed in a new prison poem, Romancer prepares for action. He soon discovers that there is neither wall nor guard under the window, and the expedition loses meaning for him. Poet meanwhile realizes that if he escapes, his now popular freedom poetry will lack motivation. Consequently, Smith's persistent desire to break jail is viewed by his companions as treachery. They try to restrain him by force and, when the commotion attracts Guard, denounce him as a jailbreaker caught red-handed. Questioned by Guard, Smith "confesses": "I was trying to break into a padded cell so I could be free." [48] Curtain. No detail about the performance is known, though it was well enough received to have been repeated in both Provincetown and New York.

The evening of three short plays was so successful that the Players decided to assemble another program. However, they found themselves short of scripts. Just then, Terry Carlin, the anarchist philosopher proud of never having earned a penny, reported living with a young man who had "a whole trunkful of plays." The prospective playwright was asked to present a manuscript that night at the Cooks' house. Too shy to read his work to a group of strangers, Eugene O'Neill stayed in the other room while it was read by the assembled amateurs. The script he had submitted, *Bound East for Cardiff*, was received with enthusiasm and put on the bill, according to traditional account.[49] Harry Kemp, the hobo poet who had just joined the group, once recalled O'Neill's first appearance at a Players' meeting differently: he had read *The Movie Man* to the gathering and, not surprisingly, failed to make a favorable impression.[50] Only at the second meeting, according to Kemp, did *Cardiff* excite the Players.

Included in the bill that was to feature O'Neill's debut was Louise Bryant's first play, *The Game,* and Wilbur Steele's second, *"Not Smart."* If the significant departure in *Bound East for Cardiff* was its substitution of mood for plot, the innovation connected with *The Game* lay in its cubist set and formalized acting style; Steele's writing was better than Bryant's and his new script's drawing card was its use of local color. But the long-range import of the evening was unquestionably the O'Neill world premiere, the exhilarating experience that forged the Provincetown Players into a producing organization.[51] Indeed, it seems that inspired by this second bill that was planned for Mary Heaton Vorse's fishhouse during the last week of July 1916, Cook launched a campaign for "associate members"—in other words, subscribers.[52] Participants themselves (writers, actors, painters, and stage-hands) became "active members" upon payment of a membership fee; "associate members" acquired tickets for the remainder of the season by making a smaller contribution.

Susan Glaspell's oft-cited reminiscence reflected the entire group's feelings:

I may see it through memories too emotional, but it seems to me I have never sat before a more moving production than our "Bound East for Cardiff" when Eugene O'Neill was produced for the first time on any stage. Jig was Yank. As he lay in his bunk dying, he talked of life as one who knew he must leave it.

The sea has been good to Eugene O'Neill. It was there for his opening. There was a fog, just as the script had demanded, fog bell in the harbor. The tide was in, and it washed under and around us, spraying through the holes in the floor, giving us the rhythm and the flavor of the sea while the big dying sailor talked to his friend Drisc of the life he had always wanted deep in the land where you'd never see a ship or smell the sea.

It is not merely figurative language to say the old wharf shook with applause.[53]

Three photographs record the performance's key moments in a setting that realized O'Neill's instructions with praiseworthy simplicity.[54] A door was stage right, slightly downstage of it a wooden pail; a triple bunk ran along the back wall, parallel to the "footlights"; another three bunks projected at a thirty-degree angle toward downstage left. There, his head pointing offstage in the lowest berth, lay dying Yank—played by Jig Cook. Portholes were painted on the canvas behind the bunks, a simple bench placed in front of each. The first picture shows an early moment with eight men on stage: above Cook one lies supine, another leans on his elbow in the uppermost berth, stage right, dangling one foot over the bunk's edge; John Reed, Brör Nordfeldt (each with a pipe), and an unidentified man sit on the bench below him. Frederic Burt sits at Cook's feet, gesturing to the dying man with his left hand, toward the others with his right as if saying, "Shut your mouths, all av you. 'Tis a hell av a thing for us to be complainin' about our guts, and a sick man maybe dyin' listenin' to us." [55] E. J. Ballantine is sitting on the pail, downstage right.

The second photo is still easier pinpointed in the action, for on it the author (who in this world premiere, "sick with stagefright, spoke one line as the Mate."),[56] stands in the door wearing a sailor's raincoat, while David Carb, as the Captain, takes Yank's pulse. Burt stands at center, looking at O'Neill over his shoulder. The man in the berth above Cook lies as in the first picture, but the one in the uppermost berth, stage right, has turned his back to the audience. The scene is between the Captain's question "And how is the sick man?" and his insertion of a thermometer under Yank's tongue.[57] The third snapshot represents the play's conclusion: the dipper has fallen from Yank's fingers, Driscoll kneels at his head (definitely identifying Burt with the part), and Nordfeldt stands, hat in hand, at the door. According to the script, only Cocky is present beside Driscoll when Yank dies, yet Margaret Nordfeldt asserted that her husband played Olson.[58] Since Nordfeldt is the only one in the picture to answer the description of Olson as a "Swede with a drooping blond mustache," it may be speculated that the two parts were melded (Olson, in fact, goes to sleep half-way through the play), or that Nordfeldt doubled.

This is not the only puzzle connected with *Cardiff*. Years later Ballantine said he had directed the first O'Neill play in Provincetown, and Burt, "the only professional actor, insisted upon playing the smallest part." [59] Yet the photographs clearly identify Burt as Driscoll, one of the two leads; two eyewitnesses insist that "Rotten potatoes" (the Norwegian Paul's only line, which Ballantine attributes to Burt) was spoken by Kemp who substituted "crackers" for "potatoes"; and Ballantine, too, was on stage.[60]

Providing sharp contrast to O'Neill's realistic mood was Louise Bryant's rather stiff "morality" play, *The Game,* which inspired the most daring décor and performance style of the summer.[61] The game is one of dice, played by Life and Death for the lives of Youth (a poet) and Girl (a dancer). Life is revealed as an enthusiast, Death as a cynic; Life wins twice in a row, Youth and Girl become each other's. Heretofore plays were done without much evidence of style: frugality commanded the use of familiar furnishings; O'Neill consciously demanded realism. William and Marguerite Zorach, given a free hand with the design and production of *The Game,* wanted to have nothing to do with realism. Envisioning theatre as a living symbolic world, and undeterred by the quality of the script, they embarked on an extreme approach. They stylized every aspect of the production: the backdrop was a cubist version of the view from Provincetown harbor, the actors' movements were choreographed with "conventionalized gestures, resulting in a series of pictures that looked like Egyptian reliefs." [62]

Two photographs of the production, one from Provincetown and one from the later New York performance, demonstrate the style attempted in *The Game.*[63] The same backdrop was used. Top center, the setting sun is framed in a diamond and surrounded by triangular hills. The sun's reflection lies heavily across the sinuous lines of waves from horizon to the bottom of the drop. Ten trees, symmetrically arranged on either side of the sun, resemble ancient columns, their foliage like so many fans. Dunes and stones in the foreground are painted with childlike simplicity of line and perspective. Against this backdrop the actors appear in formal arrangements—in the Provincetown photo in one plane, in the New York picture in two. The former displays a stiff design, the latter strong dramatic focus. Yet both indicate how consistently the Zorachs' idea of Egyptian style was carried into the actors' postures and gestures. All four characters are seen in profile; their hands, if not their feet, conform to the bas-relief principle. The Provincetown picture—in which the die is visible on the floor in front of black-masked Death—does not tell a story, the New York one—with the die between symmetrically kneeling Life and Death at stage center—does present an emblem.

Judith Lewis, who modeled for many artists on the Cape, played Life; Reed, a black mask covering his skull and half his face, Death. The role of Girl was taken by the suffragette antique dealer, Helene Freeman; bare-chested Zorach played Youth. The set became a Provincetown hallmark; a lineoleum-cut based on it was used on the collective's playbills for years to come.

Wilbur Daniel Steele's second Provincetown play, *"Not Smart,"* completed the evening's fare, adding welcome local flavor.[64] Its title is a Cape Cod euphemism for being pregnant, and the witty sketch satirized the bohemians' hypocritical pose of nonconformity as their professed libertarian morality evaporates on contact with reality. Mattie, a local girl working for an artist couple, turns out to be "not smart." The man who minutes ago described her as a "splendid, deep-bosomed ox-eyed, earth-woman" is promptly suspected by his wife of being responsible. In the heated argument it occurs to neither the accuser nor the defendant that Mattie may be producing an offspring of wedlock. It is not known who was in the cast.

The third bill of the summer followed, approximately two weeks later, on August 8; it revived *Constancy* and introduced two new plays.[65] *The Eternal Quadrangle,* by John Reed, is a skillful "Shavian farce, a burlesque of the 'triangle' plays of Broadway." The plot's motor is wealthy Mr. Fortescue who, having no time for emotions, orders his wife to keep lovers. Intolerant of the frequency with which she rotates paramours, Fortescue arranges a steady affair for his wife with their butler, Archibald, who happens to be a skating champion. But Archibald is married as well, and his wife,

3   Louise Bryant's *The Game* as presented by the Provincetown Players on Lewis Wharf, summer of 1916. The backdrop is by William Zorach. Left to right: John Reed, William Zorach, Helene Freeman, Judith Lewis. (Peter A. Juley and Son, photographers)

Estelle, demands *her* rights. She is offered Mrs. Fortescue's latest cast-off lover. The dialogue is occasionally brilliant; comic scenes built on subverted conventions follow in quick succession. Even though written "in haste, to fit the needs of the Players," [66] it matches Glaspell's one-acts in wit and structure.

Reed described the setting in minute detail, but in a preamble apparently meant for distribution, mocked the scant scenery: "We call the attention of the audience to the fact that this is the most elaborate set ever attempted on any stage . . . of this size." [67] After crediting lenders of properties and costumes, the preamble concludes: "The audience is earnestly requested to remain for the second play which is respectable."

Jig Cook and Louise Bryant took the parts of Mr. and Mrs. Fortescue, Ida Rauh played Estelle, while the fancy rollerskating, which eyewitnesses were to recall decades later, was performed by Reed himself in the role of Archibald.[68]

The other new work that evening was Susan Glaspell's best short play, *Trifles,* a deftly wrought murder mystery, written at Jig's express command. "I have announced a play of yours for the next bill," he said, and she had only the stage and her imagination to depend on.

4   The Provincetown Players' New York production of *The Game,* 1916.
Left to right: Reed, Zorach, Martha Ryther-Fuller, Kathleen Cannell. (Peter A.
Juley and Son, photographers)

So I went out on the wharf, sat alone on one of our wooden benches without a back, and looked a long time at the bare little stage. After a time the stage became a kitchen . . . I saw just where the stove was, the table, and the steps going upstairs. Then the door at the back opened, and people all bundled up came in—two or three men, I wasn't sure which, but sure enough about the two women, who hung back, reluctant to enter the kitchen. . . .

Whenever I got stuck, I would run across the street to the old wharf, sit in that leaning little theatre under which the sea sounded, until the play was ready to continue.[69]

The author and Alice Hall played two neighbors of the housewife alleged to have killed her husband. Sifting a series of "trifles," they solve the case by finding the motive that remains hidden to the detectives. Robert Rogers, Robert Conville, and Cook portrayed the official investigators who lacked the feminine intuition necessary for a solution.[70]

Some time before the summer ended, the Hapgoods' *Enemies,* although not part of the known "bills," must have been performed on the wharf.[71]

As Hapgood relates in his autobiography: "Neith wrote the woman's part and I the man's, and we acted it together in the fishhouse theatre, I think Robert Edmond Jones did the settings for it as he did for Neith's *Constancy* the year before .... in spite of the careful drilling and the fact that I had written my lines myself, I could not remember them but was forced to read them from the manuscript." [72] A photograph supports his testimony. [73] It shows a single bed with a decorative cover and a couple of pillows at center stage, a table with a colonial lamp somewhat upstage and to the right, an oriental rug left of the bed. Stage left is deep and dark, only the rolled-up backdrop for *The Game* is clearly identifiable. From stage right, a light-colored curtain extends to center, allowing room for a chair behind the table. There, script in hand, sits Hutchins Hapgood, while his wife and co-author Neith stands at the far end of the bed, facing him.

Another play that does not fit the "bills" represents the collective's only known foray into children's theatre. *Mother Carey's Chickens* was written by Henry Marion Hall to provide a vehicle for the creativity of the Players' children. [74] The *Boston Post* records the fact of performance, Mary Heaton Vorse adds that the wharf theatre's "big door was opened" so this production could use "the bay as a backdrop." [75] This too, was a sea play, but instead of lovers or seamen it featured pirates, mermaids, seagulls, and, of course, storm petrels—the proliferous small sea bird popularly called Mother Carey's chickens. Professor and Mrs. Hall took charge of "drilling the little darlings . . . for weeks," and the parents formed a grateful audience. The producers "recruited a band of 'pirates,' little Portuguese boys who were delighted to march onstage with gold curtain rings in their ears and scarlet bandannas, and roar in unison a pirate song [with the refrain] in Zanzibar, ol' Zanzibar, ahoy!" [76] Professor Charles Hapgood recalled that as a twelve-year-old, he had to haul a treasure chest across the stage with his older brother, Boyce. [77] All three Hall girls were cast. Rosalys, aged three, was among the smallest seagulls who complained "of the Pirates breaking their eggs in their nests. . . . 'Addled! All addled!' they wailed waving their white net pinions up and down. . . ." [78] Second youngest Frances played a mermaid with an intricate little tail, wagged by pulling a string, which in the opening night's excitement she failed to operate. Promised a quarter if she would do better the second night—which was given by popular demand—Frances worked her mermaid's tail like a raging dragon. [79]

Leading roles were taken by Julia, oldest of the Hall girls, and Jig Cook's eight-year-old daughter Nilla; both recall details of production. Nilla was the heroine and Julia the hero—perhaps because she was the tallest. The success of opening night apparently resulted in the unplanned second performance. According to Julia,

> success went to my parents' heads . . . they let Nilla's lines fairly well alone, except to give her a lot of new cues for me, and I got a new ten pages, or more! Added to that I now changed my sex, always confusing, and this time I had also to learn a little dance! I was costumed in a rainbow-tinted veil thing. (It was the year that Isadora's pupils were running barefoot across stages dressing in veils, and there was nothing about *that* that a mother couldn't do with me!) [80]

The change was too much for the young hero and heroine; left alone on stage, Nilla

> forgot all my new cues, and knowing she was supposed to say *something* she chatted pleasantly about whatever came into her head. . . . Paralyzed with stagefright anyhow, the new cues ruined and without the slightest idea *what* lines to use I made a few vacuous remarks until a hissed command *do your dance* galvanized me into motion, and the stage once cleared of Nilla and me, my parents shoved whatever children were still (poor, good little things) at their posts, and the play went on. . . .

Nilla responded with gratitude to this long overdue explanation

> of what happened the second day! . . . This accounts for the fact that I received no scolding for talking my head off. I recall telling Mrs. Hall quite gayly . . . that I had "made up" a new play for her. She shook her head but said nothing. Cues work both ways. Not getting mine from Julia, I had apparently decided to . . . talk about a lot of things that were not part of the play. . . . I remember clearly, a kind of excited drunkenness, which took into consideration the existence of the audience and made a play for it. [81]

She contrasted this feeling with the spirit of the previous night, when "there had been no audience for me, . . . All I knew was that I was alone on the stage with Julia, that I was shipwrecked, wore a ragged little dress, and that the lines . . . were the serious, unchangeable 'part' of a real play." That attitude, she insists, the children adopted from the adults. Consequently, "the production was a work of art," attested to by "the perfect silence, and then the applause of the audience" which rewarded the first performance. That the magic of theatre infected the children is shown by Cook's report, a few weeks later: "Nilla is rehearsing a play she's made up with eight or ten kids. It has four acts, King, Queen, Giant, fairies, guards, etc. . . . with a little help—it could be made nice." [82]

Nilla returned to theatre repeatedly: during the New York season of 1925–26, in India a few years later, and in Iran after World War II.

5   During the fourth week of August the Players set a precedent to be followed for several years in New York: they combined three scripts most favored by spectators into a review bill. Featured with the summer's exciting discovery, O'Neill's *Bound East for Cardiff*, were Steele's *Contemporaries* and Cook's *Change Your Style*—the popularity of these last two probably due to their vital topics, politics and esthetics.

The season's fifth, and last, production is the best documented. It consisted of "Two Special Performances" on September 1 and 2, reviving *Suppressed Desires* and *The Game,* and bringing to the stage for the first time O'Neill's *Thirst,* the title piece of the author's first volume of plays, published in 1914.

These "special" performances, on the eve of the first formally recorded membership meeting of the Provincetown Players, coincide with an apparent change in the group's orientation from inward to outward: the August 31 issue of the *Provincetown Advocate* carried both their first "notice" (for a reprise of *Freedom* at the Beachcomber's Club) and their first advertisement. The momentum must have been gathering for a while: Edna Kenton, who wrote regular New York letters for the *Chicago Post,* was summoned by her old friend, Jig Cook, especially for the opening of *Thirst.*[83] And, perhaps before that summons was issued, the *Boston Globe* granted the Players widespread publicity. Not only did an article by A. J. Philpott (appearing there on August 13 under the title, "Laboratory of the Drama on Cape Cod's Farthest Wharf") describe the Provincetown Players as an iconoclastic artists' organization whose members are both "revolutionists" and "strongly individual in their attitude toward life"; it adopted the term "laboratory" and took it seriously. The *Globe* also ran the only known photograph of the fishhouse interior.

Because the only new play staged in this special bill was by O'Neill, and since Philpott hinted that the amateur group had considered O'Neill special, it seems warranted to connect a series of publicity seeking moves—coverage by the *Globe,* guest appearance at the Beachcombers' with a review following, finally an advertisement preceding the special performances—with the subscription campaign briefly mentioned above, as preparations for "something bigger." Sometime during the summer of 1916 Jig Cook launched this first drive for a supporting audience. According to Glaspell, "he wrote a letter to the people who had seen the plays, asking if they cared to become associate members of the Provincetown Players." Supposedly, he asked "one dollar for the three remaining bills," announcing that the group aimed to provide "American playwrights of sincere purpose a chance to work out their ideas in freedom, to give all who worked with the plays the opportunity as artists." [84] Even though Glaspell relates this after her emotional account of the O'Neill world premiere, it seems likely that Jig's offer was made *prior* to that performance, though *after* its having been scheduled. Thus the special performances would not have been part of the three bills offered for subscription.

No one knows the extent of the response to Cook's appeal.[85] What really matters, though, is that there was sufficient interest to sustain the three bills originally planned, and more that have not even been envisioned. Thus, by the end of the still amorphous collective's second summer season Jig had reasons to see his year-old leaven working, his dream about transplanting the group to New York vindicated. Before long the idea of moving was officially adopted as the plan of action.

The feverish production and publicity calendar near the close of the 1916 summer came to a climax when, on September 4, the "Provincetown Players" organized themselves at a meeting in the fishhouse. Minutes were taken, motions adopted and rejected, officers elected, and a constitution commissioned.[86] Active members present defeated a motion to call themselves "Try-out theatre," and chose the name "Provincetown Players." At O'Neill's insistence they agreed to label their prospective playhouse somewhere in Greenwich Village "The Playwright's Theatre." An executive committee, consisting of president, secretary-treasurer, and three active members, was mandated; Jig Cook was unanimously elected president, but the election of secretary-treasurer was postponed until after a constitution would determine "the duties, salary and qualifications" of such an officer.

The first two policy decisions were that no play be barred from production merely because the author was not a member, and that to become an active member one not only had to "write, act, produce, or donate labor," but also had to be elected to the group by a majority of members. Inherent in these policies were the paradoxical desires to keep the group's boundaries flexible and to maintain selective membership. The proposed constitution, along with a series of crucial resolutions, was adopted the following evening. All petty details are not recorded, but the minutes preserve the essentials of what were the guiding principles, how were they formulated, and what seemed to be the chief issues and concerns.

In addition to a draft of the constitution (presented by a committee in charge), resolutions stating the philosophy and intended modus operandi of the Players were submitted by Reed, and after discussion, "put on the minutes as the sentiment of the meeting." [87]

Why this attempt to fashion order, if spontaneity and anarchy were considered guarantees of true creativity? It seems fair to suggest that with the appearance of O'Neill and, with him, the promise of lasting works of theatre art, gradually the concern with creation for its own sake (i.e., orientation toward process) became coupled with interest in the works created (i.e., orientation toward product). Organization was undertaken for the express purpose of setting up shop in New York. Thus the "Two Special Performances" conclude the first period in the history of the Provincetown Players, and the two meetings, preparatory to the move for Greenwich Village, usher in the second.

This milestone in the collective's life is commemorated by a lengthy report in yet another newspaper article. On September 10, under the title, "Many Literary Lights Among Provincetown Players," the *Boston* (Sunday) *Post* reported in such detail and with such insight as to suggest that the unnamed author was a member of the group. A strong emphasis on O'Neill, on the plans for continuation in New York, on the name proposed and rejected at an early organizational meeting for their future theatre (Try-Out Playhouse), are especially telling. "They do it all for fun." And the writer deduced that doing it for fun results in "seeking new ways of doing things." The account mentioned that all members "are getting a 'sense of the stage' " by rotating functions, that "like the Irish Players" the Provincetowners "are trying to get away from stage convention," that "they rewrite the plays as they are being rehearsed," and that "Eugene O'Neill, a young dramatist whose work was heretofore unproduced . . . is going to be heard from in places less remote. . . ." The Players professed to be "so modern that they not only write about modern things but satirize them." They saw "no reason for stopping the intense and delightful activity of this summer. . . . Why not get a little place around Washington Square in New York—perhaps an old stable remodelled to seat two or three hundred people—and go on doing this there?"

In the midst of enthusiasm and hope there was at least one sign that everything would not be smooth. In a letter to Edward Goodman, Lucy Huffaker wrote her husband around this time commenting on "internal troubles already seething" in the group.[88] The creative impulse that carried the Players to New York was strong enough to turn these troubles into the energy needed for the experiment to take root. In the following chapter the nature of that creative impulse and of the resulting experiment will be examined.

Jig Cook:

Dionysos in 1915

 "When the wine began to show the bottom of the bowl, 'Give it all to me,' Jig would propose, 'and I guarantee to intoxicate all the rest of you.'"
Susan Glaspell,
THE ROAD TO THE TEMPLE

"... picturable ideas flowed like rippling streams from his laughing mouth."
Hutchins Hapgood,
A VICTORIAN IN THE MODERN WORLD

The man   Jig Cook's character and activity are elusive; he was and still is difficult to analyze rationally. In *The Road to the Temple* Susan Glaspell created a moving and poetic monument to Jig's visionary, intoxicating Dionysian spirit; but his contribution to American theatre has not been sufficiently evaluated. Two reasons account for this: first, the Provincetown group is discussed primarily as an adjunct to Eugene O'Neill, its major playwright;[1] and second, Cook's personality, creative efforts, and conceptual impact are perplexing. What was least tangible, his "sublime, gallant, crazy theatrical faith"[2] was apparently most valuable.

In 1915 Jig Cook was forty-two and prematurely grey. Large and robust, stubborn and volatile, disarming and gentle, scion of a pioneer Mississippi family whose name became synonymous with power and aristocracy in Davenport, Iowa; he was an anarchist and yearned to create Plato's Republic. A passionate thinker, talker, drinker, and lover, who delighted in working with his hands, Cook had studied at the University of Iowa, at Harvard, and in Heidelberg, then had taught Greek at the University of Iowa and at Stanford. He became by turns a truck farmer, an author (his *The Chasm* was, according to Floyd Dell, the "best socialist novel this country produced" prior to the thirties),[3] a candidate for Congress on the Socialist ticket, and the literary editor of the *Chicago Evening Post (Friday Literary Review)*. Through it all the thrice-married philanderer remained a frustrated builder of dream cities.[4] Fed up with the Midwest, fed up with city life, fed up with patterned pseudo-arts, with rugged individualism, hypocrisy, war, and a host of other ingredients of "right-thinking" Americanism, Cook envisioned an apocalypse: he plunged himself and a circle of close and talented friends into feverish communal creativity. The values they embraced were as American as those they rejected: they dedicated themselves to truth and beauty, to camaraderie and self-reliance, to distrust of power, and to iconoclastic questioning of established values. With Margaret Anderson, fearless editor of the *Little Review*, they believed that "art and anarchism exist in the world for exactly the same kind of reason."[5] And with Marsden Hartley they agreed that American artists "need—abjectly—an esthetic concept of our own."[6]

A visionary of modern theatre, Jig Cook can perhaps best be approached by way of comparison with the well-known English theatrical innovator of a flamboyant temper, Edward Gordon Craig. Although Craig designed only six productions in his long life, his fundamental impact was beginning to be felt through the "new stagecraft" as early as 1915. Cook, though his name is linked with many more productions in one capacity or another, was likewise more effective as a visionary than as a practitioner. His prophetic ideas— a theatre of collective ecstasy and pure space—took a longer time and a more circuitous route to penetrate the mainstream, perhaps because they were aimed toward extremes more radically at odds with underlying assumptions of Western culture. Craig carried the traditional individualistic stance to its logical extreme. He accepted Wagner's principle concerning the oneness of theatrical art, and declared it "impossible for a work of art ever to be produced where more than one brain is permitted to direct." Consequently, Craig believed the future of theatre depended on the emergence of a single Artist of the Theatre, one who had mastered all relevant crafts.[7] The increased leadership of the designer and of the visually thinking director in this century's theatre was a historical development greatly enhanced by Craig's impact.

Contrary to Craig, Cook expected the organic unity of theatre to grow from group consciousness: "One man cannot create drama. True drama is born only of one feeling animating all members of a clan—a spirit shared by all and expressed by the few for the all. If there is nothing to take the place of the common religious purpose and passion of the primitive group, out of which the Dionysian dance was born, no new vital drama can arise in any people." [8] Moreover, convinced that inspiration and intoxication, not training and craftsmanship, were the essential ingredients, Cook made a virtue of child-like spontaneity and unskilled creativity. Jig's fusion of scholarship and life style rendered palpable to him the triple province of Dionysos—intoxication, sexual rites, and theatre: different forms of release from routine and mortality—which he saw not as a social safety valve, but rather as the basic building material of a creative community. Hence his agreement with Nietzsche that the supreme human achievement was tragedy, i.e., serious theatre capable of redeeming society, and that without untrammeled Dionysian ecstasy, sublime Apollinian order was unattainable. Although the Dionysian group spirit called for a self-denial more prevalent in Eastern tradition, Cook thought he had found a Western equivalent in Plato's Republic, which he called the beloved community of life givers.

Consequently, Jig's heart was set on the realization of a beautiful paradox, a remote reflection of the glory that was Greece: if enough selfless people with manifold talents and aspirations can be forged into a cohesive group, not only will their pooled energies enhance each other, but because "the arts fertilize each other" [9] they will, by rotating artistic functions, stretch all their expressive abilities and create a total work of art while increasingly tightening their bonds. They will not then labor in isolation, but unite in creative ecstasy: a true community. Their dreams and intoxication will mingle in the harmonious union of the Dionysian and Apollinian. And the healing creative ferment will spread forth its power from the group, giving release to "our unrealized nation," and, through it, to all civilization. [10]

He was not feeling his way in a vacuum. A widening interest in group dynamics, a series of attempts at breaching social restraints, a recognition of the power of the unconscious (even the collective unconscious), along with a rejection of all systems (even Systems of Rejection) and a new fascination with Eastern and related Western mysticism and visionary intoxication—all were components of the New Irrationalism that accompanied the end of American innocence prior to the onslaught of the twenties. These ideas surfaced in intellectual and artistic centers best represented by the Chicago Renaissance and by Greenwich Village in its heyday. With a mystical certitude that the universe is conscious, Jig Cook came from Chicago to New York by way of Provincetown.

5   George Cram Cook in Greenwich Village. (Berg Collection, New York Public Library)

Driven by Dionysian obsession, Cook became the originator and the undisputed leader of the earliest theatre group on record to have consciously operated on the principle of collectivity. As part of the Provincetown Players he, along with the other members, served in the functions of the group, as actor, designer, director, playwright, stagehand, and manager.

The concept   In an essay on "Collective Creation," Theodore Shank observed that emphasis on the "cooperation of a creative collective," sometimes in combination with group living, is a response "to the fragmentation of established society," and as such, an essential distinguishing characteristic of the alternative or new theater.[11] Social fragmentation and individual alienation from society were not, of course, products exclusively of the 1960s; the idea that survival is possible only within a group structure has emerged in previous generations that have felt threatened by a cult of individualism—a salient characteristic of Western civilization that has been carried ad absurdum in the United States.

The creation of literature, painting, and sculpture is an individual act. Such a creative act does not depend on personal contact, although the work will be perceived directly, without interpreters. By contrast, the composer reaches for personal contact by providing a game plan or rite for a group that will create the work in performance. Until modern times this contact was quite direct, because many composers wrote for specific musicians who often performed under their leadership. The playwright's position throughout history was more often like a composer's than that of a writer or visual artist. Sophocles, Lope de Vega, Shakespeare, Molière, Goldoni, Goethe, and Tom Robertson each wrote for specific actors (frequently including themselves), specific theatres and audiences.

The systematic separation of composers and playwrights from performers was a disruptive phenomenon, as was the interposition of separate conductors and directors. Hector Berlioz was the first virtuoso conductor to lead various orchestras in performances of other composers' music; Georg II of Sachs-Meiningen became the first director to oversee theatrical performances without having written or acted in plays. These nineteenth-century developments logically extended the division of labor to artistic processes, making mass production possible. Thus, both a need and an opportunity for specialization came into being; theatre artists had a wider choice of more narrowly defined functions. This severing of musical and theatrical conception from actual performance was accompanied by a heightened romantic adulation of the creative artist's isolation as an exalted, redeeming condition. Parallels between the artist and the creator of the universe abounded; those who thought in this vein ranged from Goethe through Nietzsche to Ibsen.

After worship of the individual reached its apogee, the realization came that loneliness was a liability as well as an asset; biological and social determinism revealed absolute freedom as illusory, and the need for personal interaction in a social milieu was once again recognized. The study of the individual and of society thus converged about the time of the First World War. A rising interest in philanthropy and social work, in progressive education, and in the role of creative play, all showed concern with "interpersonal relations," a term first used in 1912.[12] The last disciplines to deal with this new insight—and the most fundamental in producing consequences—were philosophy and theology. Heidegger and Jaspers began elaboration of Kierkegaard's views into what later became the school of Existentialism; Jacob Levy Moreno and Martin Buber recognized the need for personal "encounter" in religion. Almost simultaneously, Moreno applied this concept to theatre and to psychotherapy, sensing that all three fields relate to the human need for psychic catharsis that depends on some sort of coming together, and finding apparent corroboration of his perception in Aristotle's *Poetics*.[13]

Theoretical acknowledgment of human interaction, indeed, interdependence, as a building block of a healthy, creative society went hand in hand with pioneering practice. Thus, Neva Boyd's pathfinding research at Chicago's Hull House, which related the effect of playground activity on the formation of creative minds, parallelled Maria Montessori's discoveries, some of which were known and applied by progressive American intellectuals before the Great War. Likewise, the emergence in 1915 of the Provincetown Players—a theatre collective, emphasizing spontaneous, amateur group creativity as an organic reaction to individual frustrations—was an autonomous manifestation of the spirit of the times. It had great affinity with Moreno who defined spontaneity in religious, theatrical, and medical terms as the key to creativity and mental health. Another parallel was provided by a group of American artists and critics who, with their eyes fixed on dadaism, advocated "a childlike spontaneity in the arts, cultivating the naivete and the unself-consciousness of folk-expression." [14]

It appears then, that a variety of existential concepts bearing on artistic and social creativity, self-expression, spontaneity, game and role playing, encounter, and group existence had all been articulated, even briefly experimented with, before the war was over. Though not unrelated to European trends, these phenomena were quite characteristic of the end of American innocence. (For a quarter century—between the early twenties and the late forties—powers inherent in these ideas were inhibited.) Upon the conclusion of the Second World War there was a period of gestation of about ten years before these forces were unleashed—coalescing, especially in the United States, into a mass movement with the energy of a tidal wave. The emphasis on sensitivity and mystic awareness, on ritual and myth, on opposition to institutions and traditions, on experience as an end in itself, and on organic, undominated collectives resulted in a "movement that was part science, part religion, part reason, part ecstasy, part therapy, part entertainment, part personnel management, and part alternative life-style." [15] Theatre or, perhaps more precisely, "the theatrical," emerged as a prominent expression of this movement.

Connections between the early, pre-1920 temblors and the recent tidal wave of collectivity and spontaneity are indirect, but traceable. Moreno revived his *Stegreiftheater* (Wien, 1921) as Impromptu Theatre (New York, 1931), with a probable impact on founders of the Group Theatre whose theatre he shared. From the playground creativity theories of Neva Boyd, Viola Spolin developed a game-centered actor training technique for the Federal Theatre (1935–1939) and beyond. Paul Sills, who employed his mother's system at the Compass (1956) and at the Second City (1959), is largely responsible for an upsurge of improvisatory theatre that took advantage of, and helped spread, certain techniques of sensitivity training. Although Buber's *I and Thou* was first published in English in 1937, it had little effect until its second American edition, twenty years later. Nor did Existentialism become a household word until Sartre's name made it so in the fifties. Research into group dynamics and group therapy, pioneered by Moreno and others in the thirties, intensified with the establishment in 1947 of the National Training Laboratory for Group Development. The explosion into mass movement occurred when Michael Murphy, primed for mysticism by a visit to an Indian ashram, founded the Esalen Center—a Western bridgehead for the human potential movement—in 1962. About the same time, the Living Theatre's communal approach to mythmaking attracted world-wide attention when, because of harrassment by the Internal Revenue Service, it went on a tour of Europe —and the revolution of encounterculture was joined.[16]

Jig Cook and J. L. Moreno were among the precursors of this revolution. They recognized how crucial trust and interdependence, spontaneity and release were in an increasingly mechanized and impersonal world; correctly identified those elements as building blocks of the theatrical creative process, and therefore focused on theatre as a uniquely suited laboratory of human emotions within the intimate group, and eventually beyond its boundaries.

It is, however, necessary to distinguish between creative collaboration, the existence of which in the theatre has rarely been questioned, and collective creation, a more recent and essentially different phenomenon. So little is documented about the collaboration, for instance, of Sophocles with his performers, we cannot know to what extent *hypokriti* and *choreutai* may have contributed to the shaping of his texts. We do know that he was eligible for the prize, they were not. Of Molière we know from *L'Impromptu de Ver-*

sailles that he determined who spoke and did what and when. But we can also tell that he tailored roles to members of the company. Examples abound both to show interdependence and to demonstrate that each creative collaboration had a leader, though, of course, not always the playwright. In a theatre collective, on the other hand, by definition no one person dominates the creative process, but all participate more or less equally and freely. To the extent that final artistic choices are made by one person more than by others, these are supposedly expressions of the group's will. By such definition Joseph Chaikin's "passive stubbornness" [17] rendered the Open Theatre a collective, whereas no matter how fully Robert Wilson helps his performers shed their habitual defenses[18] and utilizes their unique contributions, he retains final control of his operas.

When the traditional collaborative process was disrupted by the separation of playwright from performers and by the interposition of the director, the road in America (the most advanced mass-production economy) led to the production company, that most alienating form of theatrical organization. Production companies result from the producers' efforts to avoid long-term commitments in favor of exploiting fads of popular taste for the largest possible profit. Consequently, a producer assembles diverse elements of theatre— the empty shell of a building, the mechanical and electrical equipment, the individual artists and artisans—only for one particular production of unpredictable duration. Rehearsed for, at most, a month, such a "company" gives preview performances and officially "opens" only if the auguries predict fiscal success. How often they actually perform depends entirely on how consistently spectators fill the house, and that in turn depends on "presell" campaigns and reviewers' opinions. Whether a production runs for a week or a year, the artistic consequences are equally harmful. Because the sole motive is, as P. T. Barnum more than once put it, to "get them into the tent" and derive profit, artists are pressed into following the line of least resistance, repeating whatever seemed to attract the audience last time. The most successful clichés tend to be perpetuated, there being neither opportunity nor motive for the artists to develop insights into scripts, into themselves, into one another, or into their art. Without such insights there cannot exist that organic ambiance in which everyone is as concerned with the perfection of every part of the production as ones' own, which has been the traditional keystone of artistic excellence in the theatre.[19] There must exist, instead, a sense of isolation and alienation for each participant in this mechanical approach to bringing about the theatrical event. Most profoundly affected by this alienation is, naturally, the actor: denied organic contact with the human as well as the verbal and visual environment in which he is called upon to function, he must either exist in total isolation, or throw himself completely on the spectators' mercy and pander to their taste.

Because the production company was and is primarily an American phenomenon, the first and strongest (though by no means only) reaction against it, as well as the search for a *group* structure that would provide a sense of belonging for all participants in the creative process, manifested itself in the United States. Just as relevant, it was here that the cult of individualism has been carried the farthest. An important factor determining the time of the first such attempt at group participation was the sudden urgency with which, after the turn of the century, the arts clamored for new and significant forms, and, in America, for singularly American forms. So it happened that a heterogeneous group of strong individuals, each of whom had achieved something in a field other than theatre ("the arts fertilize each other"),[20] "formed a 'constellation' which later became a movement. Only in this highly concentrated atmosphere could such totally different people join in a common activity. It seemed that the very incompatibility of character, origins, and attitudes which existed among [them] created the tension which gave, to this fortuitous group of people from all points of the compass, its unified dynamic force."[21] They were seeking spontaneous, amateur, creative "*group* expression, complete within the group"[22] that would serve as leavening in the larger community to "take the place of the common religious purpose and passion"[23] in restoring peace and health to the collective consciousness.

All "groups" are not, of course, "collectives." Differences between groups of collaborating artists on the one hand and creative collectives on the other range from the subtle to the drastic; even collectives centered on identical type of leadership vary greatly, though the leader's personality and manner of functioning is a major factor influencing the style and operation of even the most democratic collective. Togetherness and gang solidarity can be achieved in leader-led groups, as in true collectives. The former are more likely to resemble a mass movement, as characterized by Eric Hoffer in *The True Believer* (New York: Harper Bros, 1951) in which participants seek to shed their individuality, in order to be absorbed into a group identity. A group composed of such weak persons either forms around or produces a powerful leader, because the members respond eagerly to strong leadership.

Individuals with a strong sense of personal worth or accomplishment on the other hand, seek a group that will enhance their own identity; they oppose strong and lasting leadership. Sufficient numbers of powerful individuals may bring about a group with rotating leadership. In any case, appropriate leaders will emerge, corresponding to the nature of participants and to the cohesive forces of the particular group. The very existence of one "group" may enhance a strong leader's creative powers, by mere availability or by actively contributing to the process; but the creativity of a "collective" (i.e., a group of strong individuals bent on fulfillment rather than self-annihilation) follows the curve of a geometrical progression instead of an arithmetical one. Consequently the collective generates a highly charged creative atmosphere, promising increased potential for discoveries and breakthroughs; concomitantly, its life expectancy will be shorter.

Because a heterogeneous theatre collective composed of strong individuals is by nature more experimental than a homogeneous leader-led group, it ought to prepare itself for dissolution or transformation after a relatively brief, explosively fertile period of activity. Like other experiments—scientific, social, or artistic—it can survive only while accusing established usage. If and when it succeeds, in the sense that its results and discoveries are accepted and become normative, its life as an accusation is in fact over: it becomes part of established usage.[24] During the experiment's lifetime the collective is alive with risk and ambiguity, as it affords release from established usage. The breakthrough accomplished, risk and ambiguity vanish along with intoxicating freedom; release gives way to restraint as novelty turns into cliché.[25]

Earnest little experimental collectives "with an inner need to dramatize and *see* what is within . . . have something precious, each unique while the *group* lasts, and not to be regretted when time scatters it." It is such groups that keep "theatre free of . . . Institutions which Church and State could use to other ends." A collective is not an institution: that is one source of its vitality. But a collective threatens to turn into an institution when its rebellion is accepted by way of popular success or by the emergence of numerous disciples. The former development means that its revolutionary approach has become established usage, to be accused by a new generation of rebels. But the second danger is more insidious, for when what was once a small young group receives a sizeable influx of disciples, the newcomers tend to form a separate generation within the collective, unable to fit the founders' mould completely. Consequently the collective will have become an institution, probably against its will, and almost certainly without recognizing that fact. And the need for little theatre collectives is *"not* to seek Institutionalism, but to throw [their] heart into an eternally wonderful present, so that theatre becomes *mystagogia* [initiation into mystery cult], the chance for individuals to see and shape worlds of their own, yet not try to *sell* them." [26] The pitfall of becoming an institution results from failure to recognize when work has gone beyond the experimental stage; has ceased to be creative; has rendered the leaven stale and the process regurgitative. An experimental collective's only assurance of longevity lies in its failure to create established usage.

The event   Upon their marriage in 1913, Jig Cook and Susan Glaspell honeymooned on Cape Cod, where they rented (and eventually bought) a cottage. As did many other rebellious intellectuals and artists, they lived alternately in the small fishermen's village of Provincetown and in the cheap walk-up flats of Greenwich Village, finding both climates congenial. Gradually a lively assortment of summer regulars were added to Provincetown's population of Portuguese fishermen and New England farmers: Mabel Dodge, the "Madame Recamier of Greenwich Village," appeared with her entourage; others who flocked to the Cape in ever larger numbers included writers and poets; painters of tradition, as Charles Webster Hawthorne's Modern Art School, and of the avant garde; social movers and shakers like Margaret Sanger, Big Bill Haywood, and Emma Goldman.[27]

As described in the previous chapter, it was here that Jig's "beloved community" seemed to materialize in the summer of 1915. In his search for a new Athens that would enrich America as a new force for human accomplishment, he had tested several groups, some with purely theoretical aims, others with practical goals.[28] More than the specific social, intellectual, or artistic focus of these groups, Cook apparently considered their manner of functioning crucial; none measured up to his standards of excellence as sufficiently "organic" or radical. The gathering this summer seemed different: the talented elite of that epoch's counterculture vibrated with energy in renewal and with unbridled imagination. Labor organizers, painters, poets, social dropouts, patrons of the arts, anarchists, suffragettes, sculptors, philosophers, and journalists—they were united in their revulsion against the burgeoning rat race, against the shoddy artistic and social endeavors of the time.[29]

The actual emergence of the Provincetown Players was "an organic thing like a plant growing." [30] Hutchins Hapgood has best captured and analyzed the atmosphere and the ideas that led from brainstorming to communal creativity:

> It was before America had gone into the War; the contagion of conflict with its old eloquence had hardly touched us. Before the year had passed everyone I knew had lost something: he saw his work with less conviction; he was shaken in his belief in any ideas he may have had; he was disturbed, rudderless, relatively hopeless. And this moral situation seemed to affect the relations between men and women—it seemed to be an element in the dissolution of many marriages; individuals losing hope also lost their union.
>
> So we poured out our disappointment and our skepticism upon ourselves, and our virtue suffered. We were less admirable human beings; responsibility had little meaning, relatively, to our imaginations.

Consequently, the summer colony fairly burst with individuals who functioned as "poison-distributing" centers: "Suspicion, bitterness, disappointment, and a certain instinct to destroy each other's personalities were revealed. In my own case. . . . I went around analyzing my friends to the point of their ultimate discomfiture, and the fact that I did it to myself didn't mitigate the offense." But, Hapgood went on, that soil of despair became receptive to the seeds of healing through spontaneous creativity:

> But in every situation that is markedly hopeless and destructive there is either the greater possibility or the actual presence of a reconstructive agency. Out of the outcast comes the new hope, out of the gutter the enkindling spirit of religious yearning, out of the moral death of the factories the energetic hope of labor organizations.
>
> And in the midst of the poison of Provincetown came the little movement which resulted in the Provincetown Players.
>
> The group who started the Provincetown Players in the summer of 1915, was composed of men and women who were really more free in all ways than many elements of Greenwich Village—free from violence and prejudice, either radical or conservative. To this relative freedom had been added, since the beginning of the War, a more conscious desire to lead their own lives and *to express themselves unconventionally*. They

felt the thought and emotion of the day was anaemic and rudderless and they felt their own souls were too.

Recalling the motivation some twenty-five years after the events, Hapgood echoed Cook's utterance on the regenerative power of collective consciousness:

> It seemed to them that, if a simple beginning of an answer to these questions was made, a step might be taken in the solution of our bigger social problems, in our deeper self-consciousness: that without self-knowledge and honest reconsideration our political and economic effort is useless. In other words, without a truthful effort for a deeper culture, all our large social purposes are impossible. The Provincetown movement was, in part, a social effort to live again—spiritually, to recover from discouragement and disappointment, *to be free of the poison of self and the poison of the world.*[31]

Their roots as widely spread as to draw nourishment from Plato's *Republic* and Thoreau's "Civil Disobedience"; Marx and Veblen, Nietzsche and Freud; Montessori and the communitarian movement—members of this intensely creative group were greatly moved by the rarified atmosphere of that "great Provincetown summer." [32] Private affairs seemed expressive of public ones, creativity in and of itself was valued highly, and in mutual support of one another's effort, competition was apparently suspended. Life promised to be "all of a piece, work not separate from play," all geared to creation, for "it would be better to be destroyed than not to create one's own beauty." [33]

> So these few persons at Provincetown. . . . were inspired with a desire to be truthful to their simple human lives, to ignore, if possible, the big tumult and machine and get hold of some simple convictions which would stand the test of their own experience. They felt the need of rejecting everything, even the Systems of Rejection, and of living as intimately and truthfully as they could; and, if possible, they wanted to express the simple truth of their lives and experience by writing, staging, and acting their own plays.[34]

Their feeling and desires led to the intuitive discovery that the medium best suited to communal and playful creative effort was theatre. Ultimately Jig made an improbable attempt to mold a tribe, form "a laboratory of human emotions" [35] in which each member is ready to sacrifice for each other and for the common goal. In the theatre, after all, a variety of inspired talent needs to unite in producing an ephemeral work of art; though the union survives only in memory, the immediacy of performance immortalizes it. Moreover, Hapgood thought, their efforts "unconsciously took the form of the play, rather than some other form, because of the lifelessness of the theatre: here was something obviously needing the breath of life." [36] In the process, Susan Glaspell observed, "drawn together by the thing we really were, we were as a new family; we lent each other money, worried through illnesses. . . . talked about our work. Each could be himself, that was perhaps the real thing we did for one another." [37] Communal creation, and communal living, brought about "something of a Renaissance. The pall hanging over us was lifted and the rays of hope and life penetrated our lives." [38]

Even though many details are blurred, the events recounted speak clearly: as the yeast of that first summer's encounter started working, ideas and plays grew in number and aspiration. Quantitative changes led to qualitative ones: the Provincetown Players organized themselves and moved on to New York with a mission. The members who formed the collective were all skilled and experienced in creative arenas other than the theatre. They knew that none of the old social institutions, none of the familiar arts could bring redemption: distinction achieved in their respective fields had left them dissatisfied. This dissatisfaction united them in action; innocence in theatre sustained their communal feeling and their faith in redemption, which they expected in this, for them virgin, arena. As innocence faded, by natural selection on the one hand and by conscious effort on the other, the group fell apart, for without professional ambition in theatre the acquisition of skills became destructive of their communal relationship—it separated, rather than united, the members. And thus, little by little, the thing they created began to die.

On the wharf, the beloved community of life givers apparently succeeded: Jig's powers of inspiration, his visionary leadership, received sufficient support from strong disparate individuals with such diverse goals as Zorach and Nordfeldt the artists, Hapgood the anarchist, Kemp the hobo poet, Reed and Eastman the revolutionaries, Mary Vorse and Wilbur Steele the writers, a couple of college professors, and others. As this organic community was overwhelmed with creative effort, habitual defenses crumbled, tensions relaxed, hatreds and rivalries were transmuted, channeled into the projects that grew out of so many encounters, and produced healing. The rewards seemed abundant: not only Mabel and Jack, Susan and Jig, Neith and Hutch—whose lives were

6 Jack Reed and Louise Bryant in Provincetown. (Author's collection)

directly affected—but the entire collective triumphed in the cleansing that occurred, in the pleasures that were derived.

Certainly, the participants looked upon their discovery of O'Neill during the second summer as the natural climax, the organic bloom of their creative urge: he was the most tangible theatrical talent emerging from the process. His appearance undoubtedly accounted for the paradoxical nature of the Players' existence: O'Neill's personal achievement was regarded as living proof of the theory of group creativity; his accomplishment was expected to further the other members' inspiration and purpose, yet his personal ambition was not to be contained by the collective, which consequently had to be repeatedly subordinated to him. It was O'Neill's idea to name the group's New York playhouse The Playwright's Theatre, he was the one author who never actively supervised productions of his plays (as the constitution demanded), and yet his scripts were the greatest lift the Players ever received, and they came to expect and to depend upon them. The seeds of destruction ripened in the supreme bloom of the collective.

It developed that the group spirit could not be transplanted to New York: collective methods proved unworkable; the free-and-easy, boozy atmosphere of cohabitation suited to the Cape did not obtain in the Village where, despite the much-touted bohemianism, people had jobs, schedules, and deadlines. Cook's constant reference to Dionysos and his triple province was unable to work its magic there. Whether the rural surrounding or the flexibility provided by leisure was more important, in Provincetown communal drinking *was* at the root of much group thought, and *did* organically lead to cathartic play production. Unless original members of the collective, especially Jig, saw the partying as a driving force of creativity, the repeated emphases all accounts place on "Provincetown parties" in Macdougal Street—first at Nanni Bailey's Samovar, later and of more importance at "Christine's" above the playhouse—remain unexplained. And so does the sober socialist Floyd Dell's scathing denunciation of "the Walpurgis night mob" over which Jig "ruled, with the aid of a giant punchbowl!" [39]

Although Jig was the group's epicenter, he received indispensable theoretical support (distinct from the organizational backing of Jack Reed) from Hutchins Hapgood. The philosophical anarchist was a firm believer in the organic group as a tool of redemption where formal and elaborate organizations have failed. In New York, when the formation of committees threatened the communal aspect of operation, Hapgood reminded his fellow Players

7   Ida Rauh and Max Eastman. European Photo, in Churchill, *The Improper Bohemians.*

that when the collective was formed they felt "the further removed from professionalism it could be left the better the social and artistic results." He asserted that "this Provincetown impulse is an expression of what is stirring in other fields to-day. It is *group* expression, complete within the group. The Community Center movement, demanding the building of social forms from within is an analogous phenomenon." [40]

The leadership   That Cook remained the centripetal force, the cohesive element of the collective—"The Grace of God is glue!" [41]—has never been questioned. The difficulty lies in defining his method of leadership. For his *chief* contribution to the group was not as actor, not as playwright, not even as director. Most Players assumed these roles in rotation, and Jig is not remembered as exceptionally talented or effective in them. Nor did he fully assume the usual responsibilities of a producer: the Provincetown Players collectively exercised those. His main function remained that of a catalyst like, more recently, Ellen Stewart (La Mama), though unlike her, he was also a participant in all aspects of production and management. For a circumscription of his role the parlance of social and religious movements holds more promise than that of theatre. "Founder," the only term applicable to Cook that has theatrical past, may serve as a bridge toward more comprehensive definitions: Jig is recalled as a spiritual leader, an inspired seer, a charismatic prophet. Other descriptions, more current today, offer themselves: a teacher-healer, therapist-facilitator, even guru.

As the sustainer of the Provincetown Players, Cook served in the manner of a spiritual inebriate who identifies himself with the creative act itself. He attacked every task with gusto, with intoxicating enthusiasm, with self-annihilating commitment, without distinguishing between small and large issues. A true believer in the group's healing power for participating individuals, he was nevertheless a personality not to be submerged. He proved quite capable of turning against a decision collectively taken, for what he thought was the collective good; in other words he functioned as a dictator as well as a prophet. A man of vision, he was determined—and usually able—to convert others; apt to engender release in others without being able to reap its benefits himself.

Repeatedly he jolted talented friends and associates who were temporarily stymied into creative projects or entire careers through minimal, spontaneous action. In her autobiography, the poet Eunice Tietjens describes Jig's presence as somber, "yet lit at moments with an almost cosmic gaiety." She recounts the moment during a party at Floyd and Margery Dell's Chicago apartment, which is etched in her memory as her spiritual rebirth: "It was George Cook who said the thing that released me, as the right thing said at the right moment has the power to do. 'You have been too much preoccupied with technique and little things,' he said. 'Your technique is good enough, but you are afraid. Take a great theme and attack it boldly. You will manage.' " [42]

Similarly, in a narrative already cited, Susan Glaspell relates how, in the summer of 1916, Jig ordered her to write a play that he had already announced for the next bill. She did not know how, she protested. " 'Nonsense,' said Jig. 'You've got a stage, haven't you?' " [43] And Glaspell was well into her best one-act play, *Trifles*. She became the group's most accomplished playwright next to O'Neill, and also one of its finest actors.

Jig continued to boost or launch careers, both in the Provincetown collective and beyond its limits. In New York, a few seasons later, a budding writer also received his inspiration from Cook. Mike Gold told of his first encounter with Jig:

> I had a play. It was a very naive one-act play—they produced it later. I walked in, and there, bent over a table in the clubroom, was a strange and impressive person . . . . twisting a lock of hair on his forehead.
>
> I sat down. Minutes passed and he didn't say a word. Then he began talking like a character in a Dostoievsky novel. I had never heard such talk before. He talked as though he had known me for years. He glanced through the play, and I told him what I was trying to do. I was an assistant truck driver for the Adams Express Company, but he made me feel like a god! He told *me* what I was trying to do. It was what he did for everyone, great, small, dumb or literate.[44]

After a few one-acts with the Provincetown group, Gold went on to write full-length scripts and was associated with The Experimental Theatre, Inc., the New Playwrights' Theatre, and the Federal Theatre Project—parallel to his nontheatrical writing and editing career.

In another instance, Cook's spontaneous solution to a casting need recruited James Light into the Players; after a few roles, he took broader responsibilities with the group, left the Columbia School of Architecture, became director of The Playwright's Theatre during Jig's absence in 1919-20, and had a long productive career in the theatre before becoming dean of the dramatic faculty at the New School.

Jig's effect upon the work of O'Neill is both too pervasive and too subtle to be documented point by point. But his recurring talk of a "theatre of pure space," of the powers of tribal magic must be added to the sources for *The Emperor Jones*. It is hardly accidental that the *The Emperor* took shape while Cook "took a break" from the playhouse: both he and O'Neill spent their time on the Cape, and when they came back, *The Emperor* was ready. Moreover, in the pure space Jig willed into existence and provided for that play with the dome he constructed over strenuous objection, the collective reached its climax. Nor did Cook's inspirational power upon O'Neill end there, not even with his departure for Greece, or from life. The final creative union of these two Nietzschean possessed ones was *Lazarus Laughed:* the Dithyramb of the Western hemisphere that Jig talked and wrote about, the one that he willed O'Neill to do.[45]

The power to activate creativity in others was Jig's essential contribution to the Provincetown Players' collective. He seemed to lack skills to carry out his own prophetic visions except through inspiring group execution.[46] His genius, then, did not reside in direct productivity, but in his capacity to stimulate others to collective creative ferment.

This talent was generally not easily assessed, and then apparently only by those whose personality or vision admitted of the tragic sense of life. Floyd Dell had been one of Cook's oldest and most intimate friends, yet publicly evaluating Jig, he failed to grasp the essence of the admired man's aura, defiantly denying the validity of tragic vision. According to Dell, in O'Neill's company (whose one-act plays he described as "superb and beautiful romanticizations and glorifications and justifications of Failure") Jig had abandoned socialism to become the disciple of "another gospel, of the beauty of failure," according to which "Failure would be Success." Dell was unwilling or unable to understand what lay under the surface of such a credo, or to tolerate the life style predicated upon it. He had been a little theatre pioneer and a model bohemian, which "had been great fun, but I could not make a religion of it, as George seemed bent upon doing." Nevertheless, Dell sensed that Jig's "vision it was that held . . . together in some kind of Homeric peace and amity" the Provincetown Players, and that only he "could have presided over this chaos and kept it from spontaneous combustion." Going one step farther, Dell glimpsed that Jig's "life was . . . hardly within his own control; it was as if he were being driven on by a demon to some unknown goal," even that Cook "had wanted to be one of the creators of the world's future." [47] But Dell would not admit (or perhaps lacked the distance to see), that Jig's indeed magnificent failure, viewed in perspective, constitutes a tragic breakthrough.

Hutchins Hapgood sensed that. In the *New Republic,* he took Dell to task for this "painful injustice" to Cook. Recognizing that Dell regarded Jig a failure partly "because Cook himself felt that he had failed," Hapgood saw far beyond that. He pointed out that

Cook produced the Provincetown Players, an organization which made a real contribution to American life; nor was this his only achievement. Those who had the privilege of knowing him well realized that Cook possessed not only an original temperament, but one which expressed itself in many ways and contributed to the success of many careers. Only a truly great book could have influenced as many lives as did Cook's remarkable personality. Although it is true that Jig Cook felt himself a failure, it was not because his books were unsuccessful: he felt the inevitable disappointment of not being able to realize his visions.[48]

In his autobiography, Hapgood ramified this assessment of Cook's personality by observing that

it was perhaps in conversation that the creative quality of Jig's imagination was most entrancingly manifested. When four or six of us, or perhaps seven or eight, were sitting with our flagon of red wine, or slowly sipped whisky, and the gentle excitement was suffused through Jig's being, then picturable ideas flowed like rippling streams from his laughing mouth. His eyes danced with the joy of ideas becoming poetic realities. The fact that he never paused an instant in quick transitions, from one flashing thought or impulse to the next, made his talk a living reality.[49].

Others had lined up on both sides of the argument. Max Eastman confessed, he could not stand Cook's "zeal for social creativeness." [50] Edna Kenton asserted, "His was the single spirit dedicated wholly to the experiment," and she probably found the motivation for that stance when she wrote "He had never fitted into modern American life, and had long since surrendered any hope of adaptation to his age. He knew the ancient Greek temper and our native Indian spirit far better than the signatures of our own time. . . ." [51] The leadership of Jig Cook has been labeled Dionysian, Machiavellian, and dilettante. Erstwhile members of the collective recall his appetite for creative work with awe, fright, and admiration. Undoubtedly, his personality, which was "too generous for his own good as an artist," [52] and his manner of leadership, which "whipped and hell-raised and praised and prayed," [53] were indispensable to the spontaneous genesis, the tumultuous existence, and to the noble nemesis of the Provincetown Players: "we shall give this theatre we love, a good death." [54] The creative chaos in which the collective existed for seven years brought a transformation into American theatre. It inevitably ripened the seeds of the group's destruction as well. The creative contradictions present in Jig himself, characterized the Players also.

The deeper level   A theatrical innovator or revolutionary is usually evaluated on the basis of theories he promulgated, principles he practiced, or both. Jig Cook's theories survive in fragments only—embodied in Province-town circulars,[55] in personal letters and reminiscences excerpted from his scattered manuscripts by Susan Glaspell. They are visionary, contradictory, at times incoherent in their fragmentation. Whatever theory Jig did not imme-diately put into practice, poured forth unrecorded during all-night brainstorms and parties, and was only occasionally jotted down on cocktail napkins. His personal practice, as far as it can be separated from that of the group he sustained, was inconsistent, and as often as not at odds with his theory. In essence, his method of leadership consisted of turning his twin vices, carous-ing and logorrhea, into magnificent, manifold, long-lasting inspiration.

For Cook, the group was not a means of creating theatre, but instead theatre became the ideal means of creating a group. Consequently of para-mount importance was the organic relationship *between* process and product: resulting works of art he considered significant only as momentarily surviving agents of communal health. As such, under optimum conditions a work might enable its creators to engender in an audience the duplicate of the very healing process that benefited them. Here lies the seminal value of Jig's ideas and the Provincetown Players' attempt at putting them into practice. Group dy-namics, social regeneration through art, and emphasis on process has proven a durable potion, which, injected into the veins of American theatre, released its active substance gradually, delivering a cumulative effect.

After Cook sailed for Greece in March 1922, the Players folded with the end of the "interim." But his infectious ideas continued, as fermenting agents catalyzing artistic and political radicals, to mature through an attempt (by James Light and Eleanor Fitzgerald in 1925) to return to the old Prov-incetown ideals, through the New Playwrights' Theatre (1926) and the Group Theatre (1930), through the Federal Theatre Project (1935–1939) to drive roots deeper and farther Off-Broadway and off-Off-Broadway, and to emerge triumphantly from coast to coast, after the example set by the Living Theatre in the turmoil of the sixties.

Nor is this the total picture. As psychoanalysis was one of the impulses in the Players' first performances, so group psychotherapy—having matured in parallel fashion—contributed to the emergence of theatre collectives.

About the time when the Provincetown Players experimented with works of art that grew from creative group dynamics, a young psychiatrist in Vienna detected apparent parallels between God-to-man and man-to-man relation-ships, and perceived them as the root of social adjustment problems as well as solutions. Jacob Levy Moreno (today best known as the inventor of two therapeutic modalities, psychodrama and sociometry) was working with the "I-Thou" concept before Martin Buber formulated it, and began applying it to psychotherapy. Unable to consider "interpersonal relations" apart from worship, he concluded that both must take the form of spontaneous personal encounter. Creativity, Moreno insisted, inevitably springs from spontaneity and is thus both precondition for, and proof of, the occurrence of true encounter, in which he thought he had discovered the fulcrum of living.[56]

As the center of active life, encounter had to be Moreno's postulated starting point for all therapy, art, and religion. Although his observations stemmed from psychoanalytic insights in conflict with Freud, they prompted theological expression first: Moreno formulated concepts for a "religion of encounter." [57] However, it was in theatre, as the only familiar social form that combined all essential ingredients, that Moreno found the effective source of profoundly spontaneous and creative personal encounter. His ideal Theatre of Spontaneity differed from his practical one in making no provision for spectators: its main stage and several auxiliary stages were surrounded by seating for "main and auxiliary actors" only, thus erasing all but temporary distinctions between performers and observers.[58]

As did Moreno, Jig Cook believed that the power of "subconscious invention" can be actively fortified by reaching a "deep level" at which "each soul can or does connect with each other" to achieve "passionate oneness" through "rhythmic ecstasy." [59] His second full-length play, which he intended to make "the imaginative impulse to the new religion," dramatized the thesis that psychic phenomena can help solve human problems. The action of *The Spring* is based on the premise that a higher order of knowledge than is now thought possible can be achieved through actively seeking and encouraging unconscious (extrasensory) communication between the living, rather than attempting to derive it from the dead, and that in the resulting exalted states of consciousness entire minds can and will absorb one another.

Moreno's gospel—for he considered it nothing less—rested on three assumptions: first, that spontaneity/creativity is "a propelling force of human progress," second, that "faith in our fellowmen's intentions" is necessary, and third, that on these two axioms "a superdynamic community" can be based. These convictions were developed in what Moreno calls his "axionormative period"—1911 to 1923—and they appear to be articulated equivalents of Jig Cook's passionate requirements of the beloved community of life givers. Moreno, moreover, "visualized the healer as a spontaneous-creative protagonist in the midst of the group" much as "persons like Jesus, Buddha, Socrates, and Gandhi were doctors and healers" [60]—surely, the model Jig aspired to realize. It is with reference to that model that he is best understood.

Yet another ideological kinship between Cook and Moreno is manifest in their common belief in the necessity of bridging the Dionysian and the Apollinian. Unlike Cook, however, Moreno seldom touched alcohol and was firmly opposed to the use of drugs to enhance creativity. Nor did Moreno believe, as Cook seems to have,

> that everything which happens in a group is salutary; . . . He also did not subscribe to the idea of Rousseau—apparently espoused by Cook— that spontaneity is a sort of "holy" aspect of human behavior, that all that is necessary is to uncover "the noble savage" in man; he thought spontaneity was something inherent in the human organism at birth but that it could become badly misshapen in the course of a person's life so as to turn pathological as in mental disturbance or illness, or in criminality, or just weakened so it could not be relied upon. Hence he introduced the apparently contradictory notion of "spontaneity train- ing" and said mankind would fear spontaneity as long as it was beyond control, as it fears fire for the same reason.[61]

Parallels between Cook's fragmentary statements and Moreno's quasi- scientific writing are probably no more than coincidences in the development of human understanding of relations between society and creativity. But if the creative process is best understood in its own peculiar atmosphere, then the intimation must be allowed that the minds of these two men shared a source of inspiration. Cook sailed for Greece and Moreno for America, but their spirit commingled in their followers: it can be detected in ideals of several groups of artists, from the Group Theatre to the Living Theatre.

Admittedly or tacitly, therapy—or at least encounter—has been the sought-after goal of many important "alternative" theatre groups of the 1960s and early 1970s. The intended range varies: some groups are content with a healing process affecting performers only; some use nontraditional means to produce a more or less traditional infectious empathy in their audience; others, not satisfied with engulfing spectators with emotions hurled from a distance—as has been done since Thespis—attempt to make their audience into physical participants as well; and yet others aim for nothing less than a violent confrontation (perhaps encounter's antagonistic equivalent?) with at times accidental, and even unwilling audiences, or with quite remote non-spectators: the national or world community.

One can hardly contemplate parallels between psychodrama and healing-oriented collective creation without venturing some conclusions about the nature and, perhaps religious, role of theatre in society. If psychodrama and theatre collectives are both based on the assumption that human existence becomes complete only in the group, whereas artists and intellectuals who create alone believe that the strongest stand by themselves, then theatre must relate more closely to the primordial, nonrationalistic elements in man. Whether those, or overlaid civilized aspects are "better" is immaterial. And, as Eric Bentley concluded, if psychodramatic therapy "improves" rather than duplicates reality, and is therefore at one remove from life, it follows that—unless, presumably, deliberately "applied"—"dramatic art is at two removes from it." [62] Where does that leave collective creation? At how many removes —or at none at all? Is all distinction between art and therapy one of degree rather than of kind? Can esthetic relationships (such as tension and harmony) that exist between process and product have a healing property as well?

For centuries, theatre critics and literary theoreticians followed Horace's standards regarding tragedy rather than Aristotle's, perhaps because, being more rigid, they seemed more comprehensible. But must one really discard Aristotle as inscrutable or as the scourge of modern man, simply because what are presumably lecture notes of his pupils provide ambiguous answers to twentieth-century questions? Perhaps the gap between the medical interpretation of catharsis (as advanced by Bernays) and the esthetic one (superbly presented by Else) is not as unbridgeable as it seems. [63]

Accepting Else's arguments that (1) "purification" and not "purgation" is meant by catharsis, that (2) the concern is with a *process* that goes forward *throughout* the play and within its structure (rather than with an *end-product* delivered *by* it), that (3) it is addressed to a normal rather than a pathological assembly, and that (4) therefore it is not of therapeutic intent, I am still disposed to argue that a bridge exists between the "structural-objective concept of the *Poetics* and the therapeutic-subjective concept of the *Politics*." [64] For I believe that because of its Dionysian religious origin the Greek tragic theatre did aim for civic purification in the sense in which similar collective functions are served by Native American tribal ceremonies, Christian Communion, and mid-century encounter or sensitivity rituals. If mind and body are an organic unit—as the Greeks believed and as we begin to understand anew—then it should not seem shocking that Dionysos' gift, release, is obtained through suffering in the theatre[65] as it is in psychotherapy or in religious redemption. Nor did Dionysian ecstasy aim to abolish the structure from which it offered release: it was accepted as temporary suspension that enabled man and community to continue living within the structure. Such "release" is akin to "salvation through grace" in Christian theology. The interaction of accusing law and redeeming gospel offers the sinner grace without repudiating the structure of law for continued existence. A parallel insight in the political arena proclaims: "Freedom thrives in the interstices of authority." [66]

More than the other arts, theatre depends on social interaction. Hence it provides, like group psychotherapy and communally practiced religion, satisfying freedoms within a social structure. Collective theatre, aiming to make spectators participants, is an extreme version, particularly suited to times of communal crisis. That was the potent message of Jig Cook, Dionysos in 1915.

The initiator of the Provincetown experiment, the yeast of this pioneer creative community, and thus the spiritual begetter of modern theatre collectives, Jig Cook has been dead for over fifty years. He is virtually unknown except to performers and spectators of *Suppressed Desires,* the first one-act comedy he wrote with Susan Glaspell. The founder and sustainer—"in the way of Atlas" [67]—of the Provincetown Players is buried in Delphi under a stone removed from Apollo's temple in tribute to him as a promoter of the modern revival of the Panhellenic Theatre Festivals that, except for unfortunate political developments in 1966, were to blossom into an international celebration of the 2,500th anniversary of Thespis' first recorded victory.

From Cape Cod
to Greenwich Village

*"...the Provincetown Theatre, ...was the
dramatic wing of revolutionary Bohemia around
the time of the First World War, ..."*
Michael Folsom, *"Introduction,"*
MIKE GOLD: A LITERARY ANTHOLOGY

1   The first works collectively created by the amorphous group
as it coalesced into the Provincetown Players were seen as spontaneous, using
no fixed stage (in fact alternating performance space with spectator space),
and satirizing topics intimately relevant to members.

One might speculate if similarly therapeutic evenings would have followed, or if indeed the ferment "might have ended there" had it not been
for the restless Dionysian zeal of Jig Cook. But he had considered theatre
an indispensable part of his cherished dream city and wanted the now demonstrated benefit extended to a wider but just as intimately participating audience community. That is largely why the first two plays *were* performed
again, in the fishhouse on Mary Vorse's wharf. All next winter, Cook carried
the idea of transplanting their "laboratory of human emotions" [1] to the teem-
ing and seething Village. His inspiration did not prove strong enough to effect
that, but did lead to a second, better organized, and more productive sum-
ber season for the collective.

In 1916 the wharf was given a sufficient overhaul to attract would-be
subscribers, who—to foster the feeling that they were part of the group—
were offered "Associate Memberships." The constitution, not to be drafted
until mid-September, made that designation permanent. [2] Hardly anything is
known of producing practices during these two summers. Although the tradition that Robert Edmond Jones "made scenery from sofa cushions" was

shown as unsupported by the scanty evidence, he very likely had a hand in staging the first two plays at the Hapgoods.[3] This second summer, too, the professional actors Frederic Burt and E. J. Ballantine joined the group on its wharf and helped introduce O'Neill to the world. Ballantine once recalled having been in charge of the first production of *Bound East for Cardiff*, but he erred so much as to cast doubt on his entire testimony.[4] How much O'Neill had to do with staging the play is not known, but the second piece on that bill was certainly not directed by its author, Louise Bryant, but by an artist couple with an original vision, William and Marguerite Zorach. *The Game* succeeded primarily through the Egyptian bas-relief style they imposed upon it. On the other hand, *Enemies* was written, produced, and acted by Hutchins Hapgood and his wife, Neith Boyce.

Evidence of the group process was provided by Jig Cook's daughter, Nilla, who was eight years old at the time and who, because of her own involvement in and continued inspiration from the Provincetown Players, remembered vividly. She had wanted to watch the adults at play, but was frustrated in part, because:

> Rehearsals were held in the living rooms of one or another of the four houses, and.... [o]nly those taking part in a given section of a play were present. This not only saved the others time, but allowed the amateurs to feel at home, to relax, to enjoy it, to live it as really their own. This system of putting sections together at the very end was carried to such extremes that I really had no idea what was in the rest of Mother Carey's Chickens. I had never seen the others rehearse. . . .[5]

Buoyed by the response of the summer colony, by discovery of a major theatrical talent in O'Neill, and also by the apparent reliability of their non-system of spontaneous collective creativity, in September the Players made ready to take their experiment to New York. They felt that such a task required formal structure, or a rite of initiation, and addressed both philosophical and organizational principles—often indistinguishable—at a series of membership meetings. Of the concepts discernible in the records of these meetings, two became the source of later conflicts within the group. One, the primacy of script and writer within the work of the collective, was manifest in O'Neill's effective insistence on naming the group's New York headquarters The Playwright's Theatre. Second, the view of amateurism as a stepping

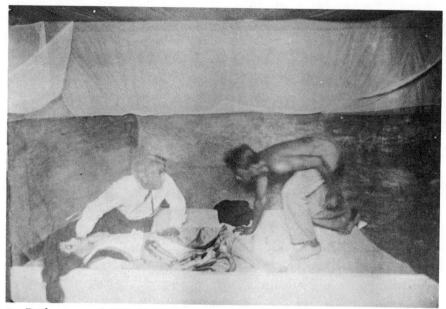

8 Performance of O'Neill's *Thirst* by the Provincetown Players on Lewis Wharf, summer of 1916. Left to right: Louise Bryant, Jig Cook, Eugene O'Neill. This was the largest role O'Neill ever played. (Yale Collection of American Literature)

stone to professionalism, was reflected in the defeated proposal, that would have named the playhouse-to-be "Try-Out Theatre." [6]

In the process of organization the group agreed that scripts would not be barred from production even if submitted by nonmembers, but that to be an active member one must "write, act, produce, or donate labor," and also be chosen by a majority. After a constitution was adopted, Reed submitted a series of significant resolutions. Accepted "as the sentiment of the meeting," [7] these resolutions articulated the basic philosophy and intended operational principles of the Provincetown Players.

Reed's preamble declares that the group's purpose is to encourage the creation of American dramas regardless of commercial value. The first few articles define play selection as collective activity exercised democratically: any member may recommend scripts for production and may refuse to read any play, but only a majority of members has the right to accept or reject a script in the name of the Provincetown Players.

Most important, the resolutions turn each playwright into his own director. They prescribe that no play be accepted unless the author is willing personally to superintend its staging. The plan of production stipulates that once a script is chosen for production, (1) the Provincetown Players' resources are placed at the author's disposal, (2) the author is given a list of nonactive members (the active members presumably knew each other), whereupon (3) he selects and directs the cast, producing the play according to his own ideas.[8]

The resolutions' final section was added to assure that the Players would remain a living, creative, democratic organism; it provided for dropping "active members" who had not participated in six consecutive bills or who in the majority's opinion had lost interest in the group's goals.

Because only members would have access to tickets, the important issue of membership classification became the main burden of the constitution, along with the description of officers and their duties. Two categories other than active membership were established: as mentioned, associate members were defined as season subscribers, while club members, upon payment of initiation fees and dues, were entitled to buy single tickets for individual bills.

Not surprisingly, the principles embodied in the resolutions and the constitution express the group's rebellion against Broadway commercialism, against the practice of tampering with the dramatists' creative work. Significantly, these very principles became the cause of friction and strife that eventually led to the group's dissolution. The crux of the Provincetown Players' theory was in fact put to the test during the first New York season and failed, though that was not discernible at that time.

2   In the old brownstone at 139 Macdougal Street, the collective's New York operation began in September 1916 amid utter chaos. That was by no means contrary to the Players' professed devotion to spontaneity, nor to the Greenwich Village environment that had been the home base of most founding members of the group.

Village life flowed from clubs, bookshops, theatres, and craftstores to bars, tearooms, and restaurants.[9] Social focus had recently shifted from lower Fifth Avenue to Macdougal Street just south of Washington Square. The central role of the Brevoort Hotel (on the corner of Fifth Avenue and Eighth Street) and of the elitist "A" Club (3 Fifth Avenue) as chief gathering places of the New World's Quartier Latin had eroded. This function was gradually taken over by the Liberal Club (137 Macdougal) and by "Polly's" (officially, the Greenwich Village Inn) in the basement immediately below.

When this establishment moved to the north side of West Fourth Street, the basement was occupied by the Dutch Oven. But a loyal clientele followed Polly Holladay and her constant companion, Hyppolite ("bourgeois pigs!") Havel, on whom O'Neill's Hugo Kalmar was later modeled. If Villagers (among them Provincetowners) wanted more privacy, they found it at Nanni Bailey's teashop, called, after its imposing functional centerpiece, "The Samovar," or at sculptor Edith Unger's "Mad Hatter." Both were located along Fourth Street toward Sixth Avenue, the former in a loft (148W), the latter appropriately advertised as being "Down the Rabbit Hatch" (150W). The Hell Hole, where Dorothy Day often accompanied Eugene O'Neill on his regular drunks, and where women were allowed to smoke in public, was located on the southeast corner of West Fourth and Sixth Avenue.

The geographical center of the Village was, of course, Washington Square. Adjacent to this landmark was the Washington Square Bookshop, operated in succession by the Boni brothers, Frank Shay, and Egmont Arens. It was first located one floor above the Liberal Club, and later at 17 W. Eighth. There was also Ira Remsen's studio and Nickolas Muray's darkroom at 131 and 129 Macdougal; *The Masses's* editorial offices in Christopher Street; and the furniture store at 17 E. Eighth operated by Sidney Powell. But it was primarily the eating and drinking establishments that defined the Provincetown Players' territory. Foremost among these was "Christine's," which began as the Provincetowners' own club and soon became a popular meeting place for local artists and artisans.

Originally situated on the third floor of 139 Macdougal Street, above the Players' first New York theatre (eyewitnesses do not distinguish this location from a later one at 123 West Third), "Christine's" was imbued with special atmospheric qualities that reflected the taste of its beloved owner—Christine Ell—and attracted the art crowd. The main room was spacious, roughly square in shape, and dark. Two long dusty windows faced the street; what natural light managed to penetrate the room was quickly absorbed by the reddish brown walls. Besides the entrance, there were two other doors: one led to a smaller dining room, another to the kitchen. Malcolm Cowley also recalls a hall bedroom at front. Saltcellars, pepper shakers, and sugar bowls graced the tables which, along with the chairs, had been painted black. A large clock encased in a wooden frame hung over the "imitation marble" mantle; O'Neill is said to have turned back its hands in a dramatic appeal to Agnes Boulton.[10]

"Christine's" was a place where Players could retreat in solitude, or mingle with nonmembers; there images and philosophies were tested and argued. Aside from providing a congenial atmosphere and renowned home-cooked meals, the "earth mother" Christine herself contributed greatly to the attraction of the club. She dispensed unsolicited solace and chastisement, and became the heroine of countless stories, some convivial, others hair-raising. Except for opening-night parties, when Jig presided over the punchbowl, Christine remained the dominant personality here. Agnes Boulton remembered that "the glory of her hair, skin, body and spirit, and the no less warming and wise sound of her laughter was the magnet that drew to her tables less vital and more frustrated souls." [11]

In this milieu, many of the Players lived in the cheap and picturesque rooming houses that stretched from Milligan Place to Bleecker Street and from Bedford Street to Washington Mews. Jack Reed rented at 42 Washington Square South, O'Neill at 38; the Nordfeldts at 135 Macdougal, Jig and Susan in Milligan Place, Edna St. Vincent Millay at 139 Waverly Place (the only street in New York that crossed itself). And when the collective anchored its creative work here, the area and its inhabitants became the breeding ground for production concepts, onstage and backstage personnel, potential subscribers, and sidewalk critics. Members and observers never belonged to a homogeneous subgroup: not all were literati, visual artists, or political animals. But these sorts of individuals mingled freely with school teachers, craftsmen, homemakers, merchants, and "street-people" in and around the pre-Victorian brownstone that became The Playwright's Theatre.

This environment and these conditions perhaps explain many of the changes their producing practices underwent. One collective process after another proved unfeasible. The first to go was play selection. Originally, meetings were held twice a week; scripts were to be read at one, discussed at the next, announced after a secret ballot as accepted or rejected at a third. However, some plays accepted were never staged, "others heaved into sight without the sanction of a formal vote." [12] After a few weeks the number of meetings was cut by half; open critique was eliminated. The friction that resulted from open discussion of each other's work probably caused this deletion as much as the amount of time members were able (or willing) to give to the mandated procedure. This is implied by the simultaneous resolution encouraging members to talk informally in the time between the meetings at which scripts were read and the ones at which they were voted upon.[13] Even this procedure soon proved untenable.

A perhaps related decision specifically permitted active members to assist an author in staging his work by making suggestions during early dress rehearsals. Thus diluting the playwrights' dominance over the creative process would seem to have strengthened the communal spirit. But by the fourth bill of the season, this aspect of collectivism was relinquished; the measure's failure may have been due to its not having gone far enough: offering criticism by the time the production is almost ready may have accomplished too little, too late.

Soon too, the first potential exception from the playwright's working as his own director surfaced, ironically in the very person of Jack Reed, the man who wrote the rule. His *Silver Spangles* was scheduled for the first bill while he was in the hospital, and arrangements were made to have it produced by proxy.[14] As it happened, the play was never staged.

The Provincetown Players now wrestled with the problem of transferring their theories about the creative process into practice. They were also beset by more mundane affairs: organization, finance, labor, and law. Not until September 19, were they certain *where* The Playwright's Theatre would be located, and what rent and construction costs they would encur. Although their first circular had already been written, it could not be printed without announcing an address or an opening date. Thus, the subscription campaign had to be delayed; whatever rehearsing there was, took place in members' nearby homes. When at last 139 Macdougal Street was leased from Mrs. Belardi, Jig was in jubilant spirits.[15] But his troubles were by no means over. To begin with, the Players' new home was not yet a theatre.

The ground floor of this typical Manhattan brownstone was twenty-four feet wide and eighty-one feet deep; it included three rooms and a narrow hall which ran the full length of the building.[16] A first reviewer described the interior as "the exact size of two parlours, dining room and butler's pantry."[17] The dining room probably housed the stage, and the pantry may be identified with the "2'6" reserved in the back for storage of scenery."[18]

Conversion of this second-class dwelling into a playhouse was accomplished by a group that included Cook and Donald Corley (an architect described as one of Jig's closest disciples), the painters Demuth, Nordfeldt, Zorach, and Joseph Lewis Weyrich among others. It is not clear what the construction entailed and when it occurred, only that it was expensive, disruptive, and threatened trouble with the law. After referring to a double door that "provided the demarcation between stage and auditorium," Deutsch and Hanau relate that "early in that first season the Players decided to do

away with the irksome wall between front and back parlours." [19] Susan Glaspell remembers, however, that the work was done *before* the season began,
for when she arrived in New York, her "first glimpse of Jig" was in the
midst of building materials, as he negotiated with "an impersonal-looking
person from the building department" who was accompanied by an Irish policeman. Moreover, Glaspell believed that Jig was using up $200 (four-fifths
of the "capital from Provincetown") for "putting in a steel girder," so a
partition could be torn out and a stage provided.[20]

 Removal of this wall was the most important, though not the only, alteration executed by the Provincetowners. The way was now cleared for the
installation of a stage and seating. According to Kenton, the stage measured
fourteen by ten and one-half feet;[21] Stella Hanau remembered it as a make-
shift affair, "Merely a build up [*sic*] part of the rear room to increase visi-
bility." [22] Similarly, the audience was accommodated in a stopgap fashion.
Deutsch and Hanau describe the seats as "tiered like a grandstand, dangerous
of approach, and unparalleled for discomfort." [23] Sheaffer adds that they
were "like circus seats" and were "bare planking, narrow strip backing seats
[*sic*]." [24] As for the surroundings, "the walls were kalsomined the smokiest
of deep greys, and the proscenium arch ... was painted ... vermillion and
gold, violet and blue." [25] The first curtain has been variously described as
having been "common bag canvas," "limp," and of the "cheapest cloth."
Thus, esthetically it was "neither decorative nor opaque," but rather "trans-
parent and disillusioning." [26]

 As construction continued at 139 Macdougal Street, the circular was at
last printed. In it Jig confirmed the spontaneous origins of the group, re-
affirmed its opposition to "submitting to the commercial manager's interpretation of public taste" and its dedication to "experiment with a stage of
extremely simple resources." [27] He continued:

 All these plays were written, staged, and acted by members of the group;
and the most expensive production cost less than thirteen dollars. The
sale of seats by subscription of associate members paid for the installation of stage, seats, electric lights, curtain, costumes, and scenery.

 The success of the experiment, the interest of the audiences, and
above all the enthusiasm manifested by the group itself, persuaded the
Provincetown Players to continue their activities in New York during
the winter....

> The *Players'* Theatre remains, as it began, a stage of free dramatic
> experiment in the true amateur spirit.
>
> In order to make possible the experiment, a sufficient audience must
> in a sense be guaranteed for the season. The *Provincetown Players* are
> organized as a club in order to avoid the legal disabilities consequent
> on establishing a public theater.

Despite Cook's enthusiastic plea for financial and moral support, the subscription campaign was still faltering. The Provincetown Players could hardly
have started operation but for two momentous, last minute developments.
First, the Liberal Club, which occupied the adjoining premises of 137 Macdougal Street, above Polly's restaurant, sold them its entire theatrical equipment ("valued at $80.–") for forty dollars on condition of being allowed
occasional use of the theatre.[28] Second, Reed—almost single handedly—acquired an audience by inducing the New York Stage Society to have each of
its 200 members subscribe for two associate memberships. It probably helped
that Emilie (Mrs. Norman) Hapgood, the society's president, was the sister-
in-law of one of Jig's first allies, Hutchins Hapgood.[29] She, along with Robert Edmond Jones, another staunch supporter of the Provincetowners, had
been instrumental in the Harlem productions of Ridgley Torrance's plays.
In any case, the Stage Society subscriptions were more important than admitted
by any previous writer and probably saved the Provincetowners' enterprise
from stillbirth. According to Edna Kenton, only a misprint turned the first
season's 450 subscribers into 550 in the Players' Spring 1918 circular.[30]
Consequently, the contrast Deutsch and Hanau draw between those evenings
when the Stage Society's 400 were in attendance (to the "terror and embar-
rassment" of the Players), and those performances given for "friends and
fellow torchbearers," must be considered baseless.[31] The point is, first, that
the proportion between Stage Society's subscribers and "friends and fellow
torchbearers" was *not* 400 to 150, but 400 to 50, and second, that there
could not have been "evenings of" torchbearers—rather, these intimate supporters were likely lost among the Stage Society's perhaps more formidable
crowd.

Little wonder, then, that many Players regarded it as a miracle when
The Playwright's Theatre's first season finally began in early November.
O'Neill's *Bound East for Cardiff* was first on the program. The otherwise
withdrawn author helped erect a set very much like the one used in Province-

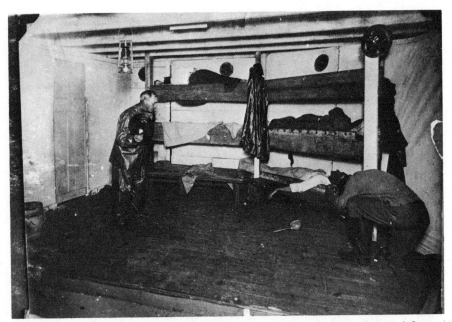

9   The Provincetown Players' New York production of *Bound East for Cardiff*,
1916. Left to right: Jig Cook (in lower berth), William Stuart, Frank Shay,
B. J. O. Nordfeldt, Harry Kemp, E. J. Ballantine, Donald Corley (in upper berth).
(Courtesy of Mrs. B. J. O. Nordfeldt)

town.[32] There is a record of the cast, but nothing is known about rehearsals
or performances. The evening's second revival, Louis Bryant's *The Game*,
was again produced by the Zorachs, who, according to the playbill attempted
"to synthesize decoration, costume, speech and action into one mood. Starting from the idea that the play is symbolic rather than representative of life,
the Zorachs have designed the decoration to suggest rather than portray; the
speech and action of the players being used as the plastic element in the
whole unified convention." [33]

A new piece by Floyd Dell completed the bill. *King Arthur's Socks*[34] is
a mockery of modern manners, superimposed on ancient legend. Although
Dell had ample experience with amateur theatricals, troublesome rehearsals
forced him to give up direction. According to the playbill the professional
actor, Teddy Ballantine, took over the reins.

For the second bill, Reed—still in the hospital—was unable to supervise
production of the revival of his comedy, *Freedom;* his function was assumed
by Arthur Hohl of the Washington Square Players. Each of the two remain-

ing plays on the bill was written by a couple; the Hapgoods and the Cooks supervised, and acted in revivals of their plays, *Enemies* and *Suppressed Desires.*[35]

A new O'Neill script, *Before Breakfast,* opened the third bill. In this Strindbergian mono-drama the author played the loquacious shrew's offstage husband of whom only "a sensitive hand with slender fingers" is seen. O'Neill disliked being his own regisseur, and although never shy to express his views on staging (in written directions, and, later, orally) shunned rehearsals whenever possible. This time his director was an unsolicited volunteer who could not be refused: his father, James O'Neill. The veteran actor, famed for thousands of appearances as the Count of Monte Cristo, had seen some of his son's plays produced in Macdougal Street. In the case of *Before Breakfast,* "Mary Pyne had the sense to do everything James O'Neill told her—grandiloquent gestures, melodramatic inflections and all. . . . As soon as he had gone, his son redirected her from the beginning to end and, . . . mumbled about his father's 'old fogey' approach." Eugene O'Neill later commented that his father "made some . . . suggestions on the acting . . . I didn't agree with, but also some I thought were fine and which the actors were glad to follow." [36]

For the first two bills the crucial production principle of the Players (making the playwright his own director) has been honored in the breach more than in the observance. In the case of the second play on the third bill, the rule was endangered in a different manner: the author, Alfred Kreymborg, was quite willing to produce *Lima Beans,* but the Provincetowners were unwilling to go along. Members voted to reject his "fantastic treatment of commonplace themes set to a stylized rhythm"—it seemed unconventional beyond their taste. Only when Reed threatened to resign, charging violation of the group's ideals, was Kreymborg's poetic playlet placed on the bill, on condition that the author "undertake to produce the play himself, with some actors outside the personnel, no one of whom believed he could impersonate the lines." Kreymborg later described his rehearsals as consisting primarily of "taking out a pencil and beating time" while the actors (fellow poets Mina Loy and William Carlos Williams joined by William Zorach) read their lines.[37] The result, according to Edna Kenton, was excellent: "two poets and a poet-painter moved and spoke in a series of rhythms so carefully worked out . . . that it seemed spontaneous play." [38]

During the third bill then (which ran the first weekend of December), the Provincetown Players continued to operate contrary to their distinctive theory of collective creativity. Some functions originally reserved for the whole group were now delegated to committees. First a revising committee was formed; its members (also known as "the consultants" in deference to protests against committees) were available to any author whose script was judged to need revision. A scenic committee and a production committee were also established, and some members vociferously objected. Hutchins Hapgood, who had already given an "address on the death which lurked in organization" when the subscription campaign got underway, again raised his voice "to prevent the gradually [*sic*] usurping of the selection of plays by any person or 'committee' within the group." [39]

The fourth bill had a play each by Nordfeldt and Saxe Commins (both now lost), and one by John Chapin Mosher; the bill was discouraging before it opened: activity and morale were both deteriorating. Already the Players wearied of obstacles in their way, and the great variety of scripts presented serious production problems. Too many sets had to be built, too many scenes changed, too many characters created, too many lines memorized. Frayed nerves resulted: actors, designers, directors, and particularly playwrights, grew insult-prone; rehearsals had to be held behind doors closed to members not involved in the particular production, and thus ended the recently introduced practice of active members proffering staging improvements to the playwright-director.[40] Had all this led to outstanding works, there would have been little danger. But bills were getting worse—scripts as well as performances declined in quality. Even Jig Cook, eternal enthusiast and constant source of inspiration, was discouraged; in a letter to his wife he complained about a depressing flow of triangle plays; concluding, "We have hardly any good, interesting plays and if we don't get them we're going to peter out." [41]

On the fifth bill, in addition to O'Neill's weakest one-act, *Fog*, there was another script by Floyd Dell. The Dell offering set off another explosion, according to Louise Bryant, because the playwright gave *A Long Time Ago* to an outsider "unconditionally to produce . . . and he wants to do it in his own way, not Ida's or Teddy's. . . ." [42] Dell blamed Cook: "when I was too busy to stage manage a play of mine, he turned it over to some new enthusiast with lunatic ideas, who put the actors on stilts, so that nothing could be heard except *clump, thump, bump!*" [43] Even though by not assuming responsibility for staging, and then waiting until the final dress rehearsal to protest, Dell was partly at fault, he saw the events as a denial of the group concept to which the Players were dedicated, and resigned his membership.

Gradually the Provincetowners grew aware of the harm caused by chaos, and recognized the need for competent direction. The group spirit was failing, adherence to the originally sacred principles of democratic selection and collective production under the playwright's supervision became the exception rather than the rule, and the incoming plays were increasingly bad. At this juncture, a competent director appeared, and the ice of amateurism, already cracking, split further open.

Ever since she had graduated from Stanford University as a drama major, Nina Moise wanted to act, but she had mostly ended up directing. Upon arrival in New York after a brief term with a stock company in Massachusetts, she was told that the Provincetown Players needed a director, and a meeting with Jig Cook in a Village restaurant was arranged. He promptly took her to the theatre, where David Pinski's *A Dollar* was in rehearsal on the diminutive stage. It appeared "quite evident that the actors didn't have much idea what to do or how to do it. . . . they had a very definite idea that anything one did in life could be done on the stage. If people stood in front of each other and bumped each other in a room, why not do it on the stage—which was exactly what they were doing." Nina Moise was almost immediately put in charge of the rehearsal. Soon, Neith Boyce, author of the second play on the bill approached her with a similar request. Finally, Susan Glaspell asked her to "please help Jig direct *Pan* in which he was playing with Edna James. I suggested he might prefer doing it himself, but she assured me he didn't and I discovered after the first rehearsal that he needed a little help. At any rate, I ended by directing that entire bill." [44]

Moise could not singlehandedly turn the performances professional even had she wished, yet her expert control made an impression on the Players, and they were never the same thereafter. Significantly, plans for next season were first broached as soon as the first bill she produced had run its course. Although answers were not promptly forthcoming, a number of questions affecting the group's future were raised at the meeting of January 31. [45] The following bill (the season's seventh) was also entirely in the newcomer's hands; it was the Players' protest against the war, included plays (now lost) by Mike Gold and Rita Wellman, along with O'Neill's *The Sniper,* and was considered an improvement over previous bills.

As a result of the measure of order she introduced into the Players' production methods, Moise's hold on the group grew stronger. At the next meeting she was asked to head the production committee; the architect, Donald Corley, was simultaneously chosen to chair the scenic committee. [46] The selection of Moise and Corley, both of whom favored a professional approach, to chairs of committees charged with practical matters amounted to an admission that the principle of group production was untenable. Before long, each of the three plays on the eighth bill was directed by a professional, Frederic Burt, Margaret Wycherley, and Nina Moise, respectively. It proved an "extraordinarily good bill" despite a weak first script, *Prodigal Son* by Harry Kemp, which had been included for lack of anything better to round out Pendleton King's suspenseful *Cocaine* and Susan Glaspell's witty *The People*.[47]

Perhaps coincidentally, a Provincetown performance was for the first time reviewed by the *New York Tribune*'s prestigious drama critic, Heywood Broun, who was apparently favorably disposed toward the group. Earlier, having read the Provincetown scripts published by Frank Shay, he concluded that the Players were running a "most efficient experimental theatre," and confessed to being particularly impressed with the work of O'Neill and Glaspell. Now, although he did not enjoy all three scripts nor all performances, Broun was amicably inclined, observing that "the setting and lighting of the plays in the tiny theatre is interesting and attractive." [48] He closed his review with the wish that the Provincetowners would find the larger theatre they were seeking for the next season, one they did not acquire until the following year.

It was during the run of this program, last but for the Review Bill, that Jacques Copeau visited The Playwright's Theatre. He judged both the plays and the performances to have been mediocre on the whole, but was "touched to the depth of his soul" by Susan Glaspell's acting in her own play, *The People*. Copeau confessed that "the simplicity of her presence" made him understand as no previous experience has "the importance of relinquishing current theatre technique, even at the price of a prolonged period of groping." [49]

The Players closed their first New York season with a stormy meeting at which—though details of the clash are difficult to discern from the minutes—matters affecting the life or death of the collective were thrashed out. This is indicated both by numerous resignations during and in the wake of the session, and by the decision to add to the paid staff a production director.[50] (Originally only the president and the secretary were paid, and in December 1916 Louis Ell was added as stage manager.) It is not clear if the production director was immediately chosen, but next season's circular named

Nina Moise—a logical promotion from the chair of the production committee.

The conflict between religious devotion to spontaneous collective theatre on the one hand, and relentless practicality on the other, was apparently coming to a head already. Some Provincetowners believed the creative community ought to operate rationally, but Jig Cook insisted that Dionysian exaltation was of the essence. He often volunteered to intoxicate the group with his own drunkenness, whether spiritual, alcoholic, or both. And intoxicate he did: without his inspiration the achievement of the Provincetown Players is unimaginable, but his enthusiasm offered no assurance of smooth sailing.

Growth

and Consequences

"We have no ambition to go uptown...."
PROVINCETOWN PLAYERS' CIRCULAR, *Spring 1917*
"Just for a week. Or maybe six plays for two weeks."
Ida Rauh

1   Evaluated as both a failure and a success, the Provincetown Players' first New York season (1916–17), had, in fact, been both. The group had tried in vain to shake up Broadway, had not attracted many outstanding dramatists, and had not entirely lived up to its proclaimed principles of collective creation and purely amateur operation. On the other hand, it had kept its head above water as a noncommercial theatre, had made a go of gathering spectators around American playwrights for whose development that support was essential, had gained the critics' attention without providing free passes, and had struck a financial balance, albeit precarious.

That year's controversial activities prefigured an ordeal of change that was to unfold throughout the Players' stormy career. Although they never stopped experimenting, they came increasingly to draw on experienced directors and to classify their efforts as successes or failures according to standards usually applied to commercial productions.[1] Yet, the core of the group continued to cling to the ideal of inspired and innocent spontaneity.

Operations were modified in subsequent seasons as the Players' composition changed ever more rapidly, with founding members becoming inactive and new recruits joining. A major element in this transformation was the growing number of paid personnel. At first only administrators were remunerated: Jig Cook and Margaret Nordfeldt, whose election to president and secretary-treasurer had occurred at the end of the second Cape Cod summer, received twenty-five and eighteen dollars a week, respectively.[2] Even before the official season began in November, President Cook was feverishly establishing the theatre: he recruited members, drafted circulars and sought out printers, acquired headquarters and equipment, supervised construction, worried about scripts and subscribers, and fanned the flames of inspiration. Secretary Nordfeldt, meanwhile, kept minutes and membership records, dispensed tickets or supervised box-office volunteers, answered the telephone and paid the bills; she was fully appreciated only after her departure at the end of the season: "we never found her equal," wrote Edna Kenton.[3]

It was not long before the need for a nonadministrative employee became clear. On December 3, 1916, Louis Ell, the ever present carpenter and fix-it man, scene technician, and occasional actor, whose wife Christine later presided over the club rooms, was hired as stage manager.[4] He was paid what the secretary-treasurer received, eighteen dollars a week. Experiences during the rest of that season primed the Players for further additions to the paid staff.

Shaken by the recent crises, the remaining members of the collective closed ranks in the spring of 1917, and began preparations for the fall before dispersing for the summer. They released a circular that looked to the future, confidently concluding that "Our audiences this year have proved that the thing we want to do is a thing others want to see done." They reasserted the Players' raison d'être: "We have a theatre because we want to do our own thing in our own way. We have no ambition to go uptown and become a 'real theatre.' We believe that hard work done in the play spirit for the pure joy of doing it, is bound to have a freshness not found in the commercial theatre."[5]

In the fall Petra Wold replaced Margaret Nordfeldt, and a fourth employee was added: Nina Moise, as production director. A modified circular, which both Cook and Kenton believed was the best the group ever issued, articulated the direction The Playwright's Theatre hoped to take:

We mean to go on giving artists of the theatre—playwrights, actors, coaches [i.e., directors], designers of set and costume—a chance to work out their ideas in freedom. . . . There are rich backgrounds of life behind the people of this group. They were accustomed to deal imaginatively with life long before they came together and began to focus their creative impulse upon their untrammelled little stage. There are more interesting things latent in their minds than anything they have yet written or acted. Their hope is greater than it was in the beginning.

We are still not afraid to fail in things worth trying. This season too shall be an adventure. We will let this theatre die before we let it become another voice of mediocrity. If any writers in this country— already of our group or still to be attracted to it—are capable of bringing down fire from heaven to the stage, we are here to receive and help.[6]

Glaspell and Cook, Rauh and O'Neill, Christine and Louis Ell, Edna Kenton and Nina Moise formed the Players' core for this second New York season (1917–18). Around them veteran members rallied when they returned to participate in productions. Wilbur Steele, Hutchinson Collins, Justus Sheffield, Ira Remsen, Rita Wellman, Otto Liveright, and Frank Shay did so with some regularity. Among new recruits Dorothy Upjohn, James Light, Clara Savage, Rollo Peters, Norma and Edna Millay, Charles Ellis, and Blanche Hays appeared most frequently. The varied personnel promised a rich harvest of creativity, much of it bearing the stamp of Jig's inspiration. His moves to recruit new talent of all kinds are impossible to document, for his inspired search was not systematic. Former companions agree that he was unflaggingly cajoling, coaxing, or browbeating anybody he thought had talent and sympathy with the cause into writing, acting, designing, or into finding others willing to participate in any fashion.[7] Cook approached Edgar Lee Masters, Padraic Colum, George Middleton, and Theodore Dreiser for scripts, drafted James Light and welcomed Edna Millay as actors, recruited Glenn Coleman and Lloyd Wright as designers.

Cook's and others' efforts to bring new blood were moderately successful. Some authors, encouraged to submit plays, were rebuffed by the membership, others withdrew already accepted scripts, sometimes in the last phase of rehearsals. Some novice actors never reappeared on any stage, others quickly "graduated" to commercial theatres. But the 1917–18 season in Macdougal Street was the better for each stalwart oldtimer or spirited newcomer. Among playwrights, O'Neill and Glaspell each had three plays produced; Floyd Dell returned with two scripts. On the fifth program The Playwright's Theatre featured its first full-length play: Cook's *The Athenian Women*. An influx of poets was manifest in plays by James Oppenheim, Maxwell Bodenheim, Mary Caroline Davies—and in the poignant appearance and abortive "season" of a splinter group that called itself the Other Players. In the realistic vein Mike Gold and Rita Wellman returned from the previous year, and Grace Potter and F. B. Kugelman represented new blood.

The second year's production schedule reflected lessons learned from the first, which had lasted just over twenty-one weeks. Programs usually had run five nights, Friday through Tuesday, with only the last two running six nights each and closing Wednesday. Four bills had followed at two-week intervals, then the time lapse between openings increased to three weeks. By way of contrast, the Fall 1917 circular promised subscribers "a new bill . . . every four weeks." Prices rose: memberships guaranteeing admission to all bills went from four to five dollars, single-guest tickets, from fifty to seventy-five cents.[8] The first program of the new season ran the customary five nights, but more spectators must have turned up than expected, for beginning with the second bill (November 30 to December 6) the run was extended to seven nights (Fridays through Thursdays), and that schedule was maintained. The 1917–18 season consisted of seven programs and even without a review bill outlasted the first by five weeks. Income from the seven bills amounted to $4,515, one-third of which came from guest tickets, according to the first surviving balance sheet.[9] Instead of indicating expenses, the document simply asserts, "All receipts . . . were consumed in putting on the seven bills of the season—nothing left on hand to cover Summer's rent."

The circular indicated numerous physical improvements that had been made on the premises before the onset of the second season, and others still in progress: "By the addition of cloak-room, lounging room, business office, scene-dock, and dressing rooms on the second floor we have enlarged our quarters. For comfort's sake last year's seats are being rebuilt and their number somewhat reduced." Backsupports for the benches proved a mixed blessing: they relieved backstrain on spectators but narrowed the seating surface.[10] How many of the new amenities were on the second floor remains unclear. Alfred Kreymborg recalled that the "box office was a table in the hall."[11] Moreover, there is evidence that some of the work upstairs was done later. The most colorful and sensitive Maecenas of the American cultural scene, Otto Kahn, had "attended the early Provincetown productions in the parlor at 139," but according to Mary Jane Matz "withheld an offer of help until" after The Long Voyage Home was produced in November 1917. At that time Jig apparently declined the banker's "proposal for a large subsidy" but accepted a contribution toward furnishing "a restaurant on the second floor of the theatre building." In addition to a "first check" this entailed "a monthly subsidy of forty-five dollars to cover the rent of the second floor."[12] A few months later, on March 23, 1918, Cook—having apparently changed his mind—turned to Kahn as a first step in a campaign for financial resources

10 O'Neill's *The Long Voyage Home,* as presented in New York, 1917. Left to right: Ida Rauh, Ira Remsen (on table), Jig Cook, and two unidentified men. (Yale Collection of American Literature)

to enable the Players to move into larger headquarters for their third New York season.[13]

The expanded club rooms were a vital component of the creative atmosphere. Under Christine's loving care active intellectual and emotional exchange was continuous. Among convivial gatherings, opening-night parties perhaps stood out, but any excuse served. Intimate carousing was a tradition with the group, the allegedly Greek origins of which are lost in the mist of Provincetown's dunes. The revels enhanced the amateur communal spirit, and provided release from creative tensions. They also served a deeper purpose, an essentially ritual function. Jig Cook's beloved community of life givers rested on the gospel of Dionysian ecstasy through intoxication. Some members (Dell, Moise, and Deeter) deplored the quasi-religious zeal with which Jig accompanied communal drinking, but they too appreciated the conviviality. Nor was the traditional punch easily resisted. It was called "fish house punch" not merely in honor of the group's first theatre in the fishhouse on Lewis Wharf, but also because it derived from a ritual potion of America's first men's club—the Fishing Company in the State of Schuylkill, otherwise known as the Fish House. A prerevolutionary victim, Philip Mackenzie, accurately described this potent punch: "I did not Know whether I was on Foot or Horseback. . . . Fish House Punch. . . . is most Exslent if taken in Moderation, but it is so Smoothe that One who does not know its Powers is Likely to take too much." [14]

The Players' recipe called for four quarts three-star Henessey brandy, two quarts rum, two quarts peach brandy, two quarts lemon juice, and ten pounds sugar—all to be stirred over an immense block of ice.[15] Conspicuously lacking are two quarts water, included by current bartender guides' version of this drink.

2   The Provincetown Players were still not acknowledging the critics, who in turn only occasionally showed awareness of the ambitious amateurs. Nevertheless, the group's chief playwright was penetrating public consciousness. "Who is Eugene O'Neill?" asked the *New York Times,* and in responding to its own rhetorical question it mentioned *The Long Voyage Home,* on the first bill in Macdougal Street.[16]

The dramatist's only sea play to unfold on dry land is set "in a low dive on the London water front" [17] and revolves around a crew member of the *S. S. Glencairn.* Oleson had long planned to exchange a sailor's life for that of a farmer, yet had squandered his pay after every voyage. Determined at last to break that custom, he is shanghaied. Alfred Kreymborg's narrative of a rehearsal at The Playwright's Theatre can refer to no other play:

> The stage, scarcely large enough to accommodate half a dozen actors, was set in a villainous bar-room, and sailors and longshoremen were roaring and cursing in the raciest language of the sea, cuffing and mawling one another and finally turning on one of their number and sandbagging him senseless. Were it not for the expert characterization of each individual part, . . . and the natural sequence of the amazing events of the plot, that business up there would remind one of an old Bowery melodrama.

Reflecting on the writings of Marlowe, Schiller, Balzac, and Hardy, Kreymborg satisfied himself that one only has to "strip away the poetry and characterization and the skeleton's nothing but melodrama," and concluded that he was "undoubtedly in the presence of a new dramatist. Suddenly he heard someone in the surrounding darkness roar instructions to the actors. 'Where do you think you are—at a tea-party?' the voice called derisively, and the company repeated the scene with redoubled pandemonium. When the house lights went up, Zorach pointed out that the voice belonged to a stocky woman, the stage director, Nina Moise." [18]

Two snapshots survive of this production.[19] One records the moment when Oleson's savings change owners: Freda (Ida Rauh) stands in the upstage right corner, with an effective gesture handing a bundle of bills to the Keeper (Jig Cook) who (center stage, his back to the audience) takes the money across the table with his left hand. His right is on Oleson, who is lying on the table and not, as the stage direction would have him, on the floor. The picture is full of suspense. Not so the second photograph, in which Cook stands behind the bar stage left, "tall, powerful" Driscoll in the open door upstage center, while three men surround the table—an arrangement that does not correspond to any of the play's action. Ira Remsen, who had designed, built, and painted the set, was playing Oleson.

Close the Book, Susan Glaspell's witty social satire, followed on the program. Her husband was the model for Peyton Root, the central character, a young instructor at a midwestern university founded and presided over by members of his wealthy, tradition-bound family who laud their revolutionary ancestors even as they denounce freedom of speech.[20] A nonconformist, Peyton is critical of the ways in which the university and the country are run. He is also in love with Jhansi, a girl who claims to be a gypsy by birth and a social outcast by spiritual obligation. The Root family is resigned to Peyton's marrying Jhansi, but determined to assimilate her: they give evidence that she is not a gypsy, but the orphan of a respectable couple, distantly related to the Roots. Outraged, Jhansi insists that respectability "in a material sense" is all the more reason to be a spiritual lawbreaker. With the same volume of genealogy that proved her lineage, Jhansi shows Peyton sufficient derogatory "fine print" about both their families to make the Roots command: "Close that Book!" The role of Peyton Root brought James Light, a student at Columbia University who roomed at 139 Macdougal Street with Charles Ellis, into active membership in the Players. He had some contact with the group before: attracted by the noise of hammering, he first jointed a craps game, then helped install benches. He passed by carrying a load of books when the play was being cast, and his professorial air got him the part. This coincidence was to prove a turning point in the lives of both Jimmy Light and the Province-town Players.[21]

The third script on the bill, James Oppenheim's philosophical *Night* (in stilted free verse), attempted to explore the eternal question of countless first plays: What is the Meaning of Life? Scientist, Poet, and Priest meditate on and discuss the question. As Woman enters with a dead child, Poet declares: "*You* are the secret of Life." None of the three can lift Woman's burden, or offer her consolation. Man enters in search of her, and though she rejects him at first, she cannot resist his plea that he needs her. As the play ends, Man and Woman exit together, baffling the abstract figures:

> The secret of life?
> He gives it to her, she gives it to him . . .
> But who shall tell of it? Who shall know it? [22]

During the first bill's run both John Corbin of the *Times* and Ralph Block of the *Tribune* mentioned the Provincetown Players, without directly reviewing the productions. Declaring the little theatre movement "the most interesting development of the past decade" Corbin praised "the tense and heartfelt realism of Eugene O'Neill," and "the sensitive feminine perceptions of Susan Glaspell." [23] Block had missed *The Long Voyage Home,* but extolled Glaspell's "light satire of the two current moralities." He commented on the "admirable bravery" of the "small but distinctive audiences" who visit the group's "artistically inelegant playhouse." [24] Oppenheim's piece occasioned no accolade, though the appearance of the actors in *Night* "in silhouette be-fore a lighted blue screen upon a simple mound that suggests a hilltop" [25] was noted as an "interesting experiment in presentation," for which Rollo Peters received credit.

The second bill (November 30 to December 6) combined two slight poetic plays with two somber realistic ones. Both bits of poetry were provided by Maxwell Bodenheim (one in collaboration with William Saphier); very brief fantasies populated by symbolic characters, they "mystified the sub-scribers and scared off the group from the repetition of such an adven-ture." [26] *Knotholes,* the joint work of the poets, opened the program. On a "road by a grave-yard" the Sleepy Mayor is being persuaded by the Jaunty Bricklayer to replace the wooden fence with a brick wall. At first, the Mayor objects: "But a wooden fence can be melted by rain and wind, and sun, until it is covered with an endless whisper. And the knotholes are like pauses in its whispering." [27] When his mind is changed by the Bricklayer, "Two ghosts leap lightly down from the fence." They do not want a brick wall, for the knotholes are "tiny windows of our moon-walled house," through which they can "sip a second life." So they seize the Bricklayer, "dance to and fro with him, spinning him about, like a top." They intend to "shake to life the dead child within" him, and as the curtain falls, they do. The cast included Bodenheim as the Mayor.

O'Neill's *'Ile,* one of the author's few plays previously produced by the Washington Square Players, followed. Mrs. Keeney, whose mind becomes deranged by loneliness, was effectively played by Clara Savage, recalled Nina Moise, the revival's director. She also praised Hutchinson Collins's portrayal of the Captain.[28] For the first time, Louis Ell received full credit for a set of scenery and he also played the small part of the harpooner—a double achievement of which he was proud.[29]

The store in Bodenheim's *The Gentle Furniture Shop* does business exclusively with old people; its proprietor, Life, employs two Sellers.[30] The first of these reveals that "the old people . . . can never buy what they want; they must take the chairs we give, or leave empty handed. Yet, they seem to delight in argument." The Second Furniture Seller defines their ware as "revery-chairs" just as two customers, Old Man and Old Woman, enter. It turns out that chairs are assigned to compensate for biases and mannerisms of each customer's life, and these corrective devices are accepted with quiet resignation. The playlet ends with the quick visit of a Young Girl. Unwilling to go to the shop for young people and heedless of rules and regulations of this one, she simply takes the chair of her choice. This time resignation is the lot of the Furniture Sellers. Except for its exposition, the symbolic miniature is quite effective.

It was followed by a portrayal of physical and mental squalor, by Rita Wellman, whose ironic war play, *Barbarians,* was part of the previous season. *Funiculi-Funicula* deals with an unmarried bohemian couple, living in a depressing Washington Square apartment with their three-year-old daughter.[31] Unproductive artists, they rationalize their failure by blaming circumstances that they have created. A doctor's visit opens the play; the child is seriously ill, but the couple subjects her "to all the excitements and nervous strains of an adult's life" instead of providing the sunlight, fresh air, quiet, and regularity she needs for recovery. The little girl is dying as her parents prepare to attend a masquerade party. To strains of the popular song, "Funiculi-Funicula," filtering from the floor above where the party is already in progress, they continue an aimless discussion of "work." Finally the mother discovers her daughter's death; she and her mate are overcome with the bathos of a Wertheriade. Ida Rauh and James Light played the poignant roles. Hutchinson Collins—O'Neill's friend from New London—provided contrast in the character of Doctor.

Opening on December 28, the third bill was notable for the New York acting debut of Edna St. Vincent Millay in the leading role of Floyd Dell's *The Angel Intrudes*. The entire program was mildly poetic. It began with a new script by Mike Gold, the truck driver turned playwright whom Cook had discovered the season before. *Down the Airshaft* has not been preserved, but its author recalled a tale from an East Side tenement concerning young Sammy Cohen who lost his job and is planning to try his fortune in the West.[32] His mother vainly pleads with him to stay, music comes down the airshaft, and Sammy talks of a mysterious call. According to Gold, Jig Cook's ocarina provided the tune; the playbill credits Louis Ell with the set and David Carb with direction.

Returning to The Playwright's Theatre, Dell was determined "to stand over my play and see that it was not mangled."[33] He borrowed the plot from Anatole France's 1914 novel, *Revolt des Anges,* in which the hero's guardian angel, Arcade, appears in human form but without human clothing when his ward, Maurice, is seducing a young woman, Gilberte. Provided with clothes, Arcade in due time replaces Maurice as Gilberte's lover. In the prologue to *The Angel Intrudes,* an earthbound angel encounters a policeman in Washington Square. In the play, Jimmy Pendleton is about to abduct fickle Annabelle, despite some second thoughts: he predicts, "you will fall in love with the next man you meet."[34] Jimmy's guardian angel enters, on holiday from heavenly life. Divested of wings and provided with a suit, Angel falls in love with Annabelle who promptly elopes with him instead of Jimmy.

In response to the casting call for an ingenue, "a slender little girl with red-gold hair came to the greenroom over the theatre, and read Annabelle's lines. She looked her frivolous part to perfection, and read the lines so winningly that she was at once engaged—at a salary of nothing at all, . . . She left her name and address as she was departing, and when she was gone we read the name and were puzzled, for it was 'Edna Millay.' " The Players were curious whether this aspiring actress was the poet whose "Renascence" they all knew. "And indeed it was she."[35] Vincent, as everybody soon called her, became a regular with the group. She submitted scripts for production, brought her sisters Norma and Kathleen, and her mother to the work of the theatre. For his prologue, Dell painted a backdrop of snowy Washington Square at night. In the foreground a plain fence stretched across the canvas, sturdy and slender posts alternating. On top of the fence the snow was clean, turning gradually dirty near the ground. Outlines of a pavilion were dimly visible in the grey background.[36] Dell shared the task of direction with Nina Moise, whose work he remembered fondly. The comedy was played straight, without the sort of winking at the audience common with amateurs. When Light asked how, in Angel's role, he should soar to the top of Washington Arch, he was told to stretch his arms forward above his head, then walk nimbly offstage. Dell claimed that Millay, who "generally did not take direction," was very amenable to his instructions in the part of Annabelle, because of a budding sentimental relationship.[37]

The third play of the evening, Glaspell's *The Outside,* is set on the Provincetown dunes, in an abandoned lifeguard station. In reality, that building was furnished by Mabel Dodge, and later served as O'Neill's abode. In the script, two hurt women inhabit the house: rich and eccentric Mrs. Patrick, and her local servant, Allie Mayo. The lady cannot bear signs of life, or having pretty things around. Allie was chosen for not having spoken "an unnecessary word for twenty years." [38] As the play begins, two lifeguards render first-aid to a drowned man. The women are unfriendly and uncooperative, but, regardless of Mrs. Patrick's hostile glance, Allie is moved to help in spite of herself. She brings coffee, and breaking silence gives her mistress a lesson: life wins, its negation cannot be sustained. The group's best actresses, Ida Rauh and Susan Glaspell, took the roles.

Surviving plays from the fourth bill (January 25–31) are both imaginative and provocative. Mary Caroline Davies's *The Slave With Two Faces* is an effective allegory whose title character is Life.[39] Ugly and cruel with those who fear him, he is beautiful and obedient to those unafraid. To become Life's master, one must command and not show fear. Of two Girls (Queens, according to the playbill) who wait for Life at the roadside, First Girl knows how to command, Second Girl wants to learn. As Life tortures a cringing group, he sees the expression of horror on Second Girl's face and as a result "from slave he becomes the tyrant." He flatters her into giving up her crown, then commands her to dance happily—instantly she grows fearful and becomes his slave. Second Girl is killed; returning, First Girl sees the victim's body, and is horrified for a moment. But as Life approaches, "She straightens up just in time to be her scornful self before his eyes light upon her." Thus she keeps Life her slave. Ida Rauh played Life, Blanche Hays and Dorothy Upjohn the Girls. A photograph shows stiffly presentational acting amidst a series of stylized cut-outs representing a grove of birches and bushes. Alfred Kreymborg composed and played a musical accompaniment.[40]

Grace Potter's *About Six* has not survived. Set in "A Disorderly Flat in New York," it was, according to James Light, a "snappy, witty domestic comedy." [41] The program's main attraction was the third item, Floyd Dell's comedy, *Sweet and Twenty,* in which Edna Millay once again took the lead. The author later confessed that in this piece, "without having the least idea that I was writing about myself and my new sweetheart, I presented a young man and a girl who, after they fall in love, find that He is interested chiefly in Socialism and She chiefly in dancing." Meeting in a cherry orchard, He and She discover that they are both being pressured by their families into buying a house each abhors; the houses turn out to be the same one. Determined not to waste love, they mutually confess and seal theirs with a kiss. A real-estate broker for both families interrupts with news that the house, and every detail of their married life has been arranged for them. Breaking into an oration on the evils of wedlock, the agent is arrested as a runaway from an asylum. He and She resign themselves to marriage. Again, Dell took the design and execution of the scenery into his own hands: "A single cherry-bough with blossoms painted on a flat blue-green backdrop, with the same branch repeated on the two blue-green screens that masked the sides of the scene, composed the cherry-orchard, in the center of which there was a bench; its simplicity, after the incredible fussiness into which the Provincetown Players had descended, made it very beautiful indeed." [42] A song Millay had composed to Dell's lyrics and sung, rendered the performance even more poetic. Though neither of her two performances in Macdougal Street was reviewed, they established Vincent's reputation as "the beautiful young actress at the Provincetown." [43]

Featuring the first full-length play at The Playwright's Theatre, the fifth bill opened in early March. *The Athenian Women* was Cook's attempt to mold into serious drama the subject of *Lysistrata*.[44] The published play's preface stated that Cook was convinced that Aristophanes, writing about a "feminine genius saving Greece by a sex-strike against the war" had a historical event and a real person, possibly Aspasia, in mind. The production

11   Performance of George Cram Cook's *The Athenian Women* by the Province-
town Players in New York, 1918. Extreme left, Ida Rauh; in front of the wall,
Jig Cook; others are unidentified. (Fales Library, Elmer Holmes Bobst Library,
New York University)

proved a formidable undertaking. The play required three sets, which would
have been necessary even for a program of one-acts, but to fill the cast of
over thirty characters demanded doubling by at least five actors. Among new
recruits who participated in the project, Samuel Eliot, Sidney Powell, and
Charles Ellis stood out. The Players even took this production "on tour":
The Athenian Women was presented at the Bramhall Playhouse under the
auspices of the Women's Peace Party of New York. Three surviving photographs show simple, effective settings which Heywood Broun considered "extremely attractive." [45] The critic found the performance occasionally moving,
although he thought it suffered "from the too obvious attempt to state present-
day problems in terms of Greece." A more serious defect was that the "part
of Aspasia [Ida Rauh] is so much better written and so much better played"
than that of Pericles (Jig Cook), "that the tingle of conflict is absent." Also
mentioned was Marjory Lacey-Baker who, in the role of Kallia, did "the
most distinctive work" by means of "an extraordinarily moving voice and an
easy grace and presence."

The Provincetowners did not prove equally hospitable to all recruits;

their laboratory emphasized content over form too strongly. The birth of the Other Players between the fifth and sixth bills was the most conspicuous result of the paradoxical attitude that reigned at The Playwright's Theatre. The first season's controversy around Kreymborg's *Lima Beans* has been recounted. The poet was not alone with his ideas; because the Players were unwilling either to incorporate the poetic fringe, or to reject it entirely, Cook and Kreymborg worked out a compromise of tolerance: the Other Players were launched. It solidified those who felt that the Provincetown Players were tied to the kitchen sink and thus "not sufficiently daring and elastic" to experiment radically with structure and language. Kreymborg became spokesman for the Zorachs and the Millay sisters, attracting additional rebels: Rihani who, as Kathleen Cannell had appeared in *The Game* a year and a half earlier; Louie Earl, "a doll-like English girl not unlike a Chelsea figurine"; the composer Julian Freedman; and Marjory Lacey-Baker, a friend of Nina Moise's who was remarkable for her diction.[46] A hybrid of *Others* magazine and the Provincetown Players, the Other Players presented an evening's fare at The Playwright's Theatre, at Kreymborg's "own expense," on four nights, March 18 through 21, 1918—causing a mild sensation. A second program was announced for the third week of April; what is more, a subscription for March, April, and May was offered at the price of seventy-five cents a month. The first bill of the Other Players, however, proved their last.

Manikin and Minikin, Kreymborg's static "Duologue in Bisque" began the evening. It was primarily a musical experiment: two puppetlike "aristocratic bisque figures" appeared through an oval frame on a mantelpiece; their exchange was accompanied by "an ancient clock whose tick acts as the metronome." [47] The author was particularly pleased with the harmony between Louie Earl's British and Marjory Lacey-Baker's Bostonian diction.[48] William Zorach provided the set.

Rihani's static dances were next, accompanied by the music of Grieg and Cui; she designed her own costume, Louis Ell prepared the set. Many years later, she recalled her contribution:

> I can't remember who invented the name of "static dances," possibly I did. . . . I never moved from one spot, all the movement was for the head, torso, arms and hands, as in certain Persian dances. In one dance, the Sphynx, I started standing and finished on the floor in the attitude of the title. At other times I began on the floor and rose to my knees

or to my feet. This was before Modern Dancers came along using the floor as an intrinsic element of the dance, so caused quite a lot of comment.[49]

Millay's "moral interlude," *Two Slatterns and a King,* followed. This poetic playlet, the author once wrote, "does exactly what it sets out to do. It is very light and slender, but it is carefully constructed, and plays well." [50] On the day the slatterns, Tidy and Slut, reverse their habitual ways, King, literally hunting for a wife, chooses between them. Perforce, his choice is wrong, so arranged by Chance who intones the Prologue, directs the action, and recites the Epilogue. Zorach played the King, Norma and Edna Millay the slatterns, and Marjory Lacey-Baker, Chance.

Another Kreymborg playlet, *Jack's House,* closed the program. Julian Freedman, billed as co-author, set it to music. In this "melo-poem," Rihani took the role of Jack, "a speaking part affording her opportunities for panto-mime," and Edna Millay played Jack's Wife. Freedman accompanied them on the piano; the Zorachs supplied curtain, set, and costumes. Millay's "com-plete . . . understanding of the pantomimic demands" apparently compensated the author for her erratic appearance at rehearsals. After worrying that "few tickets had been sold in advance," he was pleased with the show's progress: "Rihani and Edna looked and acted like puppets, the illusion being heightened by the picturesque circumstances that the former, with her stature of an over-grown boy, was two or three heads taller than the latter, who reduced Jack's large dreamy gestures to a minimum—the broad legato broken up into its component staccato bits." [51]

In the face of open skepticism by their hosts, the Other Players hoped that the "Provincetown Players were now so popular that some of their sub-scribers might come automatically to anything that held the boards of the converted stable." [52] Indeed, they had a crowded house and experienced "in-toxicating success. . . . Not only had Krimmie's investment been returned, but the company had earned several hundred dollars above the outlay." Per-haps the Provincetown Players made that profit possible by assuming over-head costs—at least they themselves had not started making money. In any case, success went to the melo-poetic company's head: moving uptown, it lost not only the profit but also the reinvested original capital. Here was a clear warning the Provincetown group was not ready to hear; three years later it too, started on the road to dissolution by taking its success uptown.[53] At the

Bramhall Playhouse, Heywood Broun summed up the accomplishments of Kreymborg's little band: "The Other Players is the latest and most ultramodern of the little theatres, with free verse dramatists, Futurist scenic artists and Cubist dancers. Its programme is a combination of plays, poems, music and dances, and it aims at the synthesis of the arts." [54]

Meanwhile The Playwright's Theatre's sixth bill was readied to open on March 29. It consisted of two new playlets and a revival. First came *The Devil's Glow,* by Alice Woods Ullman, a prolific and successful short-story writer. The script is lost, the playbill named the characters as "A Successful Author, An Unsuccessful Poet, His Wife," suggesting a triangle in a supposedly creative milieu.[55] Sidney Powell, William Rothschild, and Nina Moise made up the cast. *The Rib-Person,* Rita Wellman's third piece to be produced by the Players, was the second item. This rather badly written "Farce-Satire in Two Scenes" concerns a prostitute, upset by the general involvement with the war: even some of her colleagues have volunteered for nursing. The halting dialogue leaves in doubt whether she has been turned down for service, or just fears rejection. Her final action is to defy society by traveling to "exotic" India with a pimp and an innocent poet.[56] Ida Rauh played the lead, her companions in adventure were Justus Sheffield and Charles Ellis. To complete the evening, Wilbur Daniel Steele's highly successful *Contemporaries* was revived. No review of the bill seems to survive.

The season's last program followed on April 26, opening with F. B. Kugelman's two-character playlet, *The Hermit and His Messiah,* a shocker because an impersonation of Christ occurred in it. The action was "laid in a cave in the Carpathians inhabited by a crazy anchorite" who "knows or cares about nothing but his mysticism." [57] A Russian spy, hotly pursued and about to be captured, stumbles into the cave. As Hermit is unwilling to hide him, the "spy's eyes open with a sudden plan." [58] He "bloodies the centers of his palms" and assuming the position of crucifixion against the cave wall, reveals himself to Hermit as the Messiah, come the second time. Victorious over the anchorite's doubts, the Russian gets him to don the incriminating uniform and run into the pursuers' fatal shots. The spy then settles down to the life of a hermit. Sam Eliot played the Russian, Jig Cook Hermit.

Second on the bill was one of O'Neill's two short sea-coast plays, *The Rope.* It concerns a niggardly father's reception of his returning prodigal son. Old Bentley hid the family fortune at the end of the rope which he arranged in the barn, and on which he urges Luke to hang himself. The young man does not perceive his father's morbid joke, and nearly kills him before storming out in anger. It is the half-witted granddaughter who finds the gold and chucks it piecemeal into the ocean. No photograph of the production remains, but the director's script used by Nina Moise, and O'Neill's letters to her provide some clues.[59] A penciled ground plan on the first page shows the barn door in center, a table with two benches and a stool upstage left against the wall. A circle and a square stage right may indicate stools or bales of hay. A central location for the rope (focal point of all action) seems logical; Moise confirmed that reasoning. However, Ellis, who played Luke and provided the backdrop (which he recalled as his best painting of rocks against the sea), remembered the noose as having hung stage right—in which case it might be represented by the circle.[60]

In his first letter to the director, the dramatist gave tentative approval for editing, yet in his second he urged reinstatement of several drastic cuts. The script records the director's judicious surgery: omissions in the initial dialogue between Bentley and Annie (the slowest part of the play), effective reduction of the old man's repetitious biblical chants, and abridgment of Annie's longest speeches. O'Neill protested; he thought the cutting "spoils the rhythm." Rather, he suggested, "Make the woman talk as fast as she can in a flurry of petty, nagging rage." Moise's wise cutting seems, however, to have contributed as much to the production's success as her directing.

In the last play of the season, *Woman's Honor,* Glaspell came close to proving that woman's honor exists only in the minds of men. A young man accused of murder is unwilling to use an alibi lest he compromise the lady with whom he spent the night. A story his attorney released makes it clear Prisoner stakes his life for a woman's honor, and numerous volunteers compete to provide the alibi. Some are moved by the sacrificial bent of the accused; others consider honor a liability rather than an asset. They range from the Silly One who falls around the neck of the Lawyer instead of the defendant, to the Motherly One who offers protection and nursing. Even the most convincing contenders reveal intimately personal motivations; "she" never comes. Prisoner's disgust mounts until he blurts, "Hell, I plead guilty!" [61]

Two photographs show the simple box set of "a room in the sheriff's house." [62] In the first the women have not arrived yet, only Prisoner and his Lawyer (Clark Branyon and Justus Sheffield) are seen; the former sits at the table, the latter stands between the two doors. The second picture shows all the women (as well as Prisoner and Lawyer) in a rather interesting spatial

12   Susan Glaspell's *Woman's Honor* in the production of the Provincetown
Players, New York, 1918. Left to right: Clark Branyon, Susan Glaspell, Ida Rauh,
Justus Sheffield, three unidentified women, Norma Millay. (Fales Library,
Elmer Holmes Bobst Library, New York University)

arrangement focusing on Lawyer. Four women form a group on the left;
the Silly One (Norma Millay), "a fussily dressed hysterical woman," is easily
identifiable as the only one not in black. Glaspell (Cheated One) and
Rauh (Scornful One) are identifiable stage right. Because the script never
brings the six women together, the photo must have been posed.

3   As the seventh bill was about to open, the Players dealt with a
series of organizational matters on April 21, 1918. Along with a new circular
and tentative summer plans, the group's first surviving financial statement
was discussed.[63] In addition to $2,948 collected from members (at $5 a person, this computes to an impossible 589.6 subscribers), another $1,567.05
was gathered from over 2,000 guests. Single ticket sales thus accounted for
slightly more than one-third of total income, all of which was, in the words
of the statement, "consumed in putting on the seven bills." [64] The meeting
then ended a period of indecision that had caused severe changes in the functions and accountability of the secretary-treasurer. It was resolved to vest fiscal

responsibility in the president by combining that office with that of treasurer, and to hire rather than elect a secretary. Jig Cook was unanimously reelected to the fortified post of president. A secretary was not immediately named, but the search for someone to fill that office was not long. Emma Goldman, the well-known anarchist leader (related to members Saxe Commins and Stella Ballantine), had attended several performances at The Playwright's Theatre. One of her close associates was looking for a position and found the artistic anarchs in Macdougal Street to her liking. Thus did M. Eleanor Fitzgerald—the much-loved, tireless "Fitzi"—come to the Provincetown Players in October 1918 as secretary.[65] This small but significant expansion of paid staff injected a noticeable amount of professionalism into the amateur organization. It, paradoxically, seemed to assure the very freedom for creative expression that was the group's raison d'être but that had seemed increasingly threatened by mundane chores.

Hard upon this internally motivated change came an external jolt which caused a further shift toward more businesslike management. As had the first, so, too, the second New York season was ending with a mixed balance of cherished victories and lamented defeats. On the one hand, Glaspell and O'Neill were widely acclaimed for plays first staged by the Provincetowners, and on the other, the group itself was denied public credit. This brought to a head the awareness that their status as proud amateurs had disadvantages. After *The Rope* and *Woman's Honor* were produced by the Washington Square Players, both Heywood Broun and John Corbin paid tribute to those "semi-professionals" for the "artistic personalities they have introduced to us." [66] In a letter to the *Times* Jig Cook pointed out that four of the seven plays credited to the Washington Square Players were first performed at The Playwright's Theatre, and that Eugene O'Neill and Susan Glaspell were Provincetown Players. Calling the protest "misleading," Corbin struck a strong enough blow to alter the group's perception, because he used its self-imposed isolation as argument against public recognition. How could one credit the Provincetown Players with "personalities introduced" to the public, the critic demanded, if "performances in Macdougal Street are private?" [67]

Combined with internal competition and financial troubles, this critical comment produced changes in the group's attitude toward publicity. Policy was consequently altered as part of a transformation that accompanied the move to larger quarters and involved expansion of the secretarial staff, a "free list" for critics, the printing of posters, and a subscription to Romeike's clipping service. In other words, the Provincetown Players began consciously to seek acclaim. Although showing unmistakable characteristics of growth and maturation, and not nearly as violent as the conflict of March 1917, the ordeal of change between spring and fall 1918 was an important crisis of conscience for the entire group. If the first season had proven the doctrine of group creation unworkable, the second demonstrated the impracticability of ignoring the public. The product of creativity assumed a significance equal to that of the process.

Cook's personal concern with public recognition was further provoked when a three-column article by Edna Kenton in the *Boston Evening Transcript* failed to portray him as prime mover of the group.[68] Kenton either seriously believed in, or gave convincing lip service to, the principle of collectivism and did not give the privately acknowledged leader disproportionate tribute. But it was not true, as Jig charged in a letter, that his "work for the Provincetown Players was valued at zero," [69] for Kenton had written, "They have a producer to whom goes a larger share of their technical success than most of them know."

Even as that article appeared, Jig Cook was at work on expanding The Playwright's Theatre. His previously mentioned letter to Kahn was part of this effort, and his assumption of the treasurer's responsibilities was a preparatory move for the impending fund drive. The spring circular addressed the aims and means of this campaign when, at a time of America's deep involvement with war, it reasserted the Players' faith in creative imagination: "The social justification . . . now for makers and players of plays is that they shall keep alive in the world the light of imagination. Without it the wreck of the world that was cannot be cleared away and the new world shaped." [70]

The strongest appeal for support yet issued by the Provincetowners followed:

With no endowment, no angel, and no seeking of publicity, the Provincetown Players have been sustained through two seasons by their subscribers. Of these there were 550 the first year, 635 the second. To enlarge and improve as we now should we ought to increase this number to 1,000.

We therefore ask our Associate Members not only to resubscribe now for the season of 1918–19, but also to help extend our present membership by sending us the names and addresses of others likely to be interested in our work. We also ask that they personally place copies of this circular and subscription blank in the hands of possible new subscribers.[71]

With the "separate fund not to be drawn on for current expenses" that Jig expected in response to this appeal, he hoped to provide "a more adequate place . . . to work in." Envisioned were: a bigger and better stage; a raked auditorium with more (and more comfortable) seats; more efficient management; greater publicity; and productions of higher caliber. The Playhouse Fund was established on May 6,[72] letters seeking an auditorium with a capacity of 250 went to real-estate firms, and by May 17 the goal of a $1,700 kitty was reached by means of $1,000 contribution "from a Philadelphia admirer." [73] Although one condition set by the anonymous donor (later revealed as industrialist and art collector A. C. Barnes) had not yet been met: namely, that his donation be matched by other funds, the Players were thus able to move from 139 to 133 Macdougal Street. As such major changes in a company's history usually do, the enlarged headquarters solved some problems, but they created others.

4   The Provincetown Players' third season in New York could be called successful in terms that would appear almost conventional. Though less hectic than the second season (only five programs of new scripts, followed by two review bills), it once more brought to light new talent of all sorts, and allowed as well for new departures by known pathfinders. As it turned out, several plays, three actresses, and some unique staging methods attracted acclaim.[74] In its new location (only three doors from its previous one), The Playwright's Theatre became entrenched. The 1918–19 season, also, introduced an attractive four-page program format: its cover featured Zorach's linoleum-cut of his own set for *The Game;* the line "Under the direction of George Cram Cook" headed the inside content, officially acknowledging the collective's founder and leader; the back page listed all officers, and carried announcements of special events. Soon, too, Fitzi's workload outgrew her considerable capacity and Susan Jenkins was hired as assistant secretary. The subscription to the clipping service was begun this year as well.[75]

Meanwhile, the 1918–19 season represented a mixture of continued ex-

13 Exterior, 133 Macdougal Street. (Macgowan Papers. Department of Special
Collections, University Research Library, UCLA)

14   Interior, 133 Macdougal Street. (Macgowan Papers, Department of Special Collections, University Research Library, UCLA)

ploration and an increasing tendency to join the mainstream. Productions of almost commercial conventionality alternated with far-out innovation. This dichotomy reflected the shifting American cultural climate as well as the group's ordeal of change. With the war over, innocence was on the wane. Traditional domination by New England aristocracy had come under scrutiny, and the Bolshevik Revolution was a topic of everyday conversation. New kinds of poets were making their voices heard, new kinds of painters their visions seen. Dissent and innovation appeared side by side with older conventions still holding their own.

Edna St. Vincent Millay kicked off the Provincetown Players' season of contrasts: *The Princess Marries the Page* is a light and pretty fairy tale, entirely harmless. It was dismissed as sophomoric by the *Dramatic Mirror,* and earned Heywood Broun's praise as being visually the finest piece of the evening.[76] On the same bill, Florence Kiper Frank's *Gee-Rusalem* was a conventionally structured problem play, satirizing a range of isms, and taking particular aim at attempts to escape conformity by having its major character first embrace and then reject Judaism.[77] Sandwiched between these two was O'Neill's thus far boldest experiment with theatrical illusion. *Where the Cross is Made* not only requires an interior setting "fitted up like the captain's cabin of a deep-sea sailing vessel"[78] with an exit through the ceiling; its effect depends on the realistic appearance of three ghosts of drowned seamen. These are not visible to the captain's daughter whose mental stability is unimpaired, but are real to the insane captain, to his son when *he* gets caught up in the hallucination, and—to the audience. The Players raised "some objections . . . about the actual presence on the stage of the ghosts . . ." partly because of the technical difficulties involved, partly because some thought the concept preposterous. O'Neill, however, remained adamant. At last he said: "Everybody in the play is mad except the girl. Everyone sees the ghosts except the girl. What I want to do is hypnotize the audience so when they see the ghosts they will think they are mad too! *And by that I mean the whole audience!* Remember—'*The author shall produce his plays without hindrance, according to his own ideas.*'"[79] This was perhaps the clearest example that "just as we never considered our audiences, so Gene never . . . considered our stage in the sense, that is, of adapting his plays to it. He wrote the plays and adapted the stage to them."[80] That the author's intentions were carried out successfully is attested to by the hostile critic of the *Morning Telegraph* (November 23, 1918) who, under the headline "Only the Captain's Daughter Stays Sane," stated that anyone who would "enjoy the sensation of going mad" will "find the want supplied" in the current bill in Macdougal Street.

On another bill, the season's fifth, provocative scripts by Jack Reed and Susan Glaspell were juxtaposed. Reed's curtain raiser, *The Peace that Passeth Understanding*, was a savage attack on the shapers of the Versailles treaty. President Wilson, Premiers Clemenceau, Lloyd George, and Orlando, Japan's Baron Makino, as well as representatives of nations not party to the negotiations appear in this fantasy, the most topical piece ever staged by the Players. Reed ignored both dramaturgical conventions and physical limitation of the stage, calling for a clock that is "fifty years slow," and for dialogue "carried on by each Delegate in his native language."[81] Undeterred, the Provincetowners staged his vitriolic satire as an animated cartoon; beaverboard cut-outs of major Delegates' caricature profiles were strung on wires at various depths of the stage.[82] Small dummies of delegates not given a hearing were swept off the window sill as required by the script. This blend of Ger-

15   The Provincetown Players' production of Susan Glaspell's *Bernice*, New York, 1919. Left to right: Ida Rauh and Susan Glaspell. (Fales Library, Elmer Holmes Bobst Library, New York University)

man cabaret and Soviet agit-prop techniques was followed by Glaspell's first full-length play, *Bernice*.[83] Within a much praised and skillfully built Ibsenesque structure, it accomplished a stunning coup de théâtre: all action revolves around, and all characters are revealed through their relationship to, Bernice, who is dead before the curtain rises. Whether she killed herself or only wanted her widower to believe she did, is a question not altogether resolved until the end of the third act, when one realizes "in full measure the wisdom and beauty" of the absent heroine.[84]

Three intervening bills were less remarkable, although well enough received by critics and audiences alike, and still containing innovative attempts. Most scripts on these programs were slices of life from various ethnic backgrounds. Sympathetic as they were, critics lamented one common characteristic: lack of action. In some other context that might be seen as pure coincidence, but in this season at The Playwright's Theatre, a cause will be discerned.

A simple, potent play, Rita Creighton Smith's *The Rescue* had been performed at Harvard, a product of the "47 Workshop." [85] It concerns Anna Warden's escape from the grip of hereditary insanity. Anna is a captive of New England ancestors whose portraits dominate her sheltered life until the housekeeper, Kate, insinuates that she was conceived out of wedlock. That makes Anna feel free and relieved: "I'm not a Warden at all!" she exclaims. Now capable of leaving the house, she takes a job in New York—not suspecting that Kate has lied to set her free. Heywood Broun thought *The Rescue* "within striking distance of an idea" [86]—perhaps the one O'Neill later used as Sam Evans's hereditary insanity in *Strange Interlude*.

In *The Widow's Veil*, Alice Rostetter is as dependent on a New York Irish environment as Smith had been on Boston aristocracy.[87] This satirical comedy, in which the author distinguished herself with remarkable acting as well as writing, involves a young woman whose husband appears to be dying, and a greying widow whose life's sustenance seems to be the grief of others. Comforting her against expected bereavement, the older woman arouses the younger's vanity with a veil. So taken is the young wife with her own looks as a mourner, she cannot resist seeing herself again in the veil next morning. As her husband recovers, she is nearly caught relishing widowhood.

Rita Wellman effectively beautified an otherwise inconsequential triangle plot in *The String of the Samisen* by rooting it in Bushido legend.[88] Tama's husband and lover turn out to have been mortal enemies. Unable to comply with her lover's demand that she kill her husband, Tama substitutes herself for the intended victim. The famed dancer, Michio Itow, directed Edna Millay and Rollo Peters on Lloyd Wright's stylish set, but Heywood Broun dismissed it all as "a beautiful picture" that "does not move." [89]

The milieu of *The Baby Carriage* by Bosworth Crocker (Mrs. Ludwig Lewisohn) was the New York melting pot. Mrs. Lezinsky and Mrs. Rooney "bargain for a perambulator, which one of them is past needing and the other . . . is expecting to have use for." [90] Rounding out the ethnic circle was Mary F. Barber's *The Squealer*, a little tragedy of the Molly Maguires, Pennsylvania's rebellious miners. When Margaret Kerrigan discovers that it was her husband who, convicted and sentenced with his fellows for the killing of a boss, had squealed, she'll have nothing more to do with him. To Jim's query, "You'd sooner see me hung?" she responds, "I would." Yet when pursuers close in, she urges Jim to flee. The curtain drops on his "Not alone, Marge." [91]

All these ethnic vignettes, redolent of mood but often short on overt

16 Opening scene of O'Neill's *The Moon of the Caribbees* as presented by
The Provincetown Players, New York, 1918. On top of ladder, Charles Ellis;
beside him, Otto Liveright; at bottom of ladder, William Stuart. (Courtesy of
James Light)

action or apparent structure, materialized on the Provincetown Players' schedule this season as a distinct trend in the wake of O'Neill's favorite sea play,
one justly hailed and damned for its replacement of action with mood, *The
Moon of the Caribbees*.[92] The dramatist yearned for a director to follow in
Nina Moise's footsteps, but Ballantine was unavailable, and Thomas Mitchell
(who was to become a famous film actor) was inexperienced. (O'Neill described his direction as "punk.")[93] The realistic scene descriptions were not
complemented by the cardboard settings, nor was serious thought given to
ethnically accurate casting, and white amateurs in blackface played the West
Indian girls. In creating the proper mood the greatest impact was probably
made by the crooning of two songs by Edna, Norma, and Kathleen Millay,
with their mother Cora adding the deeper tones.[94] Squeezed in the narrow
space between the island backdrop and the beaverboard "port bulwark," the
Millays performed first a bona fide Caribbean tune, followed by a hymn to the
moon written and composed by Edna. The music was so effective, the quartet
was reinvited for *The Emperor Jones* two years later.

A very different departure from familiar surroundings was called for by *5050*, Robert Allerton Parker's social satire, cast in a futuristic science-fiction mold.[95] Inhabitants of Tropisma, "The Subterranean City of the Future" are divided into idolators and debunkers of the "Woodrovian Age." Archeologists bring the Municipal Museum such precious finds of "the classical Manhattan era" as the lions of the Public Library, and the amber liquid in a vessel sacred to the "twin gods, Haig & Haig." Culture vultures of A.D. 5050 further praise the past with references to the theatre of "the great Georgem," and to such cultic dances as "the sacred Shimmy." But the greatest admiration is reserved for a transportation system designed, in their view, to provide the population access to exhibits of contemporary art. Curators are assembling a show of rare examples of that art form: subway advertising. Detractors of this 3,000-year-old culture are revolutionaries who advocate the cause of labor, free air for the general populace, and living in the Eternal Now. Characters had such "names" as 0010, 6699, affectionately altered to "Wunny" and "Sixxy." Norma Millay (0369) recalled having fun in a hat with a halo rigged at the end of a wire.[96] Kenton called this "the first Robot play," adding that her sister, Mabel Reber, supplied round and square boxes to make "square or pyramidal costumes of pasteboard with shooting decorative angles of more pasteboard." [97]

In *Tickless Time* Cook and Glaspell held up to wholehearted ridicule their own fascination with the sundial as symbolic escape from the rat race.[98] In his Provincetown garden, Ian Joyce made a sundial to stand for Nature and Truth as expressed in "true time." As a form of sacrifice all clocks found in the house are buried at the pedestal. After evading questions as to what time it is, and persuading friends to observe "true" time at the price of missing trains or serving cold suppers in a world of "wrong" time, Ian is forced to explain the complex diagram accompanying the sundial. It turns out that his ultimate symbol of nature, the Sun, needs correction. Amidst general disillusionment the clocks are exhumed, and the sundial removed from its pedestal.

From the beginning to the end of this season the Provincetown Players struggled with problems of publicity. Halfway through the season critics were provided automatically with free passes instead of having tickets available upon request. Kenton saw this as a fundamental change of policy, in fact a betrayal of principles.[99] Yet the continuous seeking of professional recognition, as repeatedly observed, served as a constant reminder that not all individuals in the group considered their amateur status permanent. More surprising is the discovery that at least one of the iconoclastic founders harbored professional ambitions for the Players as a group. In an interview, Ida Rauh duly lectured the *Morning Telegraph*'s reporter on the theory of group creation when he made the mistake of admitting, "I thought you were the star." Near the end of the interview, however, she revealed the "ambition of the Provincetown Players ... to produce a bill of the best three plays the[y] have ever done at an 'uptown theatre.' Just for a week. Or maybe six plays for two weeks." [100] It was not to happen that way. But the season ended with two review bills, instead of the customary one. And in view of the fact that Jig Cook was about to depart for a year's "sabbatical," and Ida Rauh was to be one of the two "directors" to fill his shoes during the "Season of Youth," her announcement must have seemed momentous then, as it seems portentous in retrospect.

The Young Turks

*"I told Jig:
'Nobody's mantle descends on me.'"
Jasper Deeter in an interview,
July 25, 1963*

1   Factionalism seems endemic to movements based on belief in redemption. It was when the Provincetowners' focus began to shift from the healing *process* assumed to inhere in the ferment of spontaneous theatrical playmaking, to the presentation of *products* from the laboratory of human emotions, that the first stirrings of divergent philosophies began to surface.

Not before the third New York season (1918–19) was it grudgingly admitted that certain scripts and a few actors had won greater favor than others; only then did it become undeniable that the Players tended to classify their creative efforts in terms of success and failure, "on the basis of the criticism of Broadway." [1] But that inclination was seen earlier in a motion made at the organizational meetings in September 1916 to name the prospective New York headquarters "Try-out Theatre." The defeated proposal reflected professional aspirations that were noted in the press. [2]

Differences of opinion that emerged in planning the move from Cape Cod to Greenwich Village, grew upon arrival, and dominated by the end of the first season there. Beyond divisions caused by competitive and personal value judgments about which script, or which actor was "better," there were overlapping factions that evolved over organizational matters (viewed by some as inseparable from philosophy), and over such issues as whether theatre may (or must) deliver political messages or exist solely for art's sake. The view that the group should serve *all* kinds of artistic expression—whether oriented to social or esthetic reform or not—repeatedly prevailed, providing evidence of the healthy balance achieved by heterogeneity.

Still, ideological subgroups were formed within the collective, and the most divisive issue was that of amateurism. During the first New York season the particiaption of theatre professionals had already turned into a major issue. Over the years it was resolved by pragmatic reliance on such directors as Frederic Burt and Margaret Wycherley (March 1917), Nina Moise (January 1917–April 1918), Rollo Peters (November 1917), Thomas Mitchell (December 1918), and E. J. Ballantine (February and March 1919). Another crisis culminated in the fall of 1918 with the collective's recognition of critics, made explicit by the decision to send them complimentary tickets. As The Playwright's Theatre survived one season after another, the trend toward professionalism grew and the group's attitudes changed.

For many founders, who, as emphasized, had established their creative reputation and their economic base in arenas other than theatre, theatrical experimentation was primarily a means of addressing the broad concerns beyond personal survival that tend to dominate the latter half of adult life. Moreover, many had returned to, or remained preoccupied with, their chosen professions. Although they remained subscribers and interested "club-members," they were replaced as active Players by younger, equally talented, and perhaps more ambitious people, whose career interest lay in the theatre.

New recruits saw long-range spiritual commitments integrally related to choices of life style and vocation that characterize the earlier part of adulthood. It appeared to them that for the collective's experiment to continue, acceptance by critics and spectators (preferably in the form of ever larger numbers of subscribers) was essential. Of equal importance for young members, who thought of themselves as serving an apprenticeship with the Provincetown Players, was individual recognition. Public awareness of one's personal artistic achievement was seen as a source of psychological security, of assurance for continued learning and experimentation within a relatively free and friendly, durable company. Ambitious newcomers also hoped it would prove to be a springboard for a career. They did not think devotion to the goals of the collective contradictory to the more personal hope of using The Playwright's Theatre as a steppingstone toward critical, financial, and psychological success in their chosen profession.

Although the factor of age difference was formidable—Cook, the Nordfeldts, the Hapgoods, the Schoonmakers were fifteen to twenty years older than Bodenheim, Deeter, Light, Millay, and Vail—opposing philosophical stances taken by founders and joiners did not reduce to a "generation gap." Contrary to the aspiring group of younger members who respected (and strove to acquire) expertise, Jig distrusted theatrical know-how and considered any success resulting from it synonymous with a betrayal of principles. He continued to believe without qualification that "the gifted amateur has possibilities the professional has lost." [3]

Cook's insistence on embodying that principle raises—without bringing into doubt his role as the Provincetown Players' prime mover and sustainer—two serious questions about his leadership. The first: Had he been gifted enough to lead a group brimming with talent? received a qualified negative response from many of his coworkers who asserted that in practical matters of theatre (other than those requiring manual dexterity) Jig simply did not know what he was doing.[4] As an actor he was thought never to have gone beyond his robust, yet awkward, self. As a director he was seen as inconsistent, inarticulate, vague, and confusing. And as a playwright he appeared ineffectual except in collaboration with his wife whose skills and finesse were evident. If one remembers that even one-time adversaries, for whom Cook's memory remains holy, qualified their negative answers and stressed their belief in his inspirational and cohesive power, the assessment still leads unavoidably to the second question. Was Jig's lack of gift in the crafts of theatre at the root of his proud insistence upon remaining an amateur in the sense of ignorance of technique, despite several seasons of practical experience, rather than in the sense of willingness to try anything that would outrage commercial artists? It was insistence of the second kind that had been the initial propellent, the collective's leaven. But when Jig Cook's zeal exceeded the temperature needed for the leaven to produce rising, his inspiration lost power and turned unproductive. Thus his stance was perceived by "the young" not as enhancement, but as an obstacle to further spiritual and artistic expansion.

The crucial factor, then, was an alienation between the spiritual mentor and his disciples, a wrenching process that had been in preparation through three New York seasons. Expending all his faith and energy on others—without consistently hitting paydirt—turned Jig increasingly bitter. Not just one of the older generation, he was *the* founder and sustainer, who seemed to have given up all other ambition, and, besides the Provincetown Players, had only his dreams of recapturing Periclean Greece to live for. Consequently Cook found it increasingly difficult to delegate authority, listen to others, and temper his enthusiasms or revulsions. According to one of the younger members, he had become short-tempered, petulant at giving his time and energy to the work of others at the expense of his own creative expression.[5] He developed a phobia about conflict with Youth: he felt challenged to compete and feared defeat. Apart from childish attempts to prove his prowess through Indian wrestling and drinking bouts, Jig Cook expressed irritation with the independent views, the openly professional interest of the most ambitious and most aggressive young and talented Players.[6] Glaspell lovingly summed up her husband's problems in dealing with the group: "His instinct as an artist was for having his own way; much as he wanted to leave not one unfree spirit in the theatre, he had a peculiarly strong urge to put right a thing that was wrong. Sometimes Jig was about as true as a hurricane to the group ideal. Yet knowing the necessities of his spirit, it seems to me extraordinary how long and how patiently he gave himself to the dream of creating together."[7] But when Jig's views or attitudes were challenged, Susan was the first to defend his "extravagances" by pointing to his devotion and his powers of inspiration. After all, the Provincetown Players owed its group existence to Cook's extravagant idealism.

By the spring of 1919 younger members asserted "the need for a more ambitious organization" to replace the "personal, slightly haphazard methods of the first years," and even some dissatisfaction with "Jig's paternalism" had been expressed.[8] To cope both with the apparent dissension and with her husband's moments of depression when he doubted his own creativity, Glaspell engineered a year's absence for both of them by taking Jig at his word and insisting that he devote time to writing plays.[9]

The sabbatical Cook and Glaspell planned for the 1919–20 season was not only to relieve tensions, but also to serve as a new experiment: "Why not let the younger members have the theatre for the year and see what they do with it? . . . He had been wavering. 'We never meant to do it forever,' he said. Now that we had shown our idea, set a number of things in motion, would we rather return to our work as individuals? The theatre left small chance for Jig's writing, and took a great deal from mine."[10] Whether this particular experiment is evaluated as a success depends upon how long a perspective is taken. For the short term, the younger generation proved capable of managing the theatre with good results. In the long run, however, that record confirmed their trust in professional know-how, undermined their respect and admiration for Jig Cook, and led to the collective's disintegration.

2   The transfer of management into mostly younger hands had begun during the latter part of the Players' third New York season. Plans for the "Season of Youth" seemed to capitalize on recently achieved public acclaim[11]

and a semblance of fiscal stability, in order to continue the trend toward improved organization and efficiency. Some evidence was provided by an announcement in the season's last playbill (April 25 through May 1, 1919) that next season would commence October 31—earlier than usual. It was resolved to continue running each bill for two full weeks, but to ease the consequent overload on Louis Ell by hiring an assistant stage manager in the person of Cesare Zwaska, a regular contributor to the *Little Review*.[12]

An article on "Little Theatres," in the *Nation*, provides evidence that news of impending changes got out rather quickly; it also reveals familiarity with, and concern about, the motivation behind them:

> The voluntary character of the Provincetown Players is one of their chief assets. If they reorganize, *as is probable,* and decide to pay their actors, they must make more money, and *the need of money begets a caution in production which limits, if it does not nullify, the purely experimental character of the enterprise* . . . to justify a paid company they will be tempted to give more ambitious productions, which promise a wider appeal, and will be forced to turn, as the Theatre Guild has done, from the immaturity of the native playwright to the finished product of Europe.[13]

However, the season started well enough. The Provincetown Players' 1919–20 season did in fact open when announced; the six bills really ran two full weeks each; some of the actors began to receive salaries; but a crisis caused by the shortage of native plays erupted. The program format was retained, the phrase following "Under the direction of" was changed from "George Cram Cook" to "James Light and Ida Rauh." Rauh had been a founder, was only four years Jig's junior, and had recently become the most widely acclaimed member of the group when Heywood Broun listed her in the *New York Tribune* among the "All-American Dozen of Our Actresses" alongside Mrs. Fiske (recently retired) and Helen Hayes (youngest of the twelve).[14] Light, on the other hand, was once described as having "brought the sneering, wisecracking atmosphere into the younger part of the group and . . . discouraged Jig."[15] Wisecracking and arrogant, chief rebel Light was also talented, well educated, and dedicated to the acquisition and application of craftsmanship in the creative process. He became one of two outstanding directors to rise from the ranks of the amateur group. Although (as he admitted) his early work was largely impulsive and haphazard, he experimented boldly with production techniques.[16] His wide reading and familiarity with music, along with some expertise in the use of color and light and skilled draftsmanship (products of training in design and architecture) eminently qualified him for such experimentation.

Rauh and Light did not, of course, hold the reins alone; Charles Ellis, Edna St. Vincent Millay, Susan Jenkins, Blanche Hays, Eleanor Fitzgerald, and Edna Kenton formed the executive committee, which in turn was surrounded by a group of young and ambitious artists and intellectuals, including Lawrence Vail, Djuna Barnes, Mike Gold, Norma Millay, Jasper Deeter, Alfred Kreymborg, Helen Westley, and Remo Bufano.[17]

When, true to its promise, the youthful group began the season on October 31, the first bill was, both in the variety of scripts offered and in the critical reactions received, representative of their entire season. There was the usual innovative O'Neill play, a mystifying poetic fantasy, a dull thesis play, and a charming comedy. The thesis play, *Getting Unmarried,* by Winthrop Parkhurst, must have seemed to the Players, as to the editors of *Smart Set,* a clever treatment of marriage's chilling effect on love, but Woollcott was closer to the truth branding it "a bit of 1896 insurgency" worthy of the *Ladies' Home Journal.*[18] In it, a couple who have lived for ten years in a hell of their own making decide on a divorce, after which they expect to cohabit happily. Since "they can't live together and be *tied* and be happy," they assume that dissolving the legal bond will banish staleness from their lives once "neither can be sure the other isn't going to run off and leave." [19] This dull script received attention in performance mostly due to its lively visual setting. Norma Millay played the wife in a blue batik negligee created by Charles Ellis, her future husband. And the scenery, designed by Marguerite Zorach and realized by her husband, was "so striking" according to Kenneth Macgowan, "that it ought to ruin its play by drawing all the attention from the actors." But despite "preachers of armed neutrality for scenic backgrounds" the critic observed, "the eternal vitality of a human being on a lighted platform dominates, . . . honor to the Zorachs for reasserting it." [20]

It was Djuna Barnes's debut as a playwright with the Provincetown Players that provided the mystifying poetry: *Three from the Earth* confounded yet delighted audiences and critics alike. In this short piece, an adventuress is visited by three brothers, "peasants of the most obvious type." The dialogue reveals the uncertain identity of the boys' mother, the recent death of their father, and ends with the youngest kissing the lady on the lips, asserting she "bore him." [21] Writing in the *New York Tribune,* Rebecca Drucker was willing to accept this play as "proof that movement and light and color and semi-intelligible sounds may be fascinating in the same way as dreams are fascinating" [22]—surely an aesthetic victory. Openly admitting his inability to grasp the event on a rational level, Woollcott of the *Times* was equally impressed by "how absorbing and essentially dramatic a play can be without the audience ever knowing what, if anything, the author is driving at." [23]

Harold Chapin's *The Philosopher of Butterbiggins* was the bill's charming comedy, an exception to the group's general rule of producing untested scripts.[24] An early American casualty on the British front, Chapin had been honored in England by a Memorial Performance in 1915. This presentation of his whimsical Scottish comedy, which showed that the very young and the very old are equally helpless, was directed by the author's sister, and made memorable by the acting of Edna St. Vincent Millay and James Light as the grandfather-philosopher.

O'Neill's contribution (his last surviving one-act play except for the much later *Hughie), The Dreamy Kid,* once again challenged the Players to do the unprecedented; in this case, present a serious play on life in the black ghetto, with an all-black cast outside of Harlem. The title character, a gangster wanted for murder, is summoned to his grandmother's deathbed and in obliging her risks arrest. As the curtain closes, he prepares to fight his pursuers. Ida Rauh directed a cast she recruited in Harlem; the painter Glenn Coleman designed the set.[25] Woollcott found that the play induced "sympathy and pity for a conventionally abhorrent character," and was therefore "engrossing." [26] His comment that in the amateur environment Negro actors seemed acceptable reflected the fact that in theatre, as in other fields, unequal employment for blacks was partly due to little or no chance for training in the profession. Not bound by union restrictions, the Provincetown Players were able to take steps in breaking down the barrier. (After Gilpin's triumph the following year, O'Neill continued to provide similar opportunities under the aegis of The Experimental Theatre, Inc.) Rebecca Drucker went beyond Woollcott in appreciating the black actors whose casting, she asserted, "illumines in a great many ways the psychological values of the piece." [27]

On the whole, the season's opening bill was quite successful—and in experimental, rather than commercial, terms. A comment Drucker overheard in the theatre and cited, makes this quite clear: "This is the sixth season of their existence, and I cannot see that they have arrived at anything. They do not seem to know their own minds yet." [28] Jig Cook himself could not have improved on the critic's response: "The day in which the Provincetown Players will know their own minds is, I hope, far off. It will be the end of that buoyant experimenting that is the unique justification of their existence." Woollcott endorsed the experimental spirit perhaps more cautiously and Macgowan's comments were ultimately also positive, though marred by a condescending tone.[29]

The remainder of the "Season of Youth" was equally productive, but by no means without setbacks, conflicts, and discouragements. On the positive side must be noted the entrance of Remo Bufano and Jasper Deeter into the group; Helen Westley's debut as a director; two striking scenes designed by Ellis, and one by Jean Paul Slusser. On the negative side should be entered Ida Rauh's precipitous departure after the second bill, an episode of harrassment by the Internal Revenue Service, and the dearth of incoming American scripts, which resulted in the production of the only indisputably foreign play by the Provincetown Players.

Among new scripts, the realistic ones were overall less remarkable—none was a match for *Dreamy*: not Lewis Beach's *Brothers*, Edna Ferber's *The Eldest*, Mike Gold's *Money*, not even O'Neill's *Exorcism*. Of the crop of poetic plays several stood out: Djuna Barnes's *Irish Triangle*, Kreymborg's *Vote the New Moon*, Wallace Stevens's *Three Travelers Watch a Sunrise*, and Millay's *Aria da Capo*.

The highlights of the season may be better remembered by participants, but the record of lowlights is as well preserved. The group was plagued by an uneven flow of scripts—in quality as in numbers. No doubt, this was an old problem, as Jig Cook's complaints have indicated, but the Young Turks had heretofore only indirectly experienced it. The contacts Cook had established over the years, combined with his knack for cajoling or browbeating people into artistic contributions had often stopped the gap before. As imaginative a director as he may have become, Jimmy Light still found himself lacking that required combination of connections, skills, and tenacity. At any rate, he seems to have been driven farther into desperation by the shortage of worthwhile scripts than was beneficial for The Playwright's Theatre.

By the time of the second bill, though it featured such a masterpiece as *Aria da Capo*, it was necessary to round it out by reviving the somewhat dated and shopworn "*Not Smart*" alongside Lewis Beach's rather plodding "sardonic comedy," *Brothers,*[30] which is of interest solely for its foreshadowing of O'Neill's *Desire Under the Elms.* Beach unfolds his action in a "tarpaper shanty" where Pa is dying with resounding offstage groans, while one of his two sons, "a puttylike rubber doll whose head may be reshaped by hand" inspects a locked tin box containing the old man's will. As his brother arrives, they argue over their slim inheritance—the shack and two acres—ignoring the old man's cries for water. After recounting enough misdeeds with which each could bar the other from his legacy, their fist fight is interrupted by Pa's final sounds of agony. Tearing the key to the box off the old man, the brothers find that he left all to Ma, whom he chased off twenty years ago. The curtain falls as they prepare to burn down the hut.

With its sophisticated, symbolic treatment of a similar theme, Edna Millay's *Aria da Capo,* a musically structured poetic play, was the bill's mainstay. On an almost bare stage an apparently unbridled Harlequinade unfolds, its satire touching on a great many subjects, delicately balancing reason and caprice, until the idyll of Pierrot and Colombine is disrupted when Cothurnus rudely orders them offstage. Promptbook in hand, he summons Corydon and Thyrsis, a pair of reluctant shepherds, to act out a tragic game of ownership and patriotism, greed and war. Repeatedly protesting, they continue, with crepe paper and confetti for props, toward mutual destruction, until they fall upon one another in a final embrace. Shoving their bodies under the table, Cothurnus calls Pierrot and Colombine to resume their comedy and, after a moment's consternation, they do. In her published notes on staging, Millay specified that the Players set the scene with "cleverly utilized painted screens, the heights varying from 6 to 10 feet." [31] A rehearsal photograph shows these to have had highly stylized designs—conceived and executed with matching borders by Charles Ellis. The author directed a cast consisting of her sister Norma and Harrison Dowd as Colombine and Pierrot, Ellis and Light as shepherds, and the architect Hugh Ferriss as Cothurnus. Norma Millay and Charles Ellis recalled a sharp contrast between the realistic portrayal of the shepherds and the stylized acting of the clowns.[32]

On the third bill, a poetic play—pleasing, but no match for Millay—was sandwiched between two mediocre realistic pieces. First came Edna Ferber's *The Eldest,* which, adapted by the author from her short story by the same title, treats wasted opportunity through a "date" ironically twisted from a perspective of fifteen years.[33] Rose, the eldest, abandoned marriage plans that long ago to assume duties of her mother who had fallen ill. Meanwhile, younger siblings have grown up, continuing to be dependent on her services. Floss, the youngest, expects a caller who, chancing into the shop where she works, mistook her for Rose, whose intended he was fifteen years ago. He arrives and does not recognize Rose who, after embarrassing explications from him and cruel remarks from the family, remains alone. She silently crushes a bundle of "time-yellowed" letters, remainders of her wasted youth.

In contrast to Ferber's serious treatment of sentimental love, Djuna Barnes's *Irish Triangle* takes a cynical view of infidelity.[34] Kathleen O'Rune leads a peculiar life: her husband stays out nightly until dawn, and she has begun to act the grand lady. It turns out, she has been learning the talk and style of the Manor House upon the hill, where her man has "found her ladyship beautiful," educating his wife on his daily return. She takes pride that John has become "a better, more remembering, more observing man" and reveals the next step: a reversal of roles. For "It's a grand night coming on, and it's the moon and I will be climbing the hill, for I've nothing more to learn, but John is rare ignorant."

No doubt rooted in personal experience, Mike Gold's *Money* invokes the mood of Gorky's *Lower Depth,* transplanted to New York City's lower East Side—preserving some of the pace but none of the tension.[35] In a cellar that is a cobbler's shop by day, dormitory by night, Moisha moans and searches for his lost bundle of dollars that was to be the salvation of his family. It turns out to have been stolen, not lost—and by a fellow lodger at that. The confessed "louse" is held up as an example of the evil influence of a money-inspired rat race. The play's long-winded dialogue was not helped by the poor lighting of the stage.

Unjustly ignored by some critics and condemned by others, the fourth bill should have been hailed as a victory, weighted as it was in favor of poetry, and supported by imaginative scenery and stage business. Alfred Kreymborg's satirical election fantasy, *Vote the New Moon,*[36] begins on a bare, dark stage, to which Town Crier summons the set: four little houses (two red and two blue), and a town hall with a belfry. Burgher and Burgess pop as jack-in-a-boxes from their houses ready to elect Burgomaster by voting for Candidate, each—naturally—of his own color. By custom, the vote consists of the two citizens hammering one another over the head until one fall unconscious. The survivor's Candidate then becomes Burgomaster, enters town hall, and a moon of his color ascends the belfry. This time, though, something goes amiss during voting: as Burgher and Burgess each wield a party hammer, loudly proclaiming his color, they suddenly reverse votes. Questioned by Town Crier, the citizens admit to being tired of old moons, just as their candidates emerge to learn who's winning. They are told, instead, to repeat the campaign, and not, as usual, privately to the citizen of his own color, but facing both, and each other. As a result, Burgher and Burgess discover that color is the only difference between candidates—and they rebel. They damn the candidates, and Catfish, their mysterious overlord. Town Crier warns too late: threatening noises approach as Burgher and Burgess hammer away at the candidates, calling for a new moon—a purple one. Catfish appears bathed in purple light; citizens swallow candidates, Catfish in turn swallows them and enters town hall. From the belfry the Crier announces the new moon.

The cast included Light and Bufano as citizens, Ellis and Harry Winston as the candidates, Deeter as Town Crier. Jean Paul Slusser, "a practising and exhibiting painter in New York," was recruited by Ellis, with whom he worked in Peter Mijer's theatrical costume studio as "expert technicians in the batik process," to design the set.[37] Slusser's water-color sketch was approved by Kreymborg; it included solid-colored houses light enough to be carried on by the characters to form a curve on stage right. The town hall, its belfry topped by a fool's cap, stood stage left; a crooked lamp-post stage right is most vividly recalled by Slusser, the jog in it suggested by the author, "in the interests of keeping the mood . . . away from too ordinary a quality of realism. This ga-ga bend was faithfully built into the lamp-post, and the whole thing properly tilted and lighted had its effect on the mood of the production." Each candidate and citizen was costumed in the color of his house; Town Crier wore a particolored flowing robe, and a fool's cap. Catfish was a canvas-covered lumber-frame carried by an actor in resemblance of giant carnival masks. Papier-mache hammers and party banners effectively enlarged the puppetlike movements—Remo Bufano helped establish that style. Slusser, "a devotee of the place who saw every production of the time, usually in the first week," recalls the theatre's mood "was by no means tense or hypercritical," rather there was "a fine spirit of Come in and join us, something good is bound to happen."

Three Travelers Watch a Sunrise, by Wallace Stevens, deftly combines spectacle with philosophy in a confrontation of contemplation with reality. Three Chinese philosophers climb a hill at dawn, to contemplate sunrise. They seem unaware of a dimly visible object among the trees, which the Negro servants carrying their luggage make a discernible effort to avoid. Donning brilliantly colored Chinese robes over their business suits, the sages discuss beauty in art and life; the first and third praise seclusion, the second argues that beauty exists only with reference to life: "It is the invasion of humanity that counts." [38] Hardly audible creaks of trees punctuate the conversation which turns to the story of an Italian who disappeared on this very hill; his neighbor's daughter is said to have followed him. As the sun rises and colors the scene, it reveals the dim object as the Italian's body. The girl who crouches below it tells the wise men that he hanged himself without answering her calls. Ellis, who directed and designed the production as well as played one of the servants, enjoyed working with this script, written after a painter's heart. All was in shadow play until sunrise, which turned everything brilliantly real.

Lawrence Langner's comedy, *Pie*,[39] deals with an extramarital affair based on the incompatibility of interior decoration and cooking. Clifford Quilter has moved in with Annie Mulligan, whose apple pie he immortalizes in his latest novel (an apotheosis of marital bliss). He had deserted his wife, Diantha, an interior decorator, because she did not allow him in her rooms; thus he spent most of his time in the kitchen. Annie, their cook, pleased Cliff's palate and he pleased her by making himself useful around the kitchen. She quit because she was underpaid, and Cliff moved in with her; to keep both peace and cuisine, he is willing to divorce Diantha and marry Annie. Diantha, too, wants Annie to keep Cliff; in their "intellectual" marriage, disagreements bred dislike, but Annie can rest assured: "he'll always like your cooking." After a peaceful settlement, Diantha telephones *her* lover to report an "all clear."

Jimmy Light and the executive committee should not have taken seriously Burns Mantle's conclusion that *Pie* was the only play worth sitting through that evening. Perhaps the Young Turks felt pressure to prove themselves— Jimmy reacted "smartly to the critics' whip," threatening to "produce European dramas rather than American burlesques in the form of tragedies, comedies, and fantasies," unless incoming scripts showed improvement.[40] Certainly he believed in encouraging native talent, but must have grown impatient with the negative results, and was naturally unwilling to close the theatre. Made public the day after the fourth bill closed, his jeremiad on the lack of stageworthy American drama suggests the frustration of a junior executive unable to deliver on promises made to his superiors. Light sounded resentful, complaining that the "gaps left by the exodus of triumphant

O'Neills and Glaspells are empty and void," as though he had been victim of a deliberate walk-out. He admitted that American plays submitted to the playhouse had recently multiplied, but claimed a concomitant deterioration in quality. Unless something little short of miracle soon occurred, he warned, "the hitherto American theatre in Macdougal Street will be adulterated with translations."

No miracle occurred. Although a new O'Neill script made its way into the fifth bill, the "foreign invasion" materialized in the first and last indisputably foreign play ever put on by the Provincetown Players. Arthur Schnitzler's *Last Masks*,[41] is set in a Viennese hospital. Karl Rademacher, a journalist of about fifty who knows his days are numbered, is entertained by another patient, a young actor. To cheer the journalist, the actor suggests a method by which he believes to have cured himself: recalling adversaries from the past and telling them off nastily—in thoughts only. Inspired, Rademacher demands to see an old friend, now a celebrated author. He wrings from his physician the promise to fetch Weihgast immediately, and begins to rehearse his planned speech of invectives. The gist of the tirade is that Rademacher's seduction of Weihgast's wife makes a sham of the author's greatness. The rehearsal over, the intended victim arrives. But having vented his spleen, Rademacher has nothing more to say; he merely listens to his visitor's effluvium of pity. After Weihgast's departure Rademacher sighs to the young actor: "How pitiful they are—who must go on living."

Kurzy of the Sea is another of Djuna Barnes's Irish satires; melancholy Rory McRae, its hero, swears never to marry unless "a Queen or a Saint or a Venus, or whatever it is comes in with the tide." After much effort his father dumbfounds Rory by bringing him a scantily draped, dripping mermaid, who introduces herself as Kurzy. Recovering from fright, Rory rides off with his bride, soon to return alone. He threw her in the sea for a test, and Kurzy told him the truth: barmaid at the inn, she heard of Rory's plight during her daily swim. His story finished, Rory takes a drink and returns his mother's grey mare, "for it's a boat I shall be needing." [42]

O'Neill's *Exorcism,* which rounded out the bill, survives only in Woollcott's summary. It dealt with "a young man of substantial and correct family who is so full of contempt for it that he has walked out, head high, and fallen into the gutter." [43] So "plagued with the questioning devils within him" as to keep him from a fresh start, he swallows poison but is "yanked ... back from the brink of the grave" by drunken companions. In revival, he is a new man, "the devils have gone out of him" and he is headed for a new life on a farm in the West.

Before this program could open, instead of the hoped-for miracle, a disaster descended upon the Provincetown Players by the auditing process of the Internal Revenue Department in March 1920. Certainly, to the active members it was nothing less than a catastrophe, disrupting their activities, demanding emergency measures, and causing a two-week delay in the fifth bill's performance. To the historian, however, the surviving records generated by this shake-up afford a rare insight into the group's operation and its contact with the sustaining associate membership. It is perhaps not unfair to read signs of both moral and fiscal strength in this.

The crisis grew from the government's imposition of a War Tax on all noncharitable and noneducational institutions engaged in public entertainment. Effective as of November, 1917, money collected from admissions was taxed at a rate of ten percent. Because the Players operated as a private club (only members and their guests had access to tickets), they believed themselves exempt from this liability. A tax war over the War Tax ensued, with the Internal Revenue pressing for collection and the Provincetowners insisting that their club did not fall under the force of public taxation. Nor did they believe themselves covered by the laws on clubs, since their five dollar annual dues were below the established twelve dollar taxable minimum.[44]

After exhausting the private club argument, the Players shifted and expanded their grounds for noncompliance. They maintained that The Playwright's Theatre was not providing "public entertainment" as defined by law; rather, it qualified as an educational institution engaged in training members to write, act, and produce plays.[45] Further, the group declared itself unable to pay for reasons of poverty, sickness of officers, and disorganization (largely their own, but partially caused by the government's ambiguous position), which had prevented their collecting the tax in the first place. Much like The Living Theatre some forty years later, The Playwright's Theatre incurred trouble in part because it operated on the basis of anarchist philosophy, and partly because it was not an efficiently run business. Unlike The Living Theatre, it did not turn the government's harrassment into political confrontation or raw material for artistic work.

The Players were aided through the legalities of this tax battle by Arthur Garfield Hays, whose wife, Blanche, excelled in the costume department, and Harry Weinberger, a close associate and legal counsel of Emma Goldman. These two lawyers had previously been called upon when the organization found itself in difficulties resulting from building codes and Sunday performances. Now, first Hays and then Weinberger took up the Internal Revenue case. Their sustained arguments on behalf of the group were not entirely successful; after nearly a year of appeals (for abatements on taxes owed and penalties accrued), limited payments were made under protest as early as December 1919.[46]

The government's repeated attempts to collect money from the reluctant artists at 133 Macdougal came to a head during the spring of 1920. Investigators finally appeared on the scene: they found it much too easy to become a member, questioned the legality of the group's tax exemption as a private club, and demanded $5,000 in lieu of taxes The Playwright's Theatre should have collected on tickets sold.[47] The executive committee appealed to the membership on both sides of the curtain. Most associate members responded that they would be willing to pay the tax imposed against their current subscription. The actors, who had first begun receiving pay in January, volunteered to go without salary for the season's last two bills. Even so, the Players were left with a sizable debt to the government.[48]

Because only a portion of the relevant documents survives, and because the amounts received from members and guests, as well as amounts paid to the Internal Revenue, have been calculated in several apparently conflicting ways, it is difficult to determine precisely what was owed, what was definitely paid, and what remained in contention. Harry Weinberger's files contain the most extensive evidence regarding the tax crisis as well as other Macdougal Street economic matters. As for the tax, the Weinberger papers indicate that the Players paid the government just over $4,000, and had abatements of about $1,300 granted before the books were closed on the affair in October 1923.[49] It is clear that the Revenue Department demanded ten percent on *all* admissions, whether paid by members in the form of subscription or by guests in the form of single tickets. When the group finally began paying, it did so on the basis of ten percent on guest tickets only, not acknowledging any debt on payments made by members.[50] Eventually, the government did manage to collect some taxes on the membership income, though the percentage basis and regularity of these payments is uncertain. For the 1919–20 season, the Provincetowners appear to have paid about three percent on receipts from members; solid documentation for other seasons is lacking.

Among other financial papers in the Weinberger files are two informative balance sheets for the 1917–18 and 1918–19 seasons that show the income and expenses of the group. Based partially on estimates, the figures reveal a steady increase both in box-office receipts and in the portion deriving from nonmembers. A third balance sheet among Edna Kenton's papers (for the 1919–20 season), and numerous pieces of evidence about salaries help bring into focus the economic background of the Provincetown Players' gradual change from a purely amateur undertaking to a semiprofessional theatre. Financial gains in combination with popular and critical acclaim surely affected value judgments concerning success and failure.

According to the balance sheets, income from admissions amounted to about $4,500 during the second New York season.[51] No figure survives from the first season, but it must have been considerably lower because prices were raised for the second: subscriptions rose from four to five dollars, single tickets from fifty to seventy-five cents.[52] Receipts for the "successful" third season (1918–19) climbed to about $5,400, while for the fourth—the Season of Youth—they exceeded $10,000. Admission income was to rise dramatically during the fifth year because of the success of *The Emperor Jones*, to an astounding $26,000.

Meanwhile, the proportion of memberships and guest tickets was also changing. During the second season, guests brought in about half as much as members (or one-third of box-office income). In the third season, guests provided just over half of total admissions, while in the fourth, monies received from guests exceeded membership dues by a factor of three to one. The balance sheet for this 1919–20 season indicates a complex and impressive budget, certainly enough figures to have justified the Revenue Department's interest. There was a favorable balance of $1,630.79 after total receipts of $14,133.14 and disbursements of $12,502.35. On the credit side, memberships accounted for $5,676.11, and guest tickets for $4,972.92.[53] That, of course, meant that nonmembers appearing at the window with a member—a somewhat casual arrangement, especially if tickets were being dispensed by the anarchist "Fitzi"—provided in excess of forty-six percent of box-office revenue. By the next season, it appears that less than one-fourth the admission income was being derived from members.

Surprisingly, major expense items in these later seasons were salaries. In comparison with the first New York season, when only the president and secretary were paid the combined salaries of about $900, the 1919–20 payroll included the director, a stage manager, his assistant, and the secretary-treasurer, with a combined salary of over $5,000. According to Kenton, an assistant secretary had already been on the payroll in the fall of 1918.[54]

By the third season, each bill's run became extended from two weekends to two weeks; actors' wages were now listed as a separate item among expenses. That they were not expected to depend on The Playwright's Theatre for a living is clear from the amount: $1,524.90 in toto. Because the number of actors remains unspecified but total performance time is known as twelve weeks, each bill cost the group an average of nearly $250; if not more than ten actors were cast in each bill, that would equal an average pay of $25 for each two-week run. Jasper Deeter claims to have received only $15 for the run of *The Eldest* in January.[55]

The smallest item in that third season's budget was sixty-two dollars, earmarked for unspecified advertising. Specific reference to a public relation expenditure was Kenton's statement that the Players' subscription to Romeike's clipping service began in the spring of 1918.[56]

In view of such increased professionalization it is interesting to compare attitudes recalled by two of the younger men, both actors of professional caliber. Charles Ellis's artistic ambition lay in painting; he fell in with the Players as a designer, but found acting almost unavoidable. He tended to enjoy it, seeing it as an opportunity to employ purely technical skills to produce certain calculated (primarily visual) effects to invoke an emotional response in the audience, where Ellis thought it belonged. Eventually he was considered one of the better actors, and found it easy to earn a living in the theatre, although reserving his devotion for painting. He spoke of having barely tolerated a great deal of what he considered gibberish about motivation and the actor's true spiritual involvement in the characters' emotions, but found it easier to pretend he was emoting than to argue. Only seldom did a poetic play relieve him of what he believed was a continuous fraud imposed upon his acting.[57]

Jasper Deeter, on the other hand, was fully devoted to the theatre. Not content with Broadway's commercial approach and soon disillusioned with the Coburns' repertory company, he looked about in Greenwich Village. In April 1919 he took bit parts in Frank Conroy's production of *Shakuntala*, and meanwhile attended several Provincetown performances. There, Deeter believed, worthwhile scripts were poorly directed and indifferently acted. Consequently, The Playwright's Theatre seemed an ideal place for a young actor confident of his talents to launch a career. His acting would stand out suffi-

ciently to be noticed, and could earn him six different roles—with luck, six
favorable notices as well—a season, while his peers uptown might be tied
up in a long run. Deeter made Jimmy Light's acquaintance and agreed to
appear in Macdougal Street that coming November.[58] He was cast in every
bill of the season after that, and soon came to be regarded as a competent
director as well.

A contrast of a different sort is observable between Edward Goodman
and Helen Westley, both former Washington Square Players. Goodman had
directed regularly, including a few occasions for the Provincetowners. After
the Washington Square Players disbanded in 1917 he continued to teach and
direct in New York, and had apparently earned O'Neill's respect for, according to Deeter, it was at the author's insistence that Goodman was called in
to direct *Exorcism*.[59] When the dormant Washington Square Players reappeared after the war as the Theatre Guild, Helen Westley became a member
in good standing. While acting in the Guild production of Tolstoy's *Power
of Darkness* (January 1920), she made her first public attempt at directing
in Macdougal Street: her vehicle, Djuna Barnes's slight whimsy, *An Irish
Triangle,* was in sharp contrast with the gloomy Russian mood. She returned
to direct her second (and the Provincetowners' third) Barnes play, *Kurzy of
the Sea,* in April. [60]

The *Power of Darkness* has another connection with the Players: in it
Ida Rauh made her Broadway debut,[61] which gains added interest from the
context. Her name appeared alongside Light's as co-director for the Season
of Youth on the merit of her having been one of the group's best actresses
as well as a founder, and a very close associate of Jig's.[62] She directed two
plays on the first bill, and acted in a third, but then had nothing to do with
the second bill, and parted company with the group—not returning to act
until February 1921, although she was listed as a member of the executive
committee from the beginning of that season! She gave the removal of Jig's
name from the playbills and letterhead as the cause of her exit—though those
actions must have been taken with her knowledge.[63]

The Season of Youth ended, as had most other seasons, with a review
bill, which, for unknown reasons included only one play from the current
season: *Aria da Capo*. The two others, O'Neill's *Where the Cross is Made*,
and Dell's *Sweet and Twenty* were favorites from the two previous years,
although they had not been on the review bills. But then, subscribers were
not limited to vote for current plays. Edna St. Vincent Millay, who repeated

her original portrayal of the romantic heroine in Dell's playlet, was returned to the executive committee, which included "co-directors" Cook and Light, Eleanor Fitzgerald, Charles Ellis, Edna Kenton, and—apparently reconciled— Ida Rauh. Next fall, during the run of *The Emperor,* the Committee received three *additional* members: Glaspell, O'Neill, and E. J. Ballantine.[64]

Though their year had its share of difficulties, that was hardly news in Macdougal Street. What was a matter of pride for the Young Turks was that they carried the season to conclusion barely scathed and had both artistic and fiscal laurels to show for their trouble.

The Dome

"Nothing there but infinity and the stage, . . ."
George Cram Cook's notes cited by Susan Glaspell,
THE ROAD TO THE TEMPLE

"If we went uptown, we expanded, and
we've headed ever since for the rocks."
Edna Kenton, to Cook and Glaspell,
July 14, 1922

1   The last phase of the Provincetown Players' productive ferment began with an excitement very much like one that inspired the collective's move to New York. In the summer of 1916, the decision to establish a theatre in Greenwich Village was largely prompted by the discovery of a young playwright, Eugene O'Neill, who seemed to grow out of, and thrive in, the fertile soil of collective creativity imbued with a Dionysian spirit. Four seasons of experimentation, in the course of which twelve short plays of his were produced by the group, afforded him "prolonged preliminary freedom with stage and audience" [1] at The Playwright's Theatre. As a result the dramatist had been recognized as America's most talented even before *Beyond the Horizon* was produced on Broadway and won the Pulitzer Prize, edging out James Forbes's *The Famous Mrs. Fair*. In the summer of 1920, Jig Cook was again intent on kindling heavenly fire in the entire—and by this time, fragmented—collective. He was under the spell of a new kind of play O'Neill was writing, one that probed the Jungian unconscious of Western man and appeared to demand a vision of pure space on the tiny stage.

As the wharf remains a symbol of "that great Provincetown summer," [2] of the productive blending of disparate creative talents and energies, and of the first (and formative) spontaneous spurt of the group's accomplishments, so the dome represents the collective's second (and ultimately destructive) artistic eruption. As the former resulted in stimulating recognition, so the latter in devastating success. The wharf embodied the glory of group creativity, the dome emblematized pure space.

The Emperor Jones—the script O'Neill had been struggling with on the Cape while he and Cook absented themselves from the city's distractions—is often mistakenly analyzed as dealing with the question of race. Although the author's identification of "the primitive force" within homo sapiens with an Afro-American ex-slave is indeed rooted in the prevailing atmosphere of racial prejudice, the actual theme of the play is the blatant duality of human nature ("the beauty of the world" vs. "this quintessence of dust"). Without questioning the universality of that theme or the script's specific connection with the oft-told saga of the silver bullet, in the Provincetown context two other facts need emphasis. One is the resemblance of that duality to Nietzsche's coupling of the Apollinian and Dionysian in *The Birth of Tragedy*—a seminal book devoured and repeatedly debated by Cook and O'Neill. The other, that O'Neill's vivid interest in primitive ritual was accentuated by William Zorach who shared with the playwright a fascination with cubist features in African masks.[3]

The entire group was pleased with (but possibly also jealous of) O'Neill's Broadway success, and gratified that he chose to return to the Macdougal Street laboratory—his wish expressed in the messages he sent to the group heralding the birth of this new kind of play. O'Neill trudged across the sand dunes to read the completed script to Cook and Glaspell, and Jig's enthusiasm was instantaneous; he wanted to go back to the Village: "This is what I have been waiting for—a play to call forth the utmost each one can do, and fuse all into unity." Laying aside drafts of his own new play, *The Spring,* he hurried to the train for New York and grew prophetic: "This marks the success of the Provincetown Players. Gene knew there was a place where such a play would be produced. He wrote it to compel us to do the untried, to do the 'impossible.' "[4]

In view of what has already been said of Cook's personality, it is likely that he had urged O'Neill to write something that would be impossible to produce on Broadway. Repeatedly, when the Players experienced a slump, they had turned to O'Neill for a lift and—although grudgingly at times—he had always complied. In 1920 the situation in Macdougal Street was more complex. Broadway had at last beckoned O'Neill; whether he would switch over or not was a decision crucial not only for his individual career but also for the collective that had nurtured, and was in turn enriched by, his creative output. On the other hand, although not exactly in a slump, the group had its crises of identity, collective as well as individual. Of the latter, Cook's was of greatest concern. His sabbatical leave from the playhouse for the 1919–20 season seemed to have exacerbated the very generational conflict it was supposed to have soothed.

Members of the younger faction felt they had made good use of Jig's absence to prove that a laboratory can thrive in an organized, professional atmosphere as well or better than in an environment of spontaneous bursts of creativity that were a matter of faith with Cook. In addition to two new O'Neill scripts, their lively and successful season had introduced new plays by Edna Millay, Mike Gold, Djuna Barnes, Alfred Kreymborg, and Wallace Stevens, among others. Scheduled bills were produced on time, expenses were paid. Some of the "old-timers" got along famously with the younger group and with their palpably more professional manner of operation. Thus Millay and Lawrence Langner directed their own plays while Light took on the staging of four one-acts during the season. Directors Ballantine and Goodman brought considerable professional expertise to Macdougal Street; the Players' experimental spirit, on the other hand, offered Charles Ellis and Helen Westley their first crack at directing. O'Neill's momentary breakthrough into the mainstream, which they took pride in, was also interpreted as a victory won by a professional. When Jig Cook returned, chafing at the bit to take the lead at the Playwright's Theatre, "perhaps he felt he hadn't been missed too much," [5] nor, perhaps, did the Young Turks' success fill him with unmixed joy. Another question is, How pleased was Cook with his own productivity? He had been working on *The Spring,* while O'Neill completed *The Emperor Jones.* Rooted in American Indian traditions, which he attempted to fuse with forays into extrasensory perception, *The Spring* was notably not as successful in preserving or creating myth as *The Emperor* was.[6] And so, Jig once again threw his enthusiasm into another man's creative endeavor rather than his own.

2   On arrival in New York, Cook mobilized the Players for a new season that was to open with O'Neill's *Emperor.* The Provincetowners liked what they heard about the script (the author was still polishing it), but they grew apprehensive when Jig mentioned the mysterious "dome" as its indispensable scenic apparatus. As Edna Kenton put it:

We listened to Jig, truly a madman, telling us over and over again that we must risk our all and put in the dome for *The Emperor*. None of us had read the script yet; we took it on faith as Gene's best play. But we said, all of us, that the dome couldn't go in—not yet. We suggested putting off *The Emperor* to the second bill or the third; whenever we said that, Jig never failed to pick up his hat and walk out.[7]

The dome (often called a plaster-dome or *Kuppelhorizont*)—the projected building of which thrilled Cook, bewildered the collective, and promised to swallow up funds saved from the previous season—is a device once widely used in Europe and made famous in 1919 by Max Reinhardt's installation of one in the Grosses Schauspielhaus. It is a segment of a true dome, made of plaster, the inside of which is used as a reflecting surface to represent the horizon. A combination of vertical and horizontal curvatures can achieve an illusion of greater depth than a cyclorama hung flat, even on a shallower stage.

In addition to an unprecedented financial outlay and to seemingly unsurmountable construction problems, many Players also objected to the realization of Jig's dream because they thought that, ideal as it might be for staging some plays, it would obstruct scenery for others.[8] After extended debate among members, the executive committee finally decided *against* building the dome.[9] Cook's response was an immediate and "deliberate 'going against the group,' a reversal of executive decision." Kenton went to the playhouse to see if the script for *The Emperor* had arrived yet, and found Jig

> in a morass of steel netting and iron bars and cement and in workman's clothes, suddenly posing himself against expected attack, as troubled and astonished. I came down the aisle toward him. "There's no argument about this," he told me without preface. "I've had enough from everybody. 'The Emperor' has *got* to have a dome to play against. You see, Edna, it begins . . . thick forest at first . . . steadily thinned out . . . scene after scene . . . to pure space. . . ." It was happening, one of his hours of rare creative fancy, and, for the hour, the work dropped, he stood, in his workman's clothes, against the plastery dome, thinking aloud the values to be found and given from the playwright's brief directions of his scenes.

She thought it ironic that the foremost advocate of "the unity of the group" had reversed "the united verdict"—and in retrospect saw Jig's action as "an

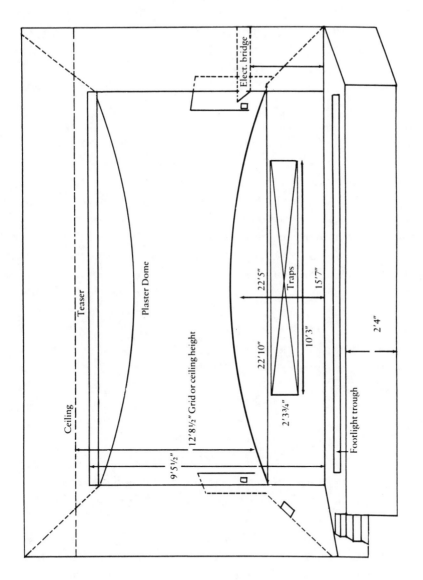

17 Diagram of the stage at 133 Macdougal Street. From Federal Theatre Project Technical Survey.

outstanding example of fine dictatorship as to purpose and, as fate would have it, to result as well." [10]

His defiant initiative taken, Cook was not deserted: certainly James Light, and probably Donald Corley as well, lent a hand to the attempted creation of "pure space." Prior to his becoming a Provincetown Player, Light had studied architecture and design; a newspaper article he wrote about the dome, and construction details he recalled shortly before his death, both carry an air of authenticity.[11] If Corley, in fact, "had drawn the plans" [12] he was unavailable to convert them into reality.

An elliptical groundplan and a circular cross section were chosen, large-grain sand was applied to the plaster surface—to provide the best combination of optimum light reflection and diffusion in the smallest space. As predicted, the "constant rate of change in the direction of [the dome's] surface" and the high count of crystalline reflective surfaces enabled the new device to create a sense of infinite space on the tiny stage as well as to produce an unlimited number of hues and degrees of saturation. Impressive though it was, the dome was to be only the first step toward Cook's second ideal, a theatre of "pure space." As far ahead of its time as the concept of a theatre of communal ecstasy, Jig's "perfect place" was to become a core of great physical expansion as well as spiritual renewal—a dream theatre he hoped would be erected in Washington Square. As excerpted by Glaspell, Cook's notes are not easy to interpret, but they conjure up images of dome-clusters foreshadowing Buckminster Fuller, or visions of Wieland Wagner's use of scenic discs.[13]

3   The Players' production of O'Neill's hypnotic *Emperor* overwhelmed subscribers and critics, and it was engulfed by a flood of spectators who had never before heard of the group. Besides the script and the lighting that created the essential atmosphere, the success was due to the superb acting of Charles Gilpin in the title role—the first time a black man played the lead in a straight play produced by a white company. Although Gilpin's talent was recognized in the reviews, he never found another vehicle he needed for its full expression.[14] The lighting effects, made possible by the dome, impressed audiences so much that they demanded encores, and attracted two designers to Macdougal Street: Robert Edmond Jones who, since sharing in

18   "Throneroom of de Emperor Jones," watercolor by Cleon Throckmorton.
(Macgowan Papers, Department of Special Collections, University Research
Library, UCLA)

the formation of the collective had become a leading American scenographer,
and Cleon Throckmorton whose talent was fully to unfold at this theatre.

Most New York critics, who did not discover *The Emperor* until the
third night,[15] responded with enthusiasm. Heywood Broun, a subscriber
who attended first nights, considered O'Neill's new work "the most interesting play which has yet come from the most promising playwright in America," and saw even its shortcomings as those of "a truly fine play." Dwelling
on the production, he observed that

> the waits between these scenes are often several minutes in length. Each
> wait is a vulture which preys upon the attention. . . . Still we have no
> disposition to say, "If only the play had been done in the 'commercial
> theatre'!" . . . "The Emperor Jones" is so unusual in its technique that
> it might wait in vain for a production anywhere except in so adven-
> turous a playhouse as the Provincetown Theatre. As a matter of fact,
> the setting of the play on the little stage is fine and imaginative and
> the lighting effects uncommonly beautiful.[16]

Within the week Broun was joined by a chorus including Kenneth Macgowan, Alexander Woollcott, Burns Mantle, Maida Castellun, and Steven Rathbun, the last two resembling advertising copywriters: "This is a rare and richly imaginative feast for lovers of true drama. No one should miss it." [17] "The first bill . . . is worth subscribing for the whole season to see. And you cannot see it unless you are a subscriber. So subscribe now and avoid the rush. Telephone Spring 8363 to secure your reservations for the evening you wish to go, and then you can pay for your subscription when you arrive." [18] Even Woollcott—generally most critical of Provincetown productions—conceded that with the dome "on their little stage they can now get such illusions of distance and the wide outdoors as few of their uptown rivals can achieve." [19]

Once again, Jig was the hero of the Provincetown Players. His devotion to O'Neill, his insistence on the dome had been right, and "it soon developed . . . that no one had been against putting in the dome—that we had all wanted it." [20] Reviews and word of mouth brought unprecedented crowds to Macdougal Street, and the bill's run was extended from the usual two weeks to almost two months.[21] When the time came to provide subscribers with a second bill on December 27, Adolph Klauber's offer to move *The Emperor* uptown for a series of matinees was regarded by most members as the well-earned reward of four courageous New York seasons. The decision to make use of the opportunity was therefore made with an overwhelming vote "one member of the Executive Committee voting NO to the end." [22] Brutus Jones continued his triumphal run at the Selwyn on Broadway—without the dome —*Tickless Time* having replaced *Matinata* as curtain raiser in order to include Jig and Susan; by May the production had become profitable "property," and in July was exported to London.

With the momentous excursion from the Village the second climax of the collective's life had peaked. In the aftermath of victory, even before it fell apart completely, the group ceased being a collective. Success went to the Players' head—not excepting Jig. The single dissenting vote was cast and the uptown venture consistently opposed by Edna Kenton alone—bookish, nonplaywright, nonactor, nonstagehand, only playreader Edna.[23] She apparently believed that the group was not ready to expand. But going along with the majority, Cook was enthusiastically for taking *The Emperor* to Broadway. Even when he regretted that decisive step, Jig seems to have been slow to draw conclusions—"All this pow-wow and meanness . . . is not going to lead to any true and beautiful work there or elsewhere. Time after time, we are brought back to the fact that the Provincetown Players would do better to stick to their own modest and intensely important job. . . . Fills atmosphere of P.P. with up-town point of view of money and notoriety" [24];—and he fell short of translating them into action.

For not only did he support similarly extending the run of *Diff'rent* at the Selwyn in February 1921; by August, Cook was eager to follow the two O'Neill plays with his own, much weaker, *The Spring*. To Glaspell he reported that Harry Weinberger and he had each put a thousand dollars into that gamble, and wondered if the Players as a group ought not to invest.[25] The point is not whether *The Spring* "deserved" to go uptown (which it did not), but that Jig Cook found himself wanting it to go, wanting to share the success that had come to O'Neill. That he was shocked by that discovery is conveyed in a letter Jig later wrote in Delphi: "Our individual gifts and talents have sought their private perfection. We have not, as we hoped, created the beloved community of life-givers. Our richest, like our poorest, have desired most not to give life, but to have it given to them. We have valued creative energy less than its rewards—our sin against our Holy Ghost." [26]

4   Until *The Emperor* became a "hit," the Provincetown Players was a revolutionary collective, a "laboratory for human emotions" taking the shape of theatre, proving that native talent can be a "transforming force" of "our unrealized nation" [27] as long as untried views and techniques were fearlessly and honestly allowed to unfold. A majority of the group believed that ignorance of theatrical routine freed them to explore open processes and to create sound products, a view Copeau had shared, and one that was to become widespread in the sixties. It is easily seen in retrospect that the time of glory was the ideal time to quit, "to go to Greece" [28] symbolically, the time to disperse—divide the leaven, multiply its power—engendering as many new creative experiments as the group had members. For the Players *had* accomplished its task when its best actors, directors, and playwrights no longer felt the need for the collective's essential offering—its amateur spirit and amateur production methods—but, having outgrown that need, came to regard as a liability what used to be an asset. What had happened, largely as the result of the Provincetown Players' career in the vanguard of the little theatre movement, was that the theatrical atmosphere had been changed to permit con-

19 "The Edge of the Forest," watercolor by Cleon Throckmorton for *The Emperor Jones*. (Norman Philbrick Library)

sideration for Broadway production of such playwrights as O'Neill, Glaspell, and others; to provide opportunities for actors like Ann Harding, Charles Ellis, and Margaret Wycherley, for directors like Jasper Deeter and James Light, designers like Cleon Throckmorton; to enter the mainstream without giving up their integrity or being swallowed up.

Gradual deviation from the original principles of spontaneity and amateurism had now run its full course: in the aftermath of public recognition, the Provincetown Players ceased to be a collective. But the abandonment of their philosophy has in the long run less significance than the breakthrough achieved by its earlier propelling force. Understood in that way, success had to mean breaking up the group or changing its ideology. But the wish to continue in an effort (and in an ambiance) that, after arduous and faltering struggle, suddenly seems proven right is deeply human. It is, moreover, questionable to what extent the group understood the meaning or impact of its own breakthrough. Even more rooted in the present than most artists, because of their stubbornly maintained innocence of theatrical tradition, members had a deliberately narrow perspective on the group's achievements. Yet, two alternatives appear to have been perceived when participants faced unexpected acclaim: continue in the manner vindicated as if nothing had changed, or turn hard-earned success into capital for professional careers. The majority seems to have taken the latter course; some consciously pursuing it, others unconsciously driven along. The Players' collective ambition was at the deepest level still unselfish: they wanted to give more playwrights, more actors, more directors, and more designers still more opportunities to try new things. So they hung on to the idea of their character as it was before they were swept away by fame. And yet, a scramble for direct personal rewards ensued—not unethically, but contrary to the group's beginnings. In this process, a sort of natural selection (previously deliberately suppressed) became unavoidable. Whereas earlier it may not have been admitted that members possessed talents of unequal force (or could not express them to the same apparent effect), in the distribution of credits—honorific or financial—comparative evaluations could no longer be shirked.

Because the claim of amateurism had not been abandoned, the matter of honorific rewards should be examined first. In view of published accounts celebrating Jig Cook as the group's hero and implying his intimate involvement in O'Neill's creation of *The Emperor Jones,* it is remarkable that the first playbill issued for the production's unusually long run does *not* list a director.[29] A later version of the program shows the statement "Directed by George Cram Cook" inserted below the line acknowledging (as in the first version) Throckmorton's "assistance in the design and execution of sets." [30] Little direct evidence is or can be available about what happened, but there are a few hints.

For one thing, during the season that began with *The Emperor* all playbills state that the Provincetown Players are "under the direction of George Cram Cook and James Light." [31] This means that Light was elevated into a position second only to the revered founder—probably as a result of his successful directorship during Cook's absence. For another, Harry Kemp relates an exchange, during rehearsals for this production, between Cook and O'Neill, in which the former's enthusiasm was allegedly cut off by the latter's "You're a rotten producer, and I came to tell you that I've reached a place where I must have competent direction." [32]

Then there is Jasper Deeter's mysterious presence. He had joined the group during the year of Jig's absence and proven himself an effective, if ambitious, actor and director. He had thought to have become Cook's right hand, and identified himself as "one of the younger men" over whose shoulders Jig dramatically threw "the great cloak he wore," designating him heir apparent.[33] In connection with *The Emperor*, Deeter is alleged to have been instrumental in procuring Throckmorton's services, and, perhaps more important, to have recruited Gilpin for the leading role after Paul Robeson reportedly turned down Cook's first appeal.[34] In an interview Deeter even claimed to have directed the play (in which he acted the strong supporting part of Smithers) "sometimes with Jig's help, sometimes directly working with Gilpin." [35] That his relations with Cook were paradoxical is indicated by Deeter's dismissal from *The Emperor*'s road company, and by his subsequent attempt to revive Jig's less than popular *The Spring* in repertory with Glaspell's well-received *Inheritors* as an abortive Spring Season.[36]

The record, at any rate, as to who deserved acclaim for directing *The Emperor*, is unclear. In the turmoil following the celebration, the line of demarcation between credit and fiscal benefit may have been thin. Lawrence Langner's *Matinata* was originally used as the curtain raiser, because the O'Neill work was not quite full-length. For the uptown run, however, it became an issue to have the short piece preceding *The Emperor* be more "representative" of the membership. Langner, founder of both the Washington Square Players and the Theatre Guild, was not thought of as a Provincetowner, and so, on pretty quick notice, *Tickless Time* was substituted. It was not regarded as a better script, but it had been written by Jig and Susan, and it had excellent roles for Jimmy Light, Norma Millay, Blanche Hays, and even Christine Ell. Thus it included a better sampling of the group—the most painful omission having been that of Ida Rauh.[37] The substitution of *Tickless Time* may seem honorific until set into the context of the Players' exploding payroll at this time.

The first evidence they were paying an author is O'Neill's letter to George C. Tyler, producer of *Beyond the Horizon*, in which he "confessed" to being so broke as to have been "forced" to request "royalties." [38] The irony should not be missed, that this occurs just after his first Broadway run and his receipt of the Pulitzer Prize. True, there is no evidence that *Tickless Time* also paid royalties, but because it went uptown, it should have. Moreover, as a result of the practice initiated during Jig's absence, some actors continued receiving remuneration—whether salaries or the number of actors increased faster is unclear: "In the cast of eighteen people Gilpin topped the list with a salary of $50." [39] Norma Millay (cast in the curtain raiser) recalled receiving her first salary, fifteen dollars a week, promptly investing it at Klauber's invitation in the uptown run, and soon having her capital tripled.[40] Granted, these payments were modest, but—ten years before the Depression—no mere pittance.

Success was also reflected in the expansion of the backstage staff: Throckmorton was now listed as technical director, presumably in command over a stage manager with two assistants (one new), and a newly added electrician.[41]

The inflow of cash confirmed Cook's suspicions that even unselfishly given dollars would tend to harm the spirit. Perhaps because the money now appeared as the consequence of a spiritual victory and as earned by hard work, the damage was greater: it triggered competition for jobs among members of the group. Success, long run, salaries, uptown, and finally the promise of a London tour completely undermined the amateur atmosphere which had become fragile long ago. Lessons of the Season of Youth without Jig's leadership were coming into sharper focus: collective creative ecstasy alone could not be relied upon as solid basis for a long-term producing organization. The nature of the experiment had to change because the original participants had either left or undergone subtle but important changes, and because all newcomers did not share all underlying assumptions.

The new situation revealed a paradox in the laboratory process, of which Jig's innocent (and in some ways, mad) creative imagination was prime mover. It not only resulted in radical breakthroughs that rendered the Provincetown achievement unique, not only spawned equally provocative departures by individuals and groups; but also nourished talented people of professional caliber and ambition for careers in traditional theatre. It is thus that the impact of visionaries, extremists out on a productive limb, often finds its way into the mainstream.

This was a bitter time for Jig Cook. "When the Provincetown Players succeeded, Jig felt they had failed" [42] was Glaspell's somewhat simplistic assessment. True, Cook was still committed to the idea that amateurism was the rejuvenating force of American theatre when others around him had outgrown that insistence as soon as they felt capable of professional caliber work. But in the success of artists with whom he had worked shoulder to shoulder, Jig also experienced a personal failure. He temporarily retired to Cape Cod and accused those caught in the race for "who goes to London" of betrayal and selfishness. And when Edna Kenton urged his return to New York in order to restore "final authority," [43] Cook acted as if he had all along opposed going uptown.[44]

Of all the Players, Jig was naturally most reluctant to see change as inevitable, and accept it. But when the London contingent had left he finally recognized the altered conditions and needs. "It is a good thing," he reasoned "that we are exporting so many of last season's personalities. There is a fairly clean slate for a new group. . . . some clean work can be done." [45] What was on his mind is indicated by a proposal he drew up for a repertory company, envisioned as functioning in his dream theatre of domes. In a public letter he wrote:

> The will to start a repertory theatre is now stirring. Two things are needed. First, the necessary capital, not to be donated, but invested in a proper building. Second, an organization that can be trusted to maintain a high artistic standard. I wish to point out that at the close of their seventh season the Provincetown Players need take only one or two short steps in order to become a repertory theatre of high interest and value. . . . Placed in a proper theatre the Provincetown Players could immediately put into repertory the best of the seventy-seven plays they have already produced. The Provincetown Players have known how to pay their way—for seven years—even when the way has cost a good deal. They should now be backed with sufficient invested capital, given a perfect place in which to work, and concentrate into the most vital theatre in the world. [46]

The appeal is couched in terms characteristic of Jig's long-range opposition to subsidy, yet it also betrays the effect of success upon his thinking: he portrays the organization as a worthwhile investment opportunity—hardly an amateur attitude. Moreover, the idea of a repertory theatre indicates a return to tradition.

Meanwhile *Diff'rent,* and its curtain raiser, Lawrence Vail's *What D'You Want,* had taken *The Emperor*'s place in Macdougal Street, and eventually followed it to the Selwyn. That bill was nothing to be ashamed of for an experimental group. O'Neill's story (a disillusioned innocent seeking her revenge) was as unconventional as his format: it required an acting ensemble to leap over a thirty year's gap between two halves of the performance. Charles O'Brien Kennedy had come from the staff of the distinguished Broadway director, Arthur Hopkins, to take command of rehearsals; the leading role had once again been given to a new member, Mary Blair. These two newcomers (one, a seasoned professional, the other a beginner) were supported by an enthusiastic group of stalwarts including Charles Ellis and Jimmy

20 Watercolor for Cook's *The Spring,* by Cleon Throckmorton. (Norman Philbrick Library)

Light.[47] Vail's piece was exploratory as well: it treated the theme of instant wish fulfillment in a surrealistic manner.[48] But no matter how interesting *Diff'rent,* how competent its cast, and how intriguing its companion piece, this production never came near duplicating the electrifying impact of the previous bill. Yet, on the waves of renown just reaped by O'Neill both on Broadway and off, *Diff'rent* also went uptown.

Jig Cook's second and most ambitious full-length play, *The Spring,* went into rehearsal at this time for the season's third bill. Just as the Provincetown Players' numbers and energies were depleted, their expectations rose once more. If the group's founder expected to match the breakthrough of his foremost protege, an anticlimax was inevitable. What followed, however, was a disaster, for the artistic effect of *The Spring* did not keep step with its ambitious plan, and the staging did not and could not remedy the mediocrity of the script. Without bringing large houses to Macdougal Street, *The Spring* went on to a series of uptown matinees where it had to close prematurely for lack of attendance. The dispersal of Jig Cook's Provincetown Players was in sight.

From Republic
to Triumvirate

1　　　　The group's dissolution, which had begun when the Players ceased to be a collective in the wake of *The Emperor*'s phenomenal success, was realized early in 1922. Although Jig Cook had waged an ultimately victorious campaign for indigenous American drama, for inoculating the country with Dionysian ferment, he fought a losing battle over *The Hairy Ape*. Not until the Provincetowners lost control over a production of their most fecund talent, Eugene O'Neill, did Cook admit to himself that the group had failed to turn his dream completely into reality. He then departed for Greece to absorb what he could from antiquity, offer a contribution to its glorious past, and die; he is buried near the navel of the ancient world.

As far as the public knew, during the first two months of 1922 the Provincetown Players were "occupied . . . with grand plans for presentation of a new O'Neill play," while leasing their theatre to the Repertory Company of Maurice Browne and Ellen Van Volkenburg (an old Chicago connection) for a production of Arthur Davison Ficke's *Mr. Faust* as the fourth bill.[1] Under that thin cover, the host organization of The Playwright's Theatre was in disarray. The road production of *The Emperor Jones* tied up a goodly portion of the group; Jimmy Light, who had gone to London but had not returned with the company, had been divested of his directorship at the beginning of the season.[2] Meanwhile, other members not on tour (e.g., Norma

Millay and Charles Ellis) had found professional opportunities that prevented their rejoining what was left of the Players' core in Macdougal Street.[3]

Cook was unable to exercise his usual magic powers of cohesion, perhaps because the bond with O'Neill had been practically severed. By January the author was nearing completion of his expressionistic play, and making private arrangements to assure professional rather than amateur production. Ostensibly this was to be realized within the framework of the Provincetown Players, or at least using the familiar Greenwich Village premises of the lapsing laboratory of human emotions. O'Neill first wanted Charles O'Brien Kennedy, a seasoned Provincetowner but also on the staff of the distinguished Broadway director, Arthur Hopkins, to head up the new production. On Kennedy's advice, the playwright chose Louis Wolheim for the title role. There seems to have been an understanding that Hopkins would take *The Hairy Ape* uptown after a run at 133 Macdougal. According to Burns Mantle, Hopkins quickly assumed control of the play, but at the author's request agreed to let the Players have it for a few weeks.[4]

O'Neill was pleased over having the production out of the Players' hands. In a letter to George Jean Nathan, he explained his plans and hopes: "Kennedy, a Hopkins man, will direct, Wolheim, a Hopkins actor, will play the lead, I hope. . . . Finally, Bobby Jones will do the eight sets, which must be in the Expressionistic method. So you can see it will not be an amateur affair but can be relied upon to achieve results."[5] And to Kenneth Macgowan he proudly announced that Hopkins himself volunteered "to help in the directing, gratis, although he had not seen the play. . . ."[6]

Kennedy, who had directed several Provincetown productions in previous years, became unavailable for some reason. This caused a delay of the opening, as well as an apparent conflict over who would direct. With his complex negotiations in jeopardy, O'Neill appears to have asked Light—just back from Europe—to fill in.[7] Cook may have already begun rehearsing, but even if not, he would rightly have felt slapped in the face. Nor was the blow lessened by the continued behind the scenes involvement of Arthur Hopkins. In a series of announcements, the *New York Tribune* followed the developments: on February 5 it held out the possibility that Hopkins would direct and Jones design; on February 12 it reported that O'Neill was "supervising rehearsals in conjunction with George Cram Cook," and on the twenty-sixth it carried the unusual statement that "James Light will be Stage Manager."[8] The playbill perpetuated the confusion, stating "Produced by The Provincetown Players" in the spot usually accorded the director.[9] Jones and Throckmorton were jointly credited with the design, while Light's name appeared, in fact, as stage manager—for the first and last time. Light later claimed that he did take over the task of directing from Cook, and that collective credit seemed preferable to naming them both.[10]

It was under the impact of these events that Jig, after participating in a series of quick, sober, and painful decisions about the group's future, bid the Players farewell in despair, exclaiming, "It is time to go to Greece!" [11] He and Susan Glaspell sailed on March 1 and on the ninth *The Hairy Ape* opened—two weeks behind the announced schedule.[12] It was, according to O'Neill in a letter to Fitzi, "really only about a one-fifth Provincetown Player production" which could not have been done at all except for outside talent called in to help.[13] Hopkins did move the play to his Plymouth Theatre on May 1, Carlotta Monterey (the future Mrs. O'Neill) replacing Mary Blair (the future Mrs. Edmund Wilson) in the role of Mildred.[14] The Players at Macdougal Street, for their part, were left wrangling with Hopkins over payment of five percent due them on the gross of the seven-week uptown run.[15]

The chief reason for calling a halt to the activity under his leadership was Jig Cook's conviction that he had failed not only as an artist, but also— and more important—as leader of the once dedicated and now demoralized group. The former of these judgments was more fully correct and its truth, certainly in retrospect, more clearly evident. Yet Cook seems not fully to have perceived it until the direction of O'Neill's play was overtly taken off his hands by an "upstart." The latter conclusion, however, is less accurate but of greater significance.

True enough, the group strayed from its charted course and fixed its sights on Broadway. More to the point, Jig himself fell victim to the popular notion of success: as an artist he failed to accept that his own experiments in playwriting resulted in essentially flawed executions of grandiose concepts; as a leader he remained blind to the fait accompli that the Provincetown Players *had* fulfilled its mission. This lack of understanding is sharply revealed by a letter in which Cook eloquently, if pathetically, analyzed the group's failure as his very own:

Three years ago, writing for the Provincetown Players, anticipating the forlornness of our hope to bring to birth in our commercial minded country a theatre whose motive was spiritual, I made this promise: "We promise to let this theatre die rather than let it become another voice of mediocrity." I am now forced to confess that our attempt to build up, by our own life and death, in this alien sea, a coral island of our own, has failed. We have failed to draw from American writers enough of the kind of plays which justify our further existence as a theatre for the production solely of American plays. But the failure is essentially more our own than America's. Lacking the instinct of the coral-builders, in which we could have found the happiness of continuing ourselves toward perfection, we have developed little willingness to die for the things we are building, for the thing we love. Our individual gifts and talents have sought their private perfection. We have not, as we hoped, created the beloved community of lifegivers. Our richest, like our poorest, have desired most not to give life, but to have it given to them. We have valued creative energy less than its rewards—our sin against our Holy Ghost. As a group we are not more but less than the great chaotic, unhappy community in whose dry heart I have vainly tried to create an oasis of living beauty.

Since we have failed spiritually in the elemental things—failed to pull together—failed to do what any good football or baseball team or crew do as a matter of course with no word said—and since the result of this is mediocrity, what one who has loved it wishes for it now is euthanasia—a swift and painless death. We keep our promise: We give this theatre we love good death; the Provincetown Players end their story here.

Some happier gateway must let in the spirit which seems to be seeking to create a soul under the ribs of death in the American theatre.[16]

Paradoxically, then, Jig's fundamental error was his unwillingness to accept popular success as an indication that the experiment had profitably been completed. He believed in a permanent state of revolution, in a continuous and ever-broadening ferment, without realizing that in such a process the original yeast cannot stay in one lump, but must dissolve and be absorbed beyond recognition for its work to be done. Cook's incomprehension was in part due to the emotional wound inflicted by O'Neill's ruthless, yet for purposes of the playwright's genius, fully justifiable, procedure.

Before departing, Cook and Glaspell met with O'Neill, Cleon Throckmorton, Kenton, and Eleanor Fitzgerald on February 23, in a final session of the executive committee. They declared an interim (i.e., suspension of activity) of one year "for the sake of our theatre," and resolved to incorporate in order to ensure "that the use of the Playhouse during the year shall be in every way in accord with *the spirit in which our organization was created.*" [17] I emphasize the phrase that indicates either an intention of a return, or a deliberate ignoring of undeniable changes. Its lack of specificity also shows that it was bound to become a battle ground.

Although no reasons for what in fact was "termination by incorporation" are enumerated in the minutes, the main two—a theoretical one and its practical twin—emerge from a series of letters from Kenton to the "Graeco-Provincetowners," which forms the majority of documentation for the rest of the story.

The corporation became a legal entity the following day with the aid of Harry Weinberger (the group's counsel in previous encounters with the law) who offered his signature to the document, apparently replacing Light as the seventh needed for incorporation.[18]

Before sailing on March 1, Cook "wrote the Provincetown valedictory," for release after the run of the season's last bill:

> For six years we have kept alive, in New York, a stage dedicated to the experimental production of plays by American playwrights. We have been unendowed from the beginning. We took our first theatre with assets of $320 and faith—literally the capital with which we ventured in the fall of 1916. We have remained unendowed. Our money assets have barely sufficed. Our faith in our adventure has survived—more than at first, we know why the great hope for the free development of a native drama rests on such stages as ours—but our faith needs quickening through "leisure," a presence which has all but gone out of the world and is surely alien to the swift coming seasons at the Playwright's Theatre.
>
> To this end therefore, the quickening of faith and the freshening of spirit—we have decided on what, mechanically looked at, from a practical standpoint, is an absurd thing—a year of rest. It is an adventure as absurd, perhaps, as our daring to believe, in 1916, that we could find our stage in New York with faith and $320. Now we dare to believe that the spirit of it will keep alive the interest in it during the "imprac-

ticable" interim of a silent year. As The Provincetown Players Incorporated we have renewed our lease on our playhouse and shall greet you there
in the fall of 1923.

To Our Playwrights

We have a frank word to say. Founded for you, committed to the
production of your plays only and with a steady flood of manuscripts
almost submerging us, we have faced notwithstanding, season after season, a discouraging lack of plays worth the doing. During our eight
seasons we have produced ninety-three plays by forty-seven American
playwrights. We have given two playwrights to America, Eugene O'Neill
and Susan Glaspell: we could have given a dozen by now if the other
ten had appeared. We have looked for them eagerly and we have not
found those among you offering us a sustained stream of freely experimental work in new dramatic forms. We do not want plays cut to old
theatric patterns but we have produced many mediocre plays because
we had nothing better to offer. We have never cared about the public's
reaction to theme and treatment but we have greatly cared about their
production values to us. We have always faced so-called "failure" as the
inevitable price of many an experiment, but we have always wanted the
experiment to be definitely "for something" which would make it,
even if it failed, a part of ultimate success. A sense of leisure in which
to work freely may make our year of rest worthwhile not only to ourselves but to you. We have received more plays this season than ever
before and a survey of the material on hand was as large a factor as
any in deciding us on a silent year.

To Our Subscribers

We have a farewell till we meet again difficult to phrase. Unendowed
though we have been, you have endowed us—first and least with your
faithfully renewed subscription checks. They have mattered—mattered
immensely, for only through them have we been able to "experiment."
They have freed us through six seasons from what would have crushed
experiment—the necessity of the box office appeal. But you have more
beautifully and most richly endowed us with sympathy, with interest,
with your presence through good bills and bad, with your appreciation,
your amusement, and your curiosity. Lacking these, our adventurous stage

must have perished. That impulse in you to escape from routine into what may freshen the spirit and that "escape" in you which brought us together will interpret the urge in us to flee from our routine for a year.[19]

3   In trying to sum up the principal reason for interring the group, Kenton was intensely personal and yet succeeded in putting the Players' demise in the perspective of their own history: "I was the one member of the P.P. who one year ago last December stood out alone against *The Emperor* going uptown—against our expanding before we could expand. If we went uptown, we expanded, and we've headed ever since for the rocks. Our interim is a direct result of that most human, and most unwise decision." [20]

That, in a nutshell, is what the two previous chapters intended to document. Kenton's statement laments the gradual deterioration of the group's original ideals, the preservation of which was the underlying theoretical reason for cessation of theatrical activities. But, although she states *why* the "Provincetown Players end their story" in philosophical terms, her observation does not illumine *how* the finale came about. The practical reason for incorporation and interim stemmed from a desire to protect the Provincetown Players' name (and perhaps the theatre and its personnel as well) from being used by artists with clearly professional aspirations who were only too eager to fill the vacuum left by Cook's departure. The wording of the Certificate of Incorporation along with a number of Kenton's letters to Greece indicate that the legal maneuver had a specific tactical goal: the prevention of nonamateur, noncollective, in a word non-Provincetown Player-like pursuits under the Players' name. There was a strong sense that the original ideal needed guarding. How prophetic that perception was, and yet how futile the action, became clear shortly.

Key personalities presumably linking theoretical and practical reasons for "termination by incorporation" were O'Neill and Light; the former covertly, the latter overtly. Kenton's letter of June 19, 1922, intimated that the purpose of the legal act was to unobtrusively oust Jimmy Light.[21] Much later, when O'Neill, Jones, and Macgowan were in fact forming The Experimental Theatre, Inc., she reported to the Cooks a conversation in which Macgowan had inquired "in regard to Jimmy's status and illegal ousting— ..." She explained that Light had given sufficient cause to justify any action against him, however drastic, "that as a matter of fact, he had gone to Europe for an indefinite stay. . . ." Further she informed Macgowan that just before incorporation, the core members of the group (which included O'Neill) had unanimously agreed to exclude Light, "that he had his trial year and failed!" [22]

It may seem odd that O'Neill would choose Jimmy to direct *The Hairy Ape,* thereby alienating Jig, and then, with rehearsals still under way, join Cook in ousting Light from the producing organization. However, one must grant that the dramatist demonstrated practical wisdom in picking whom he considered the best available director and then, to make peace with those insulted by this choice, temporarily sacrificing the director. This is especially likely since the injured parties were about to make a presumably long-term exit, thus freeing O'Neill to reestablish rapport with the "victim." Moreover, the possibility that O'Neill shared that secret with Light must not be ignored. That might explain why, on March 1, only ten hours after the *S.S. Themistocles* sailed from New York with Jig and Susan on board—and only five days after incorporation—Jimmy Light announced himself Director of the Provincetown Players.[23]

Meanwhile, Kenton's immediate task was to find an occupant for 133 Macdougal Street; a person or an organization both to satisfy philosophical criteria and to relieve the incorporated but inactive group of its overhead expenses during the interim. She encountered two kinds of difficulty. First, applicants ideologically and fiscally acceptable were few and far between. Second, and in the final analysis more disturbing, a small but determined group of Provincetowners, including Throckmorton and Fitzi, wanted to keep the playhouse open. Perhaps sensing that "interim" meant "a graceful excuse for internment," [24] this group of ambitious artists as well as job seekers was united in its desire to keep the old momentum going and the presumably advantageous association with name and location alive. In pursuing his own ambitions, James Light succeeded in gaining control over this faction.

That, of course, put Edna Kenton in a bind. Even with proxies from Cook and Glaspell she might still have found herself in the minority on the board. Yet, she had to guard the integrity of the decision, and carry it out without freedom to release the "valedictory" prior to the end of the season. Nor was she at liberty to confront Light with reasons for his ouster; that would have seemed, for lack of written evidence of and understanding behind the decision, a purely personal bias against him and his proposal. Whether she suspected a collusion between O'Neill and Light is not clear. Given O'Neill's frequent changes of mind, it is uncertain that there ever was one.

Although Kenton considered several rental possibilities, including the California Players of San Francisco who indicated an interest in using the premises, she favored an arrangement by which Edward Goodman would have taken charge of the theatre during the interim—under what aegis, her letters never state. His response, however, was not only slow in coming, it was finally disappointing: on June 2, Goodman informed her of his inability to lease The Playwright's Theatre.[25]

Alternative proposals seemed to have a common source: in one way or another, Eugene O'Neill, with his desire to make use of the playhouse in ways at odds with the intent of the new corporation, appeared as the veiled motivation behind them. O'Neill wanted a reshaped organization that could serve as an outlet for his creative drives, and he articulated this position quite clearly in a letter to Fitzi. It was "a fine experimental theatre" he was after, with "new blood, lots of it." [26] Because what transpired a year and a half later was begun in essentially that spirit, O'Neill must be credited with extraordinary foresight, powerful tenacity, or perhaps both. Whether an early bid by Kenneth Macgowan, who eventually became the playwright's partner in The Experimental Theatre, Inc., to continue "the group with me as overlord" was promoted by O'Neill can only be surmised. But the dramatist did openly suggest collaboration between the Provincetown remnant and Arthur Hopkins.[27]

In early May, Light also made an alternative offer to keep the theatre in business on such terms that it have no ties with the Provincetown Players. Again, the suspicion that O'Neill was not far behind cannot be entirely dismissed. In fact, the playwright wrote Fitzi that he supported Light's plan, even as he displayed impatience over the whole question: "Let anyone rent the theatre who can pay the rent. That's the way I feel about it. I don't want to hear about it again for a year. But if Jimmy should be able to organize a group to take over, I think—in spite of Jig's probable objections—that he should be encouraged to do so." O'Neill's only reservation in backing Light was in regard to the use of the Provincetown Players' name.[28]

In all these tentative possibilities, Fitzi wanted to play (or believed herself playing) a vital role.[29] As secretary-treasurer for the past four years she was, to be sure, a natural recipient of proposals, and she appears to have been easily swayed or sweet talked. Whether Kenton's analysis, that Fitzi was most concerned about retaining her job,[30] was correct, or whether she was motivated by devotion to an ideal—it is beyond doubt that the Provincetown Players were Fitzi's only solid point of reference after the deportation of Emma Goldman and Alexander Berkman in 1919 left her without even a vestige of her long association with the anarchist cause. Furthermore, the link between political and artistic anarchism must have been both personally and ideologically satisfying. Fitzi had first been introduced to the group by Stella Comminsky Ballantine, wife of the actor and Emma Goldman's niece; Jig's ideal community and his methods of leadership harmonized with her beliefs. Macdougal Street became nearly a home for Fitzi, and anarchism did not prevent her from introducing a certain stability and comparative efficiency into the organization. Whatever her deep-seated motivations, she remained pivotal in negotiations and operations for a long time to come.

Meanwhile Glaspell's *Chains of Dew* completed an unsuccessful run, Goodman's discouraging reply had arrived in answer to the suggestion that he take charge of the theatre during the interim, and the "valedictory" circular was mailed to subscribers and released to the press. On June 16, newspapers reported the Provincetown's "interim." The *Tribune* neatly, if perhaps unwittingly, summed up the Players' ambivalent predicament, describing them as a group "who produced drama in the byways of Greenwich Village and then sent it to Broadway." [31] On July 10, Kenton closed a deal subleasing the playhouse to Alice Kauser for a year, charging her $400 over the $3,600 the group was paying its landlords, in consideration for the equipment the Players had installed in the "store, first floor, and basement" at 133 Macdougal Street.[32] The history of the Provincetown Players as a producing organization had concluded.

4   But a band of dedicated people would not have it so, and their motives cannot be simply dismissed as having been selfish or opportunist, even if personal fortune played a part in them. Whether Jig's ideals for theatrical experimentation appeared to them as needing some modification or as totally absurd, and whether their values and intentions have been validated or not, these people were no more content with the decadent Broadway commercialism than the original rebels, the Provincetown Players. They wished to create a producing organization that would build on the achievements and insights gained by the terminated group, occupy the same

premises and appear identical to the public, and yet differ from the predecessor both in the approach to experimentation and in a more nearly corporate operation. In meetings and negotiations, in personal and legal arguments over an extended period, Eugene O'Neill, Kenneth Macgowan, James Light, Eleanor Fitzgerald, and Cleon Throckmorton formed a more or less united front against Edna Kenton, who also represented Susan Glaspell and George Cram Cook. Harry Weinberger, who was cast in the role of mediator, often ended up siding with the business-oriented majority.

As the end of the announced interim drew near, the drive for reestablishment became perceptibly stronger, and even without records one must assume preparations were going forward all year. Although they took diametrically opposing stances regarding the future organization, Cook and O'Neill had apparently come to an identical conclusion independently: radical change was needed. For his part, O'Neill wanted to "absolutely reorganize from top to bottom. . . ." He declared that "it is all Jig's fault . . . he drove all our best talent, that we have developed, away from the theatre for daring to disagree with him —this in a supposed group democracy!" Consequently, O'Neill's solution was: "New blood—lots of it—or death." [33] Likewise, Jig Cook thought "there is no hope for us again without a virgin slate." [34] As can be expected, however, his reasons for total change were not O'Neill's. He believed the root of the trouble was money and moral laxity: "We spoiled ourselves with pay—and motherhood . . . where only the heart of the spirit may be listened to." Ironically, these former brothers in Dionysos secretly accused one another of egotism, and both envisioned a tabula rasa that would replace collectivism with tyranny. Perhaps it was easier to be open and direct about it from Parnassos than from the Cape Cod sand dunes, for Jig made no bones about it: "If I am ever again to play that game there shall be absolute tyranny—and the tyrant unquestionably me. A questioned tyrant is bad to deal with." O'Neill was more cagey about it, though it became increasingly clear that by supporting Macgowan as director he really wanted a dictator.

By September 1923 it seemed as if Macgowan was ready to take over theatre, name, and corporation—lock, stock, and barrel—and to gain control by adding members to the original signatories until, presumably, he had acquired a majority.[35] O'Neill voiced no objection to such "macgowanization" of the Provincetown Players, Inc., and even Kenton first saw no reason to worry about the integrity of the name. But Glaspell left no doubt as to where she and Cook stood: "Our own feeling remains what it was—that the P.P.

was a unique group with a very definite reason for existing, and that a quite other thing should have a quite other name." [36] As letters to and from Greece crossed in the mails (it took about ten days each way), Kenton finally realized that Macgowan would merely be an administrative agent for O'Neill, who "stood for a straight handover to Macgowan." [37] Macgowan's version was that the dramatist "suggested that I be the dictator, but I said no, let's have a triumvirate of you, Bobby Jones and myself, and if there's disagreement, I'll settle it." [38] But in several letters, Harry Weinberger repeatedly refers to Macgowan as a "Mussolini dictator," and describes his proposed functions as follows: "He would have the absolute control of the theatre and everything but own it. He said he wants Fitzie for the front of the house and Throck as technical director. As far as the rest of us are concerned, we leave him fully alone except to the extent he calls on us." [39] Judging from the three possible options O'Neill put before the corporation, he seemed willing to hitch his wagon to Macgowan regardless of the use of the Provincetown name. The three options were:

1. To turn over the theatre to Macgowan with the name Provincetown.
2. Go on without the name.
3. Provincetown to go on with Macgowan absolute director.[40]

When in his absence the other directors (Kenton using proxies from Cook and Glaspell) decided on the third option and added Jones and Macgowan as members of the corporation, O'Neill appeared to be reversing himself. He wired Weinberger:

> MY STAND IS STILL THAT KENNETH SHOULD CARRY ON AS ENTIRELY ORIGINAL IDEAS WITH NEW NAMES TO FIT NEW POLICY AND THAT PROVINCETOWN PLAYERS SHOULD LEASE THEATRE TO HIM AS LAST YEAR TO KAUSER STOP AS FOR THE OLD PLAYERS GOING ON IN ABSENCE OF JIG SUSAN ON [*sic*] SITZIE [*sic*] WITHOUT NEW PLAYS NEW BLOOD NEW POLICY OR A DIRECTOR IN SIGHT I AM CERTAINLY OPPOSED WILL BE DOWN IN A WEEK ALL REGARDS GENE[41]

The conclusion Kenton conveyed to Greece was that,

> The close association of his name and fame with the P.P. is galling. . . . This is an impression, not a quotation. . . . The theatre is his theatre, and the last thing he wants is the P.P. name—won't in fact have it.
>
> Bobby Jones will—should—do nothing but his part, and we know

where Gene's values lie. The whole thing is on Kenneth's shoulders and he is not strong. . . . He's got a strong aid in Jimmy though, who will be all over the place.[42]

Consequently the triumvirate of Jones, Macgowan, and O'Neill decided on a "new" name: in an effort to have their cake and eat it too, they proposed calling themselves the Provincetown Play*house*. Kenton thought that would suffice for "history" to distinguish the group under the leadership of Jig Cook (who had died of an infection on January 14, 1924), from the triumvirate's enterprise:

> In '23 the Players became the Playhouse; it's a small line of demarcation, but it is a line and a definite one. The name of the Provincetown Play-house does mark, historically, the passing of the old organization of the Players. It has not been the Provincetown Players this year. I mean that in doing any history of the PP for Jig's part of it, such as we talked of, there could be a final paragraph: "Because a number of the old workers in the Players went in with the new group, under a new directorship etc. and the old name for the Theatre was retained. But the new group inevitably brought new etc. and with the end of their eighth season the PP passed." Or words to that effect.[43]

Glaspell disagreed. Returning to America after Jig had been ceremoniously buried by the Greek government and celebrated with Olympic games in the ancient custom—she fought an unpleasant battle to preserve the memory of her husband's achievement. In her penultimate letter on the subject, she made herself abundantly clear; she objected to the destruction of the old image of the Players, to its gradual supplanting by an entirely different one. She began by opposing very emphatically the use of the word "Provincetown" in the new organization's name:

> It savors a bit of wanting to profit by a thing and at the same time saying "We don't owe nothing to nobody."
>
> Since you are not Provincetown Players I do not think you should call yourself Provincetown something else and let people go on calling you Provincetown Players. And since you are not the Provincetown Players I do not see why you should add members to our organization.
>
> There was never a more simple organization than the PP. It seems to me there never was a more cumbersome one than you who call yourselves

21   Susan Glaspell in Greenwich Village. (Berg Collection, New York Public Library)

P. Playhouse. We never went in for patrons and this and that kind of stock. We wrote plays and put them on. We did that for a while because we felt like doing it, and we stopped because we were not sure we felt like going on doing it. That's that. And I wish it should stay at that.

Now one thing more. Hard to say, but while I am at it, I'm going to get it said. In a telephone conversation with Kenneth I said just a word or two about it, and apparently did not make myself clear. I said I felt no awareness of background. Perhaps the members of the old organization who are also members of the new may know what I mean.

There was a man named Jig Cook. He gave some eight years of his life to creating the P. Playhouse. If it had not been for him there would not be that place in which you now put on your plays. He worked until he had worked himself out, and then he went away, and he died. You are profiting by what he did and you have forgotten him. . . . There was no mention of Jig on the new Program, nor when the play for which he put in the dome was revived. It is not a spirit that will ever make the kind of place he made. . . .[44]

Her moving appeal was not heeded. The triumvirate, although it incorporated as The Experimental Theatre, Inc., continued to call its theatre the Provincetown Playhouse and labeled its published programs "the Provincetown Playbill." Even as it alienated members of the original core, the corporation sought to make itself known as one with the old group. Glaspell became enraged when Kenton's right to hold common stock was questioned. On May 31, she resigned "from the new organization into which membership in the Provincetown Players may have carried me." This was her final letter on the subject; it included a sustained defense of Kenton, whose otherwise elusive role throughout the organization's checkered existence it clarified: "And do you remember; Fitzie—and don't you remember, Throck—the nights Edna has sat over there reading plays no one else would read, and this in years when it wasn't a job for her? The rest of us either had jobs or had plays to put on. Edna, more than any other, loved the thing itself. She gave us freely of an intelligence money couldn't have bought." [45] Glaspell further asserted that Edna had saved the group "more than once from unwise divergence," had attempted to preserve "something for Jig to return to." Now she was being treated "abominably," and it was more than Susan could bear. She concluded with a terse farewell: "Fitzie, and all of you, for this letter is for all of you, from very deep down, I am through." This last statement signaled the demise of the Provincetown Players.

Displaying remarkable acumen, Kenton envisioned an already cited final paragraph of the "history of the Provincetown Players for Jig's part of it." Her epitaph lacks only limited amplification to become the fitting conclusion to this chronicle:

BECAUSE A NUMBER OF THE OLD WORKERS IN THE PLAYERS WENT IN WITH THE NEW GROUP, UNDER A NEW DIRECTORSHIP consisting of Robert Edmond Jones, Kenneth Macgowan, and Eugene O'Neill, THE OLD NAME FOR THE THEATRE WAS RETAINED. BUT THE NEW GROUP while its contribution to American theatre is significant, BROUGHT NEW purpose, new organization, new modus operandi, and new spirit along with it, AND WITH THE END OF THEIR EIGHTH SEASON THE PROVINCE-TOWN PLAYERS PASSED.

Conclusions:

The Provincetown Perspective

"Groups like ours are about to inherit the whole duty of dramatic man."
PROVINCETOWN PLAYERS' CIRCULAR, *Fall 1920*

"... by a hair's breadth I miss being a transforming force in the theatre of our unrealized nation...."
George Cram Cook, "Nilla Dear," GREEK COINS

1   Just one month before the extinction of the Provincetown Players became public knowledge in June 1922, Ludwig Lewisohn declared that "the present as well as the future of our theatre is still, as it has been for some time, firmly in the hands of the Provincetown Players, the Neighborhood Playhouse, Mr. Arthur Hopkins, and the Theatre Guild." [1] In eight seasons' existence—two Cape Cod summers and six Manhattan winters—the collective coalesced and disintegrated, accomplishing both more and less than it had set out to do. The Provincetown Players had proved the possibility of producing American drama of artistic (and *therefore* of social) significance in a theatre dependent on direct audience support, but it had failed to retain its original innocent, communal, amateur spirit.

The Players' success lies in having provided "artists of the theatre ... a chance to work out their ideas in freedom," [2] and in having helped to shape an American theatre in which it was possible at last for "playwrights of sincere, poetic, literary and dramatic purpose" [3] to be heard. From 1915 to 1922 the group had maintained a laboratory where aspiring artists learned the crafts of theatre in order to rejuvenate its art; and where spectators were enabled to become part of the creative process. It had experimented with unknown playwrights, actors, designers, and directors, as well as with new *kinds* of drama, scenery, acting style, production methods, and management procedures.

The group had not, on the other hand, turned into the Platonic beloved community of life givers imbued with Dionysian ecstatic intoxication that its founder, Jig Cook, had envisioned. Nor had it remained a band of uncompromising dilettantes, creating everything collectively. Therefore, in terms of the intensely personal theory of Jig Cook, the Provincetown Players had failed.

The need to publicize performances and organize subscription audiences had surfaced by their second summer. In the fall of 1916 came the admission that methods of play selection, as originally conceived, were untenable. The deduction that division of labor would increase efficiency and improve artistic results, followed. Next, the need for a salaried stagehand became pronounced, and, before the first New York season was over, the demand for artistic direction grew considerably. During the second winter season the recognition of critics proved inevitable, and in the course of the third, the Players' desire to demonstrate their theatrical accomplishments uptown was publicly uttered.[4]

Most members who differed on ways and means continued to cooperate, but not Hutchins Hapgood, the anarchist who believed that death lurks in organization and that no function of the Provincetown Players as a whole should be "usurped" by committees or individuals. Moreover, Hapgood remained convinced that theatre ought to be a social regenerative organ rather than an end in itself, and as the group's actions seemed to move away from that philosophy, he ceased to be active. Floyd Dell, Max Eastman, and John Reed, who considered theatre as but one weapon in the class struggle—and Alfred Kreymborg and William Zorach, who saw in it an extension of the visual arts and poetry, were in turn disappointed when the Players proved unwilling to serve any cause except the theatre's.

Throughout the group's existence tensions developed between those who persisted in upholding the pristine principles, and those who emphasized the resulting works of art—regardless of whether they had been created in faithful adherence to a philosophy of collective and spontaneous creation.

No one denied that amateur spirit and group creativity were valid principles at the outset, but to some it soon appeared necessary for ideals to change with circumstances. It was one thing to see an ignorance of theatrical craft as a means of injecting fresh imagination into the art and of opening doors to new ideas; quite another to insist upon continued ignorance despite accumulated experience. It was one thing not to aim for popular success; quite another to regard it as evil. It was one thing not to cater to critics; quite

another to snub them. There was great difference between abandoning anti-
quated and sterile conventions, and insisting that works of art must not
create their own new conventions. The temptation was great to think of avant-
garde work as neither conforming to, nor rejecting, established artistic norms,
but rather as creating something totally fresh. Poets have, of course, always
created new words, but have rarely written entire poems in a new language.
Eventually, the recognition came to The Playwright's Theatre that artists cannot be totally uninhibited by conventions surrounding them. They may, and
the Provincetown Players did, create a theatre with professed ignorance of
tradition. But how long could they remain ignorant? Did they have to be
blind to the very conventions established by the works of art they created in
order to deserve the designation of "avant garde"? That was not an acceptable proposition.

As members grew more numerous and more experienced, they increasingly became convinced that professional know-how does not have to be an
enemy, but can be a helpmate. To Jig Cook, as to some other founders, that
was high heresy. The continuous conflict, in which amateurism suffered one
kind of defeat after another, was a logical consequence.

2   The singular breakthrough of the Provincetown Players was manifest first and foremost in its manner of operation. Essentially, the group
functioned as a distinctive little theatre, fully demonstrating characteristics
that Dickinson had astutely observed as salient: in three successive small
buildings converted into theatres, it presented original plays in an intimate
way; it subsisted on a shoestring; it operated as a guild of artists; and its
source of sustenance was an alliance with a subscription audience.[5] It was also
dedicated to seeking a better system of values—in the broadest possible sense.
In addition, it was the only little theatre with the avowed purpose of producing exclusively American plays and including the dramatist in the environment of collective creativity, an environment in which members refreshingly
rotated functions.

The Provincetown Players' perspective on themselves, their goals, and
accomplishments is best seen in a series of manifestos. The majority of these
were official circulars, published and distributed by the collective. Others were
incorporated in newspaper and magazine stories (occasionally written by a
member) or in private correspondence.

As clearly pronounced by these documents, the primary aim of the Players from inception to "interim" was the staging of original American plays. This proved to be the operating principle most consistently adhered to. Its chief corollary was the provision of opportunities for American playwrights to take charge of the production of their scripts. This was realized to a lesser degree. Implied in these two objectives was the demand for freedom (the author's as well as the theatre's) from all but artistic considerations.

The second basic goal that emerges from these statements was experimentation in every aspect of theatrical creation and management. The frequently used metaphor of a laboratory signals the Players' dedication to bringing forth a new *kind* of theatrical art, characteristics of which are unpredictable. "Experiment" or one of its derivatives, appears to be the most often used word in descriptions of the group.

As important in these documents as *what* the collective wanted to accomplish was the question of *how* these aims were to be reached. In this domain the emphasis lay on a collective spirit permeating every aspect of their work. Extending their insistence on undominated individual freedom to create, and on seeking new forms, the Players wanted to eliminate stress within the group along with external pressures upon it. They believed that the sheer joy of work done in the spirit of play would assure that each could best do his or her own spontaneous creation. Consequently, the Provincetown Players remained a very loose-knit organization, with a generally anarchistic, collective working relationship.

Nor did the Players leave the *why* of their activity unstated. The manifestos articulate the collective's perception that theatrical art has a spiritual, even religious function as a regenerating force in human society. Although in a large part this force was seen as mystical and intangible, it was also manifested in a strong current of social and political advocacy and protest.

As a summary of scripts, productions, and personalities shows, the Players functioned as a most fruitful and daringly provocative theatre. It was most characteristically American not only on account of its devotion to native culture and talent, but primarily for its innocent, straightforward, and irreverent discarding of hollow traditions; its determination to eschew trodden paths in favor of breaking new ones; its dedication to expressing individual creativity through an organic group spirit; and its zealous guardianship of the right to dissent within the group as well as beyond its confines.

Roots of the rebellious Provincetown Players were deeply and firmly in

American forms of radicalism. Hence came the potent communal feeling of the founders which, though it gradually faltered in methods of theatrical production, was preserved in the convivial gatherings in the club rooms ("Christine's"), and in the close companionship many members maintained as long as they lived and that survived among children of erstwhile Players. Hence also the casual unconcern for building regulations, blue laws, fire hazards; uncomfortable seats and city noises that might elsewhere have distracted spectators; hence the nonchalant combination of plays with clashing philosophies or styles within certain bills; hence the light rejection of sizable subsidies, or of an offer by Charlie Chaplin to appear as a "walk-on"; hence the free mingling in the club rooms of artists, laborers, merchants, housewives, schoolteachers and Village bums—many of whom considered The Playwright's Theatre their second home although they might never have been active members of the group.[6]

At no time during its existence did the Provincetown Players have a clear cut organizational pattern, though from the first there was an executive committee that included "officers." Apart from Jig Cook's cohesive spiritual inebriation, the institutional fulcrum—as far as there was one—resided in the secretary-treasurer, especially after Fitzi assumed that post in 1918. An anarchist of long standing, an "Irish beauty-liar" who radiated warmth toward everybody but kept indifferent account books, Fitzi was hardly a solid center.[7]

It was in the nature of things that the Cape Cod summer seasons were run on an informal basis. The public was informed mostly by word of mouth, although printed handbills, announcements in the local *Advocate,* and reports in two Boston papers were not likely to have been accidents.

In New York, the group initially tried to center its activity on the nucleus gathered in Provincetown, but soon found some adaptation to metropolitan conditions imperative. As well as the recruitment of a subscription audience, this included dissemination of news about its activities by means of printed circulars and, when possible, through newspapers and periodicals. Although the Players' contact with the press was not systematic, neither was it totally defiant: eventually they made use of a clipping service.[8]

The subscription audience of The Playwright's Theatre for the first New York season consisted almost totally of the Stage Society; only in the following year did it win a wider base of support. Review bills, composed of favorite scripts and productions, which subscribers determined by direct vote, strengthened the bond between associate and active members. Nor was there ever a gulf separating the two categories whose adherents freely mingled in the stimulating fellowship of the club rooms upstairs or around the corner. When a casting need arose, anyone on or near the premises was drafted without an official change of category or membership fee. Review bills also served to introduce prospective subscribers, and demonstrated the Province-town Players' capacity to function as a repertory company to a limited degree, because roles in revived scripts were often taken by others than their origina-tors. On the other hand, by virtue of a continuity due to a more or less solid core of active members familiar with past productions, revivals—even with substitutions made in the original cast—were staged with comparative ease, whether in the framework of a review bill, a regular bill, or in emergencies demanding quick change in the program.

Business affairs remained chaotic throughout the group's lifespan, yet management became more efficient with accumulated experience and growing staff; consequently the atmosphere became more businesslike to the detriment of the collective spirit. Although finances stayed shaky as time passed, budgets grew larger: salaries for two part-time officers in the first year did not amount to much, but by 1921-22 there were at least half a dozen steady employees, and actors were paid with some regularity during the last two seasons and a half. In fact, Provincetown Players were able to invest their savings, both individually and as a body, into uptown runs of three of their productions.

Growing funds—used to cover salaries, production and administrative expenses—came predominantly from increasing numbers of spectators. One sign of this was the trend toward longer running bills. The Players began with two three-night weekends for each bill in 1916, gradually extended the weekend, and in 1919-20 successfully ran six bills each for two full weeks.[9] By whatever reasoning infrequent raises in the price of subscriptions or single admissions were instituted, they were never proportionate to outlay. Occa-sional fund drives did not materially affect the operating budget because they were geared to such specific goals as the move from one theatre to another, the furnishing of club rooms, and the installation of the dome. Additional presentation of a few bills outside Macdougal Street headquarters may have generated a little income, but served primarily to raise funds for the host organization, providing only indirect revenue by attracting new subscribers.

It is regrettable that the Provincetown Players' venture to make experi-mentation pay periodic dividends (both artistic and financial), by taking ef-fective productions to Broadway, did not reach fruition until applied by its successor, The Experimental Theatre, Inc. Still it is significant that during their last two seasons the Players attempted to keep one foot in Broadway's door and to penetrate its indifference with some of the best results of their laboratory. Nor was this effort based on mistaken principles, only—as Kenton had pointed out—the group did not prepare itself for the expansion demanded by such undertaking. For if the ferment of this laboratory was to become "a transforming force" in the body of "our unrealized nation" then it was certainly a valid goal to export its leaven in order to infect a larger segment of the public and to avoid becoming part of a closed clique of innovators who set examples only for each other. That the attempt misfired, that it wreaked havoc with some basic philosophy, and that it finally led to the expiration of the group was nevertheless no accident.

Sober planning simply was not in the nature of the Provincetown Players any more than it was in the nature of Jig Cook, its founder. If there was a continuous flaw in the group's operation, it was its consistent unpreparedness for the consequences of its action. In fact, the lack of sober planning was probably the single aspect in which the group had remained totally and impulsively amateur. Had that not been so, had it failed ultimately to preserve some of its precipitous spontaneity, the Provincetowners' laboratory could not have produced the direct impact nor the long-range influence it did. It was this essential characteristic that destined the Players' uptown excursions to failure, and yet this was the feature they had to export at the expense of self-destruction. Subsequent innovative groups either followed the pattern and perished while carrying their vitalizing transfusions into the mainstream (as did the Group Theatre), or adapted so fully to the mainstream as to become indistinguishable and thus wither into insignificance (as did the Theatre Guild).

The Provincetown Players had traveled the road from amateurism toward professionalism, from utter spontaneity toward long-range planning, and from ecstatic communal creation toward collaboration burdened with natural friction, during a period of about five and a half years. Their journey was haltingly, and in part unwillingly and unconsciously made, and never completed. As a group, they never became fully professional, never commercially and soberly businesslike, nor fiercely competitive with one another. A greater or lesser remnant of Jig Cook's anarchistic dream—the beloved community of life givers—was too deeply implanted and rooted in the hearts even of the "young sneerers" to be so soon dislodged.

Change was first forced upon the group by the urban environment, and by physical, legal, and financial conditions beyond their control of which they knew nothing when they began, and to which they adapted gradually. Subsequent modifications were in large part the result of more subtle pressures—first and foremost of which was the perhaps unwelcome, but ultimately inevitable, enlightenment that flowed irresistibly from accumulated experience. In other words, the artistic conditions operating in theatrical creative processes, of which the Players deliberately wished to remain ignorant and innocent, nevertheless made their marks upon them. There also emerged an adversary relationship as "members of the collective" gradually became "collaborating individuals." Part of this contentiousness was motivated by broad philosophical issues and social concerns, part of it, however, directly related to division of creative labor in the theatre—even when the labor was rotated. Finally, the unexpected and unprepared-for success released individual participants almost totally from their communal bonds—ironically, in a sequential burst of spontaneous reactions.

The Provincetown Players' effort to create as a group, to unite in purifying feverish ferment, was very much part and parcel of the last bloom of American innocence. With the onslaught of the twenties that bloom was wilting and it soon died. It was altogether fitting that the collective, conceived in innocence, should end its life with the twenties; its last two years are the record of a courageous struggle to postpone the inevitable. But when the bloom dies, it gives life to the fruit; the yeast that gives rise to the ferment does not vanish, it sustains life in the form of bread. So did American innocence, and so did the Provincetown Players.

3   The immediate and tangible results of the Provincetown Players' lively laboratory were the scripts, productions, and personalities it presented. From the perspective of drama alone, it was the single most fruitful American theatre prior to the Second World War: it introduced more native playwrights, had a greater impact on audiences and critics, and a longer life than any other similar group. Playwrights' theatres, wrote Kenneth Macgowan, "have usually lacked physical facilities and financial capital. They have had to seek long for an audience that cared to submit itself to the unknown work of unknown authors. Only one group has accomplished what it set out to do. . . . This is the celebrated Provincetown Players." [10]

Chiefly known for having given Eugene O'Neill a chance to mature into a dramatist of stature by providing virtually unlimited freedom for experimentation, the group had in fact done much more than that. It had encouraged and accelerated a general transformation of American playwriting from mere craft into art, and it did this by offering the same opportunity for experimentation to any potential dramatist willing to take a risk, and by introducing legitimate drama that treated subjects of broader range and in styles of greater variety, than had ever reached the American stage before. In this way the Provincetown Players had belatedly brought about in the United States what European little theatres under the leadership of such men as Antoine, Brahm, Grein, and Falck accomplished decades earlier: it built a bridge from *pieces bien faites* and similar manufactured goods to art theatres of striking originality. It might have achieved still more, had it attracted, or more actively sought out, talented and enterprising writers in greater numbers.

The only foreign play produced by the group, according to its "official" records, was Schnitzler's *Last Masks*. However, for the sake of completeness one must add that Wied's *Autumn Fires* was on a bill during Jasper Deeter's "unofficial" Spring Season of 1921. Finally, although Pinski is considered a Yiddish dramatist, his *A Dollar* was counted American for treating a local subject from a recent immigrant's point of view.

In eight seasons, the Provincetown Players produced ninety-seven plays by forty-seven American authors, the vast majority of which would not otherwise have reached theatre-goers or critics. O'Neill heads the list not only because he is the foremost, but because he offered the largest number of plays for production, fifteen altogether. Susan Glaspell, a gifted and highly polished, witty, and sensitive writer was a close second with eleven titles; Cook had a hand in five plays, on two of which he collaborated with her. The roster continues with Neith Boyce Hapgood, Floyd Dell, Alfred Kreymborg, Rita Wellman, who wrote four plays each; Djuna Barnes, Michael Gold, Edna St. Vincent Millay, John Reed, three plays each; Maxwell Bodenheim, Lawrence Langner, John Chapin Mosher and Wilbur Daniel Steele, two plays each. Most influential among those who had only one play presented by the Players are Lawrence Vail, Edna Ferber, Harry Kemp, Mary Caroline Davies, Pierre Loving, Evelyn Scott, Wallace Stevens, and Theodore Dreiser. Some scripts became memorable in performance without propelling their author to a notable career. Pendleton King's *Cocaine*, Alice Rostetter's *The Widow's*

Veil, and Lawrence Vail's *What D' You Want?* are most prominent in that category.

The Players were unafraid to produce plays treating social or racial groups, exploring universal problems, and by doing so they invited polemics. Potential troublemakers included Djuna Barnes's Irish satires, O'Neill's treatment of a black gangster in *The Dreamy Kid* (*The Emperor Jones* is sometimes still analysed as demonstrating the Negro's "savagery"), Dreiser's study of degeneracy in *The Hand of the Potter,* Gold's *Money,* and O'Neill's *The Hairy Ape;* the last has been interpreted both as a Socialist rabble-rouser and as a condescending view of the proletariat. Merely the presentation of plays that outraged solid citizens by scorning or subverting standards of language (*Three from the Earth, The Hairy Ape, The Verge*), mores (*Cocaine, Getting Unmarried*), or of sentiments (*Dreamy Kid, The Hand of the Potter*), qualified the Provincetown Players as a daring experimental group, and prompted Conrad Aiken to call it "almost the only theatre in America which has been willing to experiment, and to experiment courageously, with new authors and untried ideas. . . . without such advancing fringe of integrity and individualism the American theatre would be immeasurably poorer." [11]

Not only did the Provincetown Players stage new kinds of plays, they evolved for each its own peculiar performance style. Because some of the earliest scripts had homegrown topics, these often called for naturalistic or realistic production of the simplest sort. Their novelty lay not in the evocation of visual imagination but in the courage and skill with which they touched on bohemian morality (*Constancy, "Not Smart"*), on current political events (*Contemporaries*), or dominant cultural fads (*Change Your Style, Suppressed Desires, The Eternal Quadrangle*). Even later seasons abounded in plays that, though treating significant issues, moods, or relationships, were set in realistic interiors that did little to visually stimulate spectators. When directions called for a mud hut (*The Sniper*), a tarpaper shanty (*Brothers*), a Greenwich Village apartment (*The Angel Intrudes, Funiculi-Funicula*), the antechamber of a courtroom (*Woman's Honor*), or a family living room (*Close the Book, The Eldest*)—such sets were easily taken care of, but few so effectively solved as the simple living room created with curtains and standard set pieces for *Bernice.* An odd exception was provided by *Getting Unmarried,* in which a domestically conceived scene was played against a provocatively spectacular set.

Most of O'Neill's short pieces were also easily outfitted with shabby walls and furnishings, although occasionally they required a backdrop to conjure up imaginatively a mood such as the polar sea (*Fog*) or the tropical one (*Thirst, Moon of the Caribbees*). In the case of the *Moon of the Caribbees* and *The Rope*, the production's mood greatly depended on delicately established rhythms and sound effects. Only three O'Neill plays made exorbitant demands on the Provincetown Players in the way of production: *Where the Cross is Made*, which in addition to the presentation of ghosts required exits through the ceiling; *The Emperor Jones*, for which the dome was put in; and *The Hairy Ape*, which demanded a succession of eight expressionistic sets and lighting effects.

At the other end of the scale were poetic plays that called forth imaginative performance techniques as well as striking sets. The first and one of the most effective of these was *The Game*, a rather weak allegory in verse, enlivened by means of a bas-relieflike pantomime, set against a backdrop flirting with cubism. A forceful effort to create a fantasy style had failed in the case of Dell's *A Long Time Ago*, where royal costumes were patterned on playing cards, but the production was ruined by an attempt to raise the actors to superhuman height by means of wood-blocks tied under their shoes in pseudo-Greek fashion. *Lima Beans* depended on rhythmic and melodic performance. The allegorical characters of James Oppenheim's poetic *Night* were enhanced by appearing as silhouettes against a deep-blue sky. A similar shadow effect in the first part of *Three Travelers Watch a Sunrise* was sharply contrasted with brilliantly colored costumes and lights toward the end of the play.

The production of *Vote the New Moon* not only made use of the play's inherent color scheme by creating decor and costumes in blue, red, and purple, but added oversize properties and marionettelike movement to emphasize the grotesque quality of the election procedure that the play was satirizing. A more directly topical political message was served in *The Peace that Passeth Understanding* by the substitution of profile cutouts and dummies for actors. The performance of *Aria da Capo*, with its use of crepe paper, confetti, and decorative screens, reinforced the tension between the dialogue's deadly subject and delicate style. *The Slave With Two Faces*, a comparatively successful poetic allegory, effectively combined simplified costumes with highly conventionalized acting and with scenery in a fairy-tale style. The production of *5050* followed the author into the future with fantastic costumes, and *The String of the Samisen* combined the talents of Rollo Peters, Lloyd Wright,

Michio Itow, and Edna St. Vincent Millay for a delightful excursion into oriental conventions.

Jig Cook's second full-length play, *The Spring*, also put the designer to the test: between the prologue and the first act, the untouched natural beauty in which Namequa's spring is situated has to give way to a colonial mansion with attendant encroaching civilization without rendering the rocky landscape unrecognizable. Cleon Throckmorton recalled having sketched part of the scenery on the dome and enraged some purists. The few surviving photographs of the finished set lend his account no visible support. More demonstrable is the effect by which Throckmorton provided Susan Glaspell's haunting *The Verge* with a set representing Claire's tower, twisted like "no masonry has ever been." In the foreground the proscenium arch is filled by what resembles the glass-supporting framework of a giant terrarium (greenhouse). Stage right the head of a spiral staircase emerges from below. In the background, stage left, two men stand in front of a brightly lit cot; the remainder of the stage is cast in strangely patterned light achieved, according to Throckmorton, by a strong lamp (seen suspended from the ceiling) that held an intricately cut grillwork in front of the light source.

4   The Provincetown Players made its long-range impact in part through personalities who matured in its laboratory, and in part through principles that grew in its ferment. In some cases personalities are hardly separable from principles, in others, no connection at all is evident. Nevertheless, people who forged the group and were in turn shaped by it constitute an important aspect of the Players' impact—both on the narrowly defined Village environment and on the broader cultural milieu of America. In the free mingling of artists and intellectuals with their more ordinary neighbors resided much of the group's strength. Visual images, moods, and actions of future performances (as well as many a cast and crew) emerged in the convivial atmosphere so characteristic of Greenwich Village in its heyday. Artists who experimented in the Players' laboratory of human emotions were part and parcel of the same crowd as the potential spectators of their experiments. Many people whose names occur on the playbills as transient or recurring participants went on to lives and careers that cannot be traced, or that show no relation to their brief activity as Provincetown Players. But

they, too, added to the ferment, carried it wherever they went, and became a durable and potent contribution of the group to the mainstream. When those who once coalesced to give the Players life scattered, they enriched the very soil from which they had come. The strange amalgam of Macdougal Street worked in mysterious ways.

Many participants and observers brought their careers to fruition in fields remote from theatre; their connection with the group nevertheless made an indelible—if not always readily identifiable—imprint on their professional lives. Writers and poets such as Lucian Cary, Mina Loy, and Samuel Foster Damon continued to learn primarily about the craft of writing even if in Macdougal Street they served as actors, but they carried away with them a keener sense of visual awareness. Working in three dimensions on a stage perhaps contributed to William Zorach's change of emphasis from painting to sculpture; Hugh Ferriss's acting gave him a feeling for space that surfaced in his architectural visions; and Saxe Commins certainly became an editor because of the contact he made with O'Neill through the Players. It is more difficult to assess what the economist Karl Karsten, the educator and publishing executive Ordway Tead, or the biographer Robert Allerton Parker may have gained from the group.

For those whose arena of activity was primarily the theatre, the Provincetown experience was more crucial. Mary Blair, Charles Ellis, Ann Harding, Luther Adler, and Ida Rauh were among the actors who made their debut with the Players; James Light, Helen Westley, Jasper Deeter were among the directors. But Theron Bamberger might not have become a producer, Harrison Dowd an actor, Samuel Eliot a professor of drama, had they not been for a time Provincetown Players. Some of these people consciously or instinctively applied nonconformist methods to their theatre work, others joined the mainstream.

In addition to the playwrights already mentioned, who profited greatly from Jig Cook's Provincetown, many others were more indebted to the group than the group was to them. Of those, Ida Rauh, Jasper Deeter, and Mike Gold joined John Howard Lawson in 1926 to form the Workers' Drama League, which gave rise to the New Playwrights' Theatre and other organizations. In 1923 Jasper Deeter founded the Hedgerow Theatre in Pennsylvania. For thirty-three years the Hedgerow gave America a true repertory operation; of the two-hundred and ten plays presented there, fifty were world premieres. James Light, Eleanor Fitzgerald, and Cleon Throckmorton head the list of those Players who worked with the group's successor, The Experimental Theatre, Inc. After that venture, Light held major responsibilities in the Federal Theatre, directed at home and abroad, and eventually served as dean of the dramatic faculty at the New School. Fitzi went on to work for the Theatre Union, the Group Theatre, the Federal Theatre and the New School's Studio Theatre. At the New School, too, both Fitzi and Light worked with Piscator. And "Throck" designed for the Theatre Guild, founded an exemplary scenic supply house, later organized and headed the entire design-technical operation of the Federal Theatre Project. In that first national theatre venture in the United States, some other Provincetowners (notably the playwrights Glaspell, Kreymborg, and Gold), bore major administrative and creative responsibilities as well.

Whether or not directly traceable to the group's practice or to subsequent careers of its members and supporters, a number of the principles that had been manifested in the Provincetown Players' activity came to infuse the work of several influential theatre companies. The activity of the Workers' Drama League, and the New Playwrights' Theatre both nurtured seeds of political radicalism that had sprouted at The Playwright's Theatre, and encouraged new playwrights. Instead of Jig Cook's anarchist collectivism the Group Theatre followed a more or less socialist model after 1931. The Theatre Union (begun in 1933) traveled from amateurism to professionalism while allowing the voices of new dramatists and new segments of the population to be heard. The Federal Theatre Project institutionalized many goals and characteristics of little theatres (including the Players' unique emphasis on native talent, pertinent issues, and new values), through a national network. Its uneven combination of esthetic and political radicalism as well as its mixture of professional expertise with innocently zealous amateurism echoed the Provincetown on a much larger scale. The Playwrights' Producing Company (1938–1960) sought noncommercial opportunities for native dramatists, yet become a profit-making organization.

Although off-Broadway unfolded immediately after the Second World War, combining artistic freedom with commercial solvency, two groups most readily compared and contrasted with the Provincetown Players—the Living Theatre and the San Francisco Mime Troupe—did not take shape until the sixties. With its emphasis on poetry and anarchy, the Living Theatre combined esthetic and political revolt more systematically than the Provincetowners. So, too, was its communalism intended to be more extreme and self-conscious.

Yet, if notebooks for *Paradise Now* give a true picture of the Living Theatre's creative processes, then Judith Malina and Julian Beck ended up dominating and manipulating the anarchistic collective more deliberately and overtly than any one leader ever did The Playwright's Theatre.[12]

The Mime Troupe's political stance since 1970, on the other hand, is more homogeneous and focused than the Provincetown's aspired to be. Nevertheless, its artistic modus operandi is quite comparable. Joan Holden's articulate statements about how flexible collectivism works in the Mime Troupe could well be a description of the Players' actual (as opposed to desired) operations.[13] Thus, since becoming a collective, the Troupe "never moved to abolish the writer, the director, or the designer, but only to allow more people to play those roles." Involving the audience did not for them take the shape of insistence on physically molesting spectators or dragging them into improvised action, but—as in Macdougal Street—of allowing their responses *as spectators* to influence various aspects of a production during its run. Nor is the Mime Troupe dogmatic in its observance of spontaneity; its use as an important tool in rehearsals is preceded by professional methods and criteria at auditions, and followed by careful recording of both lines and business that emerge in the process. As does its division of labor, so the Troupe's collectivism remains flexible; everyone does not have to do everything. Artistic and managerial functions rotate within reason; staff members make suggestions which are developed by members most skilled in the appropriate area of responsibility. Holden is candid about two major apparent drawbacks of the collective process, which are not usually admitted: that "style is the most difficult thing to achieve collectively" (perhaps a prime reason for its failure with the Players), and that large doses of gloom and nastiness, rather than pure bliss, pave the road of collective creation.

Ultimately, the greatest tribute to Jig Cook and his Provincetown Players is that their impact is too pervasive to be documented conclusively. Their leaven has been absorbed by American theatre, and the ferment continues. Immediately upon the group's dissolution, the battle about its name and playhouse planted seeds of confusion as to where "The Provincetown Players" ended their work. That confusion had been perpetuated by Helen Deutsch and Stella Hanau, authors of *The Provincetown: A Story of the Theatre,* which deals with three different organizations. But the lines continued to be blurred: many other groups inhabited the theatre Cook and his companions willed into existence. Even today, Provincetown Playhouses operate both in

Macdougal Street and on the Provincetown beach. Those who carried on—whether in harmony or discord with the original group's spirit—believed with Jimmy Light that "An empty theatre would be the lousiest monument to Jig Cook." Cook's restless Dionysian inspiration is certainly best served and preserved by any vigorous theatre that produces American works by unknown, imaginative, and provocative artists.

Appendix A

Chronology

Summer Season 1915

[Late Summer— July 15?] [1]	Hapgoods' house 621 Commercial St. Provincetown	First Bill *Suppressed Desires* George Cram Cook Susan Glaspell
		Constancy Neith Boyce
Thu., Sept. 9	Lewis Wharf [2] 571 Commercial St. Provincetown	Second Bill *"Change Your Style"* George Cram Cook
		Contemporaries Wilbur Daniel Steele

Spring–Summer Season 1916

Sun., Mar. 5	Liberal Club 137 Macdougal St. New York	*Suppressed Desires*
Shortly after Mar. 5	Ira Remsen's Studio 131 Macdougal St. New York	*Suppressed Desires*

Thu., July 13	Lewis Wharf [3]	First Bill
		Winter's Night Neith Boyce
		Freedom John Reed
		Suppressed Desires
[Sometime between Mon., Jul. 24 & Fri., Jul. 28] [4]		Second Bill
		Bound East For Cardiff Eugene O'Neill
		The Game Louise Bryant
		"Not Smart" Wilbur Daniel Steele
Tue., Aug. 8		Third Bill
		Constancy
		The Eternal Quadrangle John Reed
		Trifles Susan Glaspell
[Sometime between Mon., Aug. 21 & Fri., Aug. 25] [5]		Fourth Bill (Review)
		"Change Your Style"
		Contemporaries
		Bound East For Cardiff
Date Undetermined		Children's Bill
		Mother Carey's Chickens Henry Marion Hall
Date Undetermined		*Enemies* Neith Boyce Hutchins Hapgood
Wed., Aug. 30	Beachcomber Club's First Annual Minstrel Show Provincetown	Guest Appearance *Freedom*

Fri., Sept. 1 & Sat., Sept. 2	Lewis Wharf	Special Bill *Thirst* Eugene O'Neill *The Game* *Suppressed Desires*

1916–1917

Fri., Nov. 3—Tue., Nov. 7 (five days)	The Playwright's Theatre[6] 139 Macdougal St. New York	First Bill *Bound East For Cardiff* *The Game* *King Arthur's Socks* Floyd Dell
Fri., Nov. 17—Tue., Nov. 21		Second Bill *Freedom* *Enemies* *Suppressed Desires*
Fri., Dec. 1—Tue., Dec. 5		Third Bill *Before Breakfast* Eugene O'Neill *Lima Beans* Alfred Kreymborg *The Two Sons* Neith Boyce
Fri., Dec. 15—Tue., Dec. 19		Fourth Bill *Joined Together* Bror Nordfeldt *The Obituary* Saxe Commins *Sauce for the Emperor* John Mosher
Fri., Jan. 5—Tue., Jan. 9		Fifth Bill *Bored* John Mosher

	A Long Time Ago Floyd Dell
	Fog Eugene O'Neill
Fri., Jan. 26—Tue., Jan. 30	Sixth Bill
	Pan Kenneth MacNichol
	Winter's Night Neith Boyce
	A Dollar David Pinski
Fri., Feb. 16—Tue., Feb. 20	Seventh Bill
	Ivan's Homecoming Irwin Granich[7]
	Barbarians Rita Wellman
	The Sniper Eugene O'Neill
Fri., Mar. 9—Wed., Mar. 14 (six days)	Eighth Bill
	The Prodigal Son Harry Kemp
	Cocaine Pendleton King
	The People Susan Glaspell
Fri., Mar. 30—Wed., Apr. 4	Ninth Bill (Review)
	Barbarians
	The People
	Cocaine
	Suppressed Desires

1917–1918

Fri., Nov. 2—Tue., Nov. 6 (five days)	First Bill
	The Long Voyage Home Eugene O'Neill

Close the Book
Susan Glaspell

Night
James Oppenheim

Fri., Nov. 30—Thu.,
Dec. 6 (seven days)

Second Bill

Knotholes
Maxwell Bodenheim
William Saphier

'Ile
Eugene O'Neill

*The Gentle Furniture
Shop*
Maxwell Bodenheim

Funiculi-Funicula
Rita Wellman

Fri., Dec. 28—Thu.,
Jan. 3

Third Bill

Down The Airshaft
Irwin Granich

The Angel Intrudes
Floyd Dell

The Outside
Susan Glaspell

Fri., Jan. 25—Thu.,
Jan. 31

Fourth Bill

*The Slave With Two
Faces*
Mary Caroline Davies

"About Six"
Grace Potter

Sweet and Twenty
Floyd Dell

Fri., Mar. 1—Thu.,
Mar. 7

Fifth Bill

The Athenian Women
George Cram Cook

Mon., Mar. 18—Thu., Mar. 21 (four days)		Other Players' Bill
		Manikin and Minikin
		Alfred Kreymborg
		Rihani's *Static Dances*
		Two Slatterns and a King
		Edna St. Vincent Millay
		Jack's House
		Alfred Kreymborg
Fri., Mar. 29—Thu., Apr. 4 (seven days)		Sixth Bill
		The Devil's Glow
		Alice Woods
		The Rib-Person
		Rita Wellman
		Contemporaries
Sat., Apr. 13 For the Women's Peace Party of New York State	The Bramhall Playhouse 138 East 27th St. New York	*The Athenian Women*
Fri., Apr. 26—Thu., May 2		Seventh Bill
		The Hermit and His Messiah
		F. B. Kugelman [Frederick Kaye]
		The Rope
		Eugene O'Neill
		Woman's Honor
		Susan Glaspell

1918–1919

Fri., Nov. 22—Thu., Nov. 28		First Bill
		The Princess Marries the Page
		Edna St. Vincent Millay

		Where the Cross is Made Eugene O'Neill
		Gee-Rusalem Florence Kiper Frank
Fri., Dec. 20—Thu., Dec. 26		Second Bill
		The Moon of the Caribbees Eugene O'Neill
		The Rescue Rita C. Smith
		Tickless Time George Cram Cook Susan Glaspell
Fri., Jan. 17—Thu., Jan. 23		Third Bill
		From Portland to Dover Otto Liveright
		5050 Robert A. Parker
		The Widow's Veil Alice L. Rostetter
		The String of the Samisen Rita Wellman
Fri., Feb. 14—Thu., Feb. 20		Fourth Bill
		The Baby Carriage Bosworth Crocker
		The Squealer Mary F. Barber
		"*Not Smart*"
Mon., Feb. 24 & Tues., Feb. 25	Friendly House of Brooklyn	Fourth Bill repeated
Fri., Mar. 21—Thu., Mar. 27		Fifth Bill
		The Peace that Passeth Understanding John Reed

		Bernice
		Susan Glaspell
Fri., Apr. 11—Thu.,		Sixth Bill (Review)
Apr. 17		*The Widow's Veil*
		Night
		Bound East For Cardiff
		Woman's Honor
Sat., Apr. 19—Thu.,	Recital Hall	*The Widow's Veil*
Apr. 24 (six days)	828 Broad St.	*The Angel Intrudes*
	Newark	*Tickless Time*
Fri., Apr. 25—Thu.,		Seventh Bill (Review)
May 1 (seven days)		*The Rope*
		The Angel Intrudes
		Cocaine
		Tickless Time

1919–1920

Fri., Oct. 31—Thu.,	First Bill
Nov. 13 (fourteen days)	*The Dreamy Kid*
	Eugene O'Neill
	The Philosopher of
	Butterbiggins
	Harold Chapin
	Three From The Earth
	Djuna Barnes
	Getting Unmarried
	Winthrop Parkhurst
Fri., Dec. 5—Thu.,	Second Bill
Dec. 18	*Brothers*
	Lewis Beach
	Aria Da Capo
	Edna St. Vincent Millay
	"Not Smart"

Fri., Jan. 9—Thu., Jan. 22		Third Bill
		The Eldest Edna Ferber
		An Irish Triangle Djuna Barnes
		Money Irwin Granich
Fri., Jan. 30—Wed., Feb. 4 (five days) For the Society for Ethical Culture	Y.M.C.A. Brooklyn	Third Bill repeated
Fri., Feb. 13—Thu., Feb. 26 (fourteen days)		Fourth Bill
		Vote the New Moon Alfred Kreymborg
		Three Travelers Watch A Sunrise Wallace Stevens
		Pie Lawrence Langner
Fri., Feb. 27—Tue., Mar. 2 (five days) For the Benefit of the Rand School Library		Fourth Bill repeated
Fri., Mar. 26—Thu., Apr. 8 (fourteen days)		Fifth Bill
		Last Masks Arthur Schnitzler
		Kurzy of the Sea Djuna Barnes
		Exorcism Eugene O'Neill
Fri., Apr. 23—Thu., May 6		Sixth Bill (Review)
		Where the Cross is Made
		Aria Da Capo
		Sweet and Twenty

1920–1921

Mon., Nov. 1—
[Sat., Dec. 25]⁸
(fifty-five days)

First Bill

Matinata
Lawrence Langner

The Emperor Jones
Eugene O'Neill

Mon., Dec. 27—Fri.,
Jan. 28
(moved to Princess
Theatre Jan. 29)

The Selwyn
Theatre
42nd St. West of
Broadway, New York

Tickless Time

The Emperor Jones

Mon., Dec. 27—
[Thu., Jan. 27]
(thirty-two days)

Second Bill

What D'You Want?
Lawrence Vail

Diff'rent
Eugene O'Neill

Mon., Jan. 31—Fri.,
Feb. 4
(moved to Princess
Theatre Feb. 5)

The Selwyn
Theatre
42nd St. West of
Broadway, New York

Diff'rent

Mon., Jan. 31—Sun.,
Feb. 20
(twenty-one days)

Third Bill

The Spring
George Cram Cook

Mon., Feb. 28—Sun.,
Mar. 13
(fourteen days)

Fourth Bill

Love
Evelyn Scott

Mon., Mar. 21—Sun.,
Apr. 10
(twenty-one days)
Additional perfor-
mances on Wed., Apr.
13 and Sat., Apr. 16

Fifth Bill

Inheritors
Susan Glaspell

Mon., Apr. 25—Sun.,
May 15

Sixth Bill

Trifles

Grotesques
Cloyd Head

*The Moon of the
Caribbees*

"Spring Season"

Wed., May 18—Sun.,   *Inheritors*
June 5

Wed., June 8—Fri.,   *The Widow's Veil*
July 1   *Aria Da Capo*

                                                           Autumn Fires
                                                           Gustav Wied

1921–1922

Wed., Sept. 21—Sat.,   The Princess   *The Spring*
Oct. 1   Theatre
                         39th St. near Broadway
                         New York

Mon., Nov. 14—Thu.,   First Bill
Dec. 1 (eighteen days)   *The Verge*
Additional matinees   Susan Glaspell
presented by the Theatre
Guild at the Garrick
Theatre, 65 W. 35th St.
Tue., Dec. 6—Fri.,
Dec. 16 (eleven days)

Mon., Dec. 5—Sun.,   Second Bill
Dec. 18 (fourteen days)   *Hand of the Potter*
                                               Theodore Dreiser

Mon., Jan. 9—Wed.,   Third Bill
Jan. 25 (seventeen   *A Little Act of Justice*
days)   Norman C. Lindau

                                               Footsteps
                                               Donald Corley

                                               The Stick-Up
                                               Pierre Loving

Mon., Jan. 30—Mon.,   Fourth Bill
Feb. 13 (guest   *Mr. Faust*
appearance of The   Arthur Davidson Ficke
Ellen Van Volkenburg-
Maurice Browne
Repertory Company)

Thu., Mar. 9—Sun., Apr. 16 (thirty-nine days)	Fifth Bill *The Hairy Ape* Eugene O'Neill
Thu., Apr. 27—Mon., May 15 (eighteen days)	Sixth Bill *"Chains of Dew"* Susan Glaspell

Appendix B

Dramatis Personae:

an annotated who was who

Almost every book about the twenties and the decade preceding it, whether biography or memoir, literary history or sociological study, popular or scholarly, is strewn with dozens of names intended as milestones or indicators of a milieu. Often, however, not even an explanatory phrase or adjective accompanies these names: they are expected to work their magic unaided. For specialists of one sort or another, certain names will indeed perform such a function, but the uninitiate without some guidance will not know even where to look them up and will be frustrated. Let two examples suffice. Henrietta Rodman is invoked as the founder or patroness of the Liberal Club, a prime mover of the prewar Greenwich Village spirit. That she was a high school teacher who broke the traditional dress code and championed the right of teachers to become mothers, is never mentioned, nor that this activity earned her front-page notoriety in the *New York Times.* "Bobby" Edwards is apostrophied as the "Bard of Bohemia," without reference to his exotic ukuleles or to his founding the *Quill*—an outlet for poets and writers rejected elsewhere.

The purpose of this appendix is to spare readers some frustration. Some famous, some infamous, and some obscure founders, participants, and friends of the Provincetown Players will herein be identified by their chief interests and activities as well as by certain vital data; where possible, their salient characteristics will also be described, but completeness proved an elusive goal. As a reminder, some well-known members and friends of the Provincetown Players are listed without descriptive paragraphs.

BERENICE ABBOTT (b. 1898)   Born in Springfield, Ohio, Abbott is a photographer. After attending Ohio State University, she studied sculpture in New York, switched to photography and, with Man Ray in Paris during the twenties, was "the semi-official portraitist" of the "intelligentsia of the Quarter." In 1929 she returned to New York, did portraits for *Fortune* magazine, and began to document New York City in photographs. Abbott taught at the New School for Social Research and published *A Guide to Better Photography* in 1941. She received an award honoring her artistic contributions to New York City in October 1979.

COURTNEY ALLEN (1896–?) Born in Norfolk, Virginia, Allen was an illustrator and model builder. He worked for the art department of the *Washington Times,* took night courses at the Corcoran School of Art, and later attended the Provincetown Art School. With fellow artists, Allen operated a coffee shop called the Sixes and Sevens on the Lewis Wharf in Provincetown. A free-lance illustrator for the *Saturday Evening Post, Collier's, Cosmopolitan,* and other magazines, Allen was also adept at sculpting, painting, and carving.

EDWARD J. BALLANTINE (1888–1968) Born in Edinburgh, Scotland, Ballantine was a character actor and director. He came to the United States with Mrs. Patrick Campbell's production of *Pygmalion* in 1914, and acted in the Provincetown Players first production of O'Neill's *Bound East for Cardiff* on Cape Cod. He directed Floyd Dell's *King Arthur's Socks* on their opening bill in New York. He also directed and acted in O'Neill's *S.S. Glencairn* in 1929, appeared on Broadway in *Alien Corn* (1933), *The Moon is Down* (1942), *King Lear* (1950), and *Redemption* with John Barrymore. After 1964 he lived in London, where he died.

THERON BAMBERGER (1894–1953) Born in Philadelphia, Bamberger worked on various newspapers there before moving to the New York *Globe.* In the late 1920s he was city editor of the *Evening Post,* and in 1935 mounted his first Broadway production, *Fly Away Home.* His most successful show was James Gow Arnaud d'Usseau's *Tomorrow the World* (1943), which ran for sixty-two weeks. For years he wrote for the Sunday drama section of the *New York Times.*

DJUNA BARNES (b. 1892) Born at Cornwall-on-the-Hudson in New York, Barnes was educated at home, and began writing at an early age for *The Magazine* and the *Little Review.* In 1915 she published *The Book of Repulsive Women;* the Provincetown Players produced her plays in 1919–20. She wrote for the *Dial,* and published many volumes of poetry and fiction; her prose was compared to James Joyce.

MARY BLAIR (1895–1947) Born in Pittsburgh, Blair graduated in the Carnegie Institute's first acting class. From 1918–1930 she played leading roles in New York and on tour. After her initial experience of acting O'Neill in *Diff'rent* with the Provincetown Players in 1921, she also appeared in his *The Hairy Ape, All God's Chillun Got Wings,* and *Desire Under The Elms.* The critic Edmund Wilson was her second husband. In 1935 she was stricken with tuberculosis and spent her last years in a Pittsburgh sanitarium.

MAXWELL BODENHEIM (1893–1954) Born in Hermanville, Mississippi, he had no formal education, spent his early years in the army and as a hobo, and had published poems in the *Little Review* by the time he was twenty-one. Part of the Chicago literary revival, Bodenheim had his plays performed, and continued to be a success with such books as *Minna and Myself, Introducing Irony,* and *Advice.* After Minna Schein divorced him in 1938, his alcohol habit changed the once sought-after poet into a bothersome bum who sold poems on the street for the price of a drink.

NEITH BOYCE (1872–1951) Born in California, Boyce was a prolific feminist author. She moved to Greenwich Village and wrote short stories and novels characterized by "a restless search for life's purpose." She wrote *Constancy,* one of the first two plays presented by the Provincetown Players. Married to Hutchins Hapgood (q.v.), Boyce never recovered completely from the loss of their eldest son in 1919, and lived a private life in Provincetown until her death.

LOUISE BRYANT (1890–1936) A novelist and short-story writer, Bryant became fascinated with the political changes in Russia through John Reed (q.v.), whom she married in 1916, and with whom she traveled to Russia during the later part of the Revolution. Her books, *Six Red Months in Russia* and *Mirrors of Moscow,* give a personal account of the early leaders and the chaos of the Bolshevik movement. She later married William Bullitt, the first U.S. ambassador to the Soviet Union.

REMO BUFANO (1894–1948) Born in Italy, Bufano was an author and puppeteer. He moved to the United States with his parents in 1897 and was raised in the Village. He performed with puppets as a child, and during his teens took minor roles in plays by O'Neill, Kreymborg, and Millay. He became well known for his marionettes that toured with famous orchestras. Bufano built puppets of all sizes for *Alice in Wonderland, Jumbo,* and *Cinderella;* wrote books on puppetry and plays for marionettes. He died at fifty-four in a plane crash near Mt. Carmel, Pennsylvania.

FREDERIC L. BURT (1876–1943) Born in Lincoln, Nebraska, Burt was a New York actor and later a Hollywood film actor. He acted in *Bound East for Cardiff* in 1916 and produced *The Prodigal Son* in 1917 for the Provincetown Players. His home was in Carmel, California. His wife, Helen Ware, who died in 1938, was also an actress. Burt died at sixty-seven at Twentynine Palms, California, after a long illness.

KATHLEEN EATON CANNELL (1891–1974) Born in Utica, New York, Cannell was a dance critic for the *Christian Science Monitor.* Briefly married to the poet, Skipwith Cannell, she originated "static dances" during World War I which, under the stage name Rihani, she "performed in tiny night spots in the village." Cannell also became a member of the Other Players. Paris Fashion Editor and

Fashion Correspondent for the *New Yorker* during the Nazi Occupation, she covered German Press Conferences there for the *New York Times*. She received a PEN grant for furthering the cause of literature.

DAVID CARB (b.1885?) Of the several plays he wrote, only Carb's collaboration with Walter Pritchard Eaton, *Queen Victoria,* is known to have been staged on Broadway in 1922.

LUCIAN CARY (1886–1971) Born in Kansas, Cary began working as a reporter for the *Chicago Tribune* in 1910. From 1913 to 1914 he succeeded Jig Cook as literary editor for the *Chicago Evening Post,* then became acting editor for the *Dial.* A founder of the Provincetown Players, he contributed short stories to *Collier's* and *Saturday Evening Post.* One, "Saturday's Millions," was made into a motion picture in the 1930s. Cary was also gun editor for *True Magazine* for twenty years.

GLENN COLEMAN (1881–1932) Born in Springfield, Ohio, Coleman studied at the New York School of Art, and ushered at Carnegie Hall. A painter and lithographer whose favorite subject was street scenes, he designed sets for the Provincetown Players, won third place in a Carnegie Institute competition in 1928, and regularly contributed illustrations to leftist magazines.

SAXE COMMINS (1892–1958) Born in Rochester, New York, Commins was a dentist. His sister, Stella (who was married to E. J. Ballantine, q.v.) introduced him to the Macdougal Street group. He struck up a friendship with O'Neill and became his editor with the Liveright publishing house. When Liveright went bankrupt in 1933, O'Neill took Commins along to Random House. There Commins edited works of Faulkner, Sinclair Lewis, Huxley, Gertrude Stein, and W. H. Auden among others, and became editor-in-chief.

DONALD CORLEY (1886–1955) His study of architecture lead Corley to illustration. During the war he designed camouflage for New York Harbor. One of Jig Cook's closest disciples, Corley wrote and illustrated several books.

SAMUEL FOSTER DAMON (1893–1971) Born in Newton, Massachusetts, Damon was a distinguished poet and renowned Blake scholar. He received a fellowship from the American Scandinavian Foundation 1920–21, translated *A Book of Danish Verse* in 1922; taught English at Harvard from 1921 to 1927, then at Brown University until his retirement. He also wrote the plays, *Witch of Dogtown* (Russel Crouse Award, 1954), and *Punch and Judy* (1957).

MARY CAROLINE DAVIES. Born at Sprague, Washington, Davies was educated near Portland, Oregon, and at the University of California, where she won the Emily Chamberlin Cook prize for poetry. Her early poems expressed "girl consciousness." Between 1918 and 1927, she wrote seven volumes of poetry, including whimsical verses for children. Many of her poems deal with the subject of death. Her allegorical play *The Slave With Two Faces* was produced by Provincetown Players in 1918. She also wrote a novel, *The Husband Test* (1921).

JASPER DEETER (1893–1972)   Born in Mechanicsburg, Pennsylvania, Deeter attended Lafayette College, then studied at the Chatauqua Institute in New York. In 1919 he joined the Provincetown Players as an actor, and soon became a director. Following the success of *The Emperor Jones,* Deeter left the group and toured the midwest. In 1923, believing that repertory was the best creative environment for actors, he founded the Hedgerow Repertory Theatre in Moylan, Pennsylvania.

FLOYD DELL (1887–1969)   Born in Barry, Illinois, Dell left school at sixteen and held factory jobs until 1905, when he became a reporter in Davenport, Iowa. That position led him to the "Chicago School" of writers. First as assistant, then as successor to Francis Hackett, literary editor of the *Chicago Evening Post,* Dell built the *Friday Literary Review* into one of the best literary newspaper supplements. A socialist since boyhood, he moved to New York in 1913 and became associate editor of *The Masses,* later made major contributions to the *Liberator.* Dell's plays were produced by the Liberal Club, the Provincetown Players, and the Theatre Guild.

CHARLES HENRY DEMUTH (1883–1935)   Born in Lancaster, Pennsylvania, Demuth studied at the Drexel Institute and the Pennsylvania Academy of Fine Arts. An important member of the Stieglitz group, The Little Gallery, and the Intimate Gallery, in 1915 he took part in the forming of the Provincetown Players. Demuth was among the first diabetics to receive insulin at Otto Kahn's (q.v.) old house, by that time a sanitarium.

HARRISON DOWD (1897–1964)   Born in Madison, Connecticut, Dowd was an actor and poet. He made his Broadway debut in *Chu Chin Chow* in 1918 and played Pierrot in *Aria da Capo* with the Provincetown Players in 1919. He appeared as the Matchmaker in *The Power of Darkness* in 1920, and later performed in *Kiss Me Kate, Blood Wedding, The Visit, Our Town, Caligula,* and *The Iceman Cometh.* Dowd also played piano in various jazz bands, wrote an autobiographical novel, *The Night Air* (1950), and contributed stories and poetry to magazines.

MAX EASTMAN (1883–1964)   Born in Canandaigua, New York, Eastman taught logic and psychology at Columbia before becoming editor of *The Masses.* He participated in the founding of the Provincetown Players; later he was arrested with Floyd Dell, John Reed, and Art Young for sedition. He translated Marx and Trotsky, becoming the first American Marxist to denounce Stalinism. *Enjoyment of Laughter,* a study of the psychology of literature, and his autobiography *Enjoyment of Living,* are his best-known works. He was once married to Ida Rauh (q.v.).

ROBERT ("BOBBY") EDWARDS (1879–1948)   Born in Buffalo, New York, Edwards was an illustrator, writer, and portrait painter. He graduated in 1901 from Harvard, attended the Chase Art School and moved to New York where he became known as the "Troubador of Greenwich Village." He sang his own songs about the Village in bohemian restaurants, accompanied by "futuristic" ukeleles he made. In 1921 Edwards started the *Quill,* printing new authors who found it difficult to get published, for six years.

SAMUEL ATKINS ELIOT, JR. (b.1893) Born in Denver, Colorado, Eliot graduated from Harvard in 1912, worked as play reader and stage manager for Winthrop Ames's Little Theatre, then joined the Washington Square Players. He was director of the Indianapolis Little Theatre, the Cincinnati Art Theatre, and the Studio Theatre in New York City, then became professor of English at Smith College from 1918 until his retirement in 1961; after 1955 he also taught theatre there. Eliot edited *Little Theatre Classics, Greek Drama and Shakespeare,* among others. He lives in Northampton, Massachusetts.

CHARLES ELLIS (1893–1976) An abstractionist painter, Ellis studied at Ohio State University and at the Art Students' League in New York. For the Province-town Players he designed and executed the set for *Aria da Capo* in December 1919, then acted in many plays. In 1924 Ellis portrayed Eben Cabot in *Desire Under the Elms.* He also acted in the 1932 revival of *Show Boat,* Maxwell Anderson's *Valley Forge,* and *Key Largo* in 1939. After the 1940s he concentrated exclusively on painting. He married Edna St. Vincent Millay's sister, Norma (q.v.).

NORMA MILLAY ELLIS (b.1893) Born in Union, Maine, Norma Millay is a younger sister and executrix of Edna St. Vincent Millay. She appeared as Columbine in *Aria da Capo* and as the wife in Jig Cook's and Susan Glaspell's *Tickless Time.* She married Charles Ellis (q.v.) in 1921. In 1927 Norma sang the leading role in Mozart's *La Finta Giardiniera* for the Intimate Opera Company. She published Vincent's posthumous *Mine the Harvest* and, at the private funeral service, read her sister's "The Poet and His Book."

EDNA FERBER (1887–1968) Born in Kalamazoo, Michigan, Ferber worked as a full-time reporter for the *Chicago Tribune* and served as a correspondent during World War I. In 1924 she won the Pulitzer Prize for *So Big.* Her novels, including *Show Boat* (1926) and *Giant* (1952) depicted American life. With George S. Kaufman, she wrote plays and screen plays some of which were adapted from her novels. She died in New York.

HUGH FERRISS (1889–1962) Born in St. Louis, Missouri, Ferriss graduated from Washington University with a degree in architecture. An influential visionary, he first opposed skyscrapers, later designed cities with elevated traffic and amusement centers. He worked as a consultant on Idlewild Airport and the United Nations Building; he wrote *Metropolis of Tomorrow* and *Power in Buildings.*

ARTHUR DAVISON FICKE (1883–1945) Born in Davenport, Iowa, Ficke was a poet and author. A close friend of Floyd Dell (q.v.), he graduated from Harvard in 1904, taught English and studied law at the State University of Iowa until 1907. He then turned to poetry, contributed poems to the *New York Times,* published numerous books, including a novel based on travels in Mexico. With Witter Bynner he founded the "New School" of "spectrist poetry" which hoaxed critics in 1918. Ficke died in Hudson, New York.

M. ELEANOR FITZGERALD (1877–1955) Born in Hancock, Wisconsin, "Fitzi" became assistant editor of the anarchist magazines, *Mother Earth* and the *Blast*. During World War I, she "fought for liberation of political prisoners," such as Mooney and Billings. Her political career ended when her editors, Emma Goldman and Alexander Berkman, were deported. She became the business manager of the Provincetown Players in 1918, and a director later. In 1940 she joined the Dramatic Workshop of the New School for Social Research.

FLORENCE KIPER FRANK (1886–1976) Frank graduated from the University of Chicago and was a member of Chicago Literary Circle, associated with Carl Sandburg, Sherwood Anderson, Edgar Lee Masters, and Amy Lowell. By the time she married Jerome N. Frank (later a member of F.D.R.'s "brain trust" and a judge), in 1914, she was an accomplished poet. She wrote the plays *Joel* and *Cabined*, and was anthologized in *The New Poetry* (1956).

WALDO FRANK (1889–1966) Born in Long Branch, New Jersey, Frank was a writer. After receiving an M.A. from Yale in 1911, he worked for the *Evening Post* and the *Times*, spent a year in Germany and France, then returned to New York. With James Oppenheim (q.v.), he founded and edited 7 *Arts*, a magazine that published Robert Frost, D. H. Lawrence, and Eugene O'Neill. A critic of American society and culture, he received international renown for his lyric parables in novel form.

CHARLES S. GILPIN (1872–1930) Born in Richmond, Virginia, Gilpin appeared in variety shows and worked odd jobs. He toured with the Great Southern Minstrels, and appeared with Bert Williams and George Walker in *Abyssinia*. In 1916 he helped organize and manage the Lafayette Players, the first black dramatic "stock" company in New York, and in 1919 he appeared in John Drinkwater's *Abraham Lincoln*. In 1920 he created a sensation as the Emperor Jones. He played the role for four years and again in 1926, which paved the way for other black actors.

SUSAN GLASPELL (1882–1948) Born in Davenport, Iowa, Glaspell was a popular author of short stories, novels, and plays. In 1913 she married George Cram Cook (with whom she founded the Provincetown Players). She went to Greece with Cook but returned to America after his death, and married Norman H. Matson with whom she wrote *The Comic Artist* in 1927. She achieved highest acclaim when *Alison's House*, a play about Emily Dickinson, won the Pulitzer Prize in 1930. She became director of the Midwest Play Bureau for the Federal Theatre Project.

MICHAEL GOLD (1894–1967) Born Irwin Granich in New York, the son of poor Jewish immigrants from Russia, Gold held myriad jobs to survive. He favored proletarian ideals, became copywriter for the *Call*, a socialist daily; then assistant editor of the *Masses*, and a founder of the *Liberator*. His first plays were produced by the Provincetown Players; he later joined the Playwrights' Producing Company and was involved in the Federal Theatre Project.

EDWARD GOODMAN (1888–1962) A graduate of Columbia, he was drama critic for the *New York Press,* book reviewer for the *New York Times,* and editor of *Moods Magazine.* In 1915 he joined the Washington Square Players and taught at the American Academy of Dramatic Art until 1953. Goodman directed both stage plays and films. In 1925 he founded the Stagers who performed some seventy plays. His wife, Lucy Huffaker, had been a close friend of Susan Glaspell's.

HENRY MARION HALL (1877–1963) Born in New York City, Hall was a naturalist. He graduated from Harvard in 1899, in 1906 received a Ph.D. in Comparative Literature from Columbia, where he became an English instructor. Hall was president of the Newport, Rhode Island Audubon Society, wrote numerous books and articles on ornithology and wildlife, and won the *New York Herald-Tribune* prize for short story.

HUTCHINS HAPGOOD (1869–1944) The "philosophical anarchist" was born in Chicago. After receiving an M.A. from Harvard, he began a long and productive career as a New York journalist. He traveled extensively, wrote several books, including an autobiography, *A Victorian in the Modern World* (1939), and contributed to magazines, interpreting ideological and aesthetic aspects of the labor movement. A close friend of Mabel Dodge Luhan's (q.v.), he first suggested what became her celebrated Evenings. He married Neith Boyce (q.v.) in 1899, and they had two daughters and two sons.

ANN HARDING (1902–1981) Born Dorothy Walton Gatley in Fort Sam Houston, Texas, Harding made her debut with the Provincetown Players as Madeline Morton in Glaspell's *Inheritors* (1921), then studied acting with Jasper Deeter (q.v.) in 1922. A founder of the Screen Actors Guild, she first appeared on Broadway in 1921, and played Peter Pan in 1922. At Deeter's Hedgerow Theatre she played Candida, and Hilda in *The Master Builder.* She appeared as Nina Leeds in O'Neill's *Strange Interlude* (1929) and as Mrs. Venable in *Suddenly Last Summer* (1958). In 1963 she played Amanda in *Glass Menagerie.* Harding performed in such films as *Paris Bound* (1929), *The Girl of the Golden West,* and *The Man in the Grey Flannel Suit* (1956).

MARSDEN HARTLEY (1877–1943) Born in Lewiston, New York, Hartley was an internationally known painter of landscapes and marines whose stark and brusque paintings tend toward formalization. First exhibited in 1908 by Stieglitz, he had annual one-man shows in New York for thirty years. Hartley was also verbally articulate, a talent few visual artists can claim. He wrote *Adventures in the Arts, Sea Burial,* and *Twenty-five Poems.*

GEORGE THEODORE HARTMANN (1894–1976) Born in Hoboken, New Jersey, Hartmann was a painter and etcher. He studied in New York and in Munich; worked for the *Herald Tribune* and New York *Post* during the twenties and thirties and exhibited at the National Arts Club. He was an off-Broadway scene designer, a poster designer for major movie firms, an illustrator and jacket designer. He painted landscapes, cityscapes, and portraits.

WILLIAM (Big Bill) HAYWOOD (1869–1928)   Born in Salt Lake City, Haywood began working at nine, and gradually became a labor leader. In 1907 he rose to director of the Industrial Workers of the World, that sought to unite labor into "one big union," and to give workers ultimate control over all means of production. During World War I, Haywood was convicted of espionage with other IWW leaders. When the Supreme Court upheld the verdict, he jumped bond and sailed to Russia. Haywood, an awe-inspiring and legendary figure of his time, died of paralysis in Moscow and is buried under the Kremlin Wall near John Reed's grave.

JOHN HELD, JR. (1889–1958)   Born in Salt Lake City, Held is famous for his drawings of flappers, which were published in *Life* and the *New Yorker*. Held illustrated F. Scott Fitzgerald's *Tales of the Jazz Age* and in the thirties he wrote short stories and novels. After World War II his flapper drawings were revived in magazines.

B. W. HUEBSCH (c. 1875–1964)   Born in New York, Huebsch studied art and violin, then became music critic for the *New York Sun* before going into publishing. He started as a printer, eventually became editor-in-chief and vice president. Noted for bringing English translations of Hauptmann and Sudermann to American readers, Huebsch also published Strindberg, D. H. Lawrence, Sherwood Anderson, James Joyce, and Upton Sinclair. A lifelong activist for peace and civil rights, Huebsch was treasurer of the American Civil Liberties Union and a member of P.E.N.

EDWARD E. HUNT (1885–1953)   Born in Bellwood, Nebraska, Hunt graduated from Harvard (1910), served on the editorial staff of *American Magazine,* became one of the first American correspondents of World War I, and was soon made U.S. delegate to the Relief Commission. In 1917 Hunt became head of the International Red Cross economic rehabilitation in France, and in 1921 President Harding appointed him Secretary of the Conference on Unemployment. He wrote books on economics and war relief, including *An Audit of America* (1930) and *The Power of Industry and the Public Interest* (1944).

MICHIO ITOW (1894–1961)   Born in Japan, Itow was a dancer and choreographer who studied European dance forms in Berlin and Paris. In London he became a sensation, then went to work for the Ziegfeld Follies in New York but left after considering it "too commercial." Itow worked independently, joined the Theatre Guild's production of *Bushido,* and became well known in the twenties with John Murray Anderson's Greenwich Village Follies. In 1930 his "Players from Japan" played at the Booth Theatre. In 1948 he directed the first post-World War II Tokyo production of Gilbert and Sullivan's *The Mikado.*

NORMAN JACOBSEN (1885–1944)   Born in Cokeville, Wyoming, Jacobsen was a painter and illustrator. As a young man he contributed cartoons to *The Masses;* from 1920 to 1939 he lived abroad and painted in many parts of the world. In 1939 he settled in Salt Lake City.

SUSAN JENKINS (b. 1896) Born in Pittsburgh, Jenkins went to school with Mary Blair (q.v.), Kenneth Burke, Malcolm Cowley, and James Light (q.v.). She also attended Ohio State University with Light, whom she married in 1917 and divorced in 1922. From 1918 to 1922 she was secretary, playreader, and box-office attendant for the Provincetown Players. Later she edited a pulp magazine, and worked with Van Wyck Brooks, Alfred Kreymborg (q.v.), and Lewis Mumford, in assembling volumes of *The American Caravan.* In 1969 she published *Robber Rocks: Letters and Memories of Hart Crane, 1923–1932.*

ROBERT EDMOND JONES (1887–1954) After attending Harvard, where he became an instructor of fine arts, Jones designed costumes, traveled to Europe, and, refused by Gordon Craig, studied with Max Reinhardt. He made his mark in New York with the set for *The Man Who Married a Dumb Wife* in 1915. Breaking with the Belasco school of realism, he used light and color imaginatively. Jones was most influential in the development of modern American theatre, wrote *The Dramatic Imagination,* and became part of the triumvirate (with O'Neill and Kenneth Macgowan) that ran The Experimental Theatre, Inc.

OTTO KAHN (1867–1934) Born in Mannheim, Germany, Kahn was a capitalist and patron of the arts. He became a broker with Kuhn Loeb & Co. in 1897 and rose to the front ranks through major railroad transactions. He married, gained American citizenship and became an erudite patron. He supported free concerts during the Depression and gave paintings and cash to museums, but opera was his specialty. He brought Toscanini and Gatti Casazza to the Metropolitan Opera, reviving the demoralized company.

FREDERICK B. (Kugelman) KAYE (1892–1930) Born in New York City, Kaye was an English professor. He graduated from Yale in 1914, where he also received an M.A. in 1916 and a Ph.D. in 1917. He became Instructor of English at Northwestern University in 1917 and Associate Professor in 1926. The Provincetown Players performed his *The Hermit and His Messiah.*

HARRY KEMP (1883–1960) The "hobo poet" was born in Youngstown, Ohio. Raised by his grandmother next to the train yards, Kemp was enchanted by the mystique of hobo life and left home at sixteen. He traveled for most of his life, and as a struggling poet was supported by friends. After his involvement with the Provincetown Players, he continued to write and produce plays with little theatre groups. His wife, Mary Pyne, was also a Player.

CHARLES O'BRIEN KENNEDY (1879–1958) Kennedy acted with John Barrymore in *Redemption* (1918), with Lionel Barrymore in *The Claw* (1921), and with both John and Lionel Barrymore in *The Jest* (1919). He directed Theodore

Dreiser's *The Hand of the Potter* (1921) at the Provincetown. He later wrote plays, and worked on the editorial staff of Samuel French, Inc. A close friend of producer Arthur Hopkins, Kennedy was one of the few people O'Neill saw in his last years.

EDNA KENTON (1876–1954) Kenton was a journalist and historian, specializing in early Jesuit history in America; she edited several volumes of letters and documents, including *The Indians of North America*, based on Jesuit documents in New France, 1610–1791. She wrote *Simon Kenton* (1930), a nonfiction account of her ancestor and of the Kentucky frontier, and later edited and wrote the introduction to *Eight Uncollected Tales of Henry James* (1949).

ALFRED KREYMBORG (1883–1966) Born in New York City, Kreymborg, an influential poet, supported himself for years by playing chess. He edited several magazines of poetry, among them *Glebe, Others,* and *Broom.* One of the Imagists, Kreymborg assembled the *American Caravan* with Van Wyck Brooks, Lewis Mumford, and Paul Rosenfeld. He organized the Other Players in 1918, and participated in the Federal Theatre Project.

LAWRENCE LANGNER (1890–1962) Born in Wales, Langner came to America in 1911, and quickly established himself as a patent lawyer. He started the Washington Square Players in 1915, and in 1919 was a founder of the Theatre Guild. During World War I he was a munitions consultant, then helped prepare patent sections of the Versailles Treaty. He worked closely with George Bernard Shaw in directing *St. Joan* and *Back to Methuselah.* Later, he founded the American Shakespeare Festival in Stratford, Connecticut.

JAMES LIGHT (1894–1964) Born in Pittsburgh, Pennsylvania, Light learned design at the Carnegie Institute 1914–15, then spent a year at Ohio State University, studying philosophy and comparative literature. He joined the Provincetown Players in 1917 and for thirteen years was a director with the Players and their successors. From 1939 to 1942 he was dean of the dramatic art faculty at the New School for Social Research. In the Federal Theatre Project, Light was first co-director in New York, then director in Philadelphia. He was equally devoted to staging experimental (Strindberg, O'Neill, Hasenclever, and cummings) and established authors (Ibsen and Shakespeare).

OTTO K. LIVERIGHT, brother of the publisher, Horace Liveright, was a literary agent whose best-known client was Sherwood Anderson. He played many roles with the Provincetown Players, and had a play produced by them.

ROLLO LLOYD (1883–1938) Lloyd was an actor, writer, and director. He directed Evelyn Scott's *Love* for the Provincetown Players in 1921. After a stage career in New York, he moved to Hollywood in 1929.

EDWARD PIERRE LOVING (1892–1956) Born in New York, Loving was a poet, news correspondent, and editor. After World War I he worked for the Havas

News Agency, *The Nation,* and *Dial.* He was on the Paris staff of the *New York Herald,* later a Washington correspondent of the International News Service. He edited *10 Minute Plays,* and with Frank Shay co-edited *Fifty Contemporary One-Act Plays.* He wrote a biographical novel of Charles Baudelaire, and translated Schnitzler's *Comedy of Words,* as well as Hölderlin's short poems.

MINA LOY (1882–1966)   Born in London, Loy was a poet, closely associated with the American Imagists, whose intellectual limitations she criticized. She published in *Little Review, Others,* and *Dial,* as well as volumes of verse, *Lunar Baedeker* and *Time Tables.* Loy's poetry was cerebral, bitterly satirical, and critical of "aesthetic commonplaces." William Carlos Williams described her as "very English, very skittish, . . . too smart to involve herself . . . with any of us. . . ." Although lauded as "one of the best poets of her time," she remains virtually unknown and scarcely read.

MABEL DODGE LUHAN (1879–1962)   Born in Buffalo, New York, Luhan was a wealthy patron of arts as well as an internationally known author. After divorcing her second husband, Edwin Dodge, she moved to Greenwich Village just before World War I, and continued her famous affair with John Reed. An unusual capacity for listening became the basis of her celebrated Wednesday Evenings. Luhan was the moving spirit behind the 1913 post-Impressionist Art Exhibition known as the Armory Show. After marrying and divorcing the painter, Maurice Sterne, she moved to Taos, New Mexico, where she continued to sponsor writers and artists, and in 1932 married Antonio Luhan, a Pueblo Indian. She wrote books about Taos; her memoirs of D. H. Lawrence are an important document.

ALICE F. MCDOUGAL (1868–1945)   Born in New York City, McDougal began a coffee business in 1907 when her first husband, a jobber in green coffee, died. Beginning with thirty-eight dollars and a coffee blend formula, she built a two and a half million dollar enterprise. During the twenties and early thirties her restaurants at various locations in Manhattan were among the most popular eating places. She retired in 1935.

HAROLD MCGEE (1900–1955)   McGee was born in Schenectady, New York. After graduating from Union College in 1920, he joined the Provincetown Players as a student actor, and after 1923 became a director of the Experimental Theatre, Inc. In 1924 he acted in O'Neill's *S.S. Glencairn.* He continued to act for twenty-five years, playing leads from *Abraham's Bosom* (1927), to *Anne of the Thousand Days* (1948).

FENIMORE MERRILL (d. 1919)   graduated from the University of Chicago and went to Harvard on a scholarship. In New York he wrote a number of plays, including *The Avenue* which was on a bill with O'Neill's *In the Zone* produced by the Washington Square Players in 1917. Merrill went to France with American Expeditionary Forces in 1918 and died at Coblenz.

THOMAS MITCHELL (1892–1962)   Born in Elizabeth, New Jersey, Mitchell worked as a reporter, wrote skits, did some acting, and by 1913 had traveled the United States with a stock company. In 1918 he directed the *Moon of the Caribbees* for the Provincetown. Mitchell made his film debut in *Cloudy With Showers* (1934). His character role in *Lost Horizon* (1936) boosted his career, and in 1939 he won an Oscar for his role as the whisky-soaked doctor in *Stagecoach.*

JOHN CHAPIN MOSHER (1892–1942)   Born in Albany, New York, Mosher was a film critic. He graduated from Williams College, served in World War I, and taught English at Northwestern University. In 1926 he joined the *New Yorker* and in 1940 he published *Celibate of Twilight,* a collection of sketches.

ALLEN WARD NAGLE (1892–1937)   Born in Norwalk, Connecticut, Nagle became a professional actor after graduating from Fordham University. He played Simeon Cabot in O'Neill's *Desire Under the Elms* with Walter Huston, and a principal role in the 1926 revival of *East Lynne.* Nagle appeared in Shakespearean repertory for years and was with the Federal Theatre before his death.

BRÖR OLSSON JULIUS NORDFELDT (1878–1955)   Born in Sweden, Nordfelt studied painting in Paris, England, and New York. He designed scenery for the Chicago Little Theatre, and was involved in the futurist movement. Besides a master printmaker, Nordfeldt is best known as a still-life and landscape painter. He settled in Santa Fe in 1926 and continued to paint and exhibit.

MARGARET DOOLITTLE NORDFELDT (1873–1968)   A homeopathic doctor with an M.D. from Boston University, she studied psychoanalysis with Jung in Zurich, then practiced in New York. She married Brör Nordfeldt (q.v.) in 1909 and divorced him in 1944 after a four-year separation. A founder of the Provincetown Players, she was the group's first secretary.

JAMES OPPENHEIM (1882–1932)   Born in Saint Paul, Minnesota, Oppenheim attended Columbia University, then became assistant head of the Hudson Guild Settlement House. A pioneer of Greenwich Village Bohemia, Oppenheim was a poet, and an editor of *Seven Arts,* until his antiwar sentiments caused financiers to withdraw their support. Loss of work made him turn a long-term interest in psychoanalysis into a profession. Influenced by Whitman, the Bible, and Jung, he wrote eight books of poetry, including the *Mystic Warrior* (1921), and an autobiography in free verse. He also published a collection of essays on psychology.

ROBERT ALLERTON PARKER (1889–1970)   Born in Alameda, California, Parker graduated from the University of California at Berkeley. A student of popular religious movements and a biographer, he wrote *A Yankee Saint* in 1935 and *The Incredible Messiah* in 1937. His *The Transatlantic Smiths* (1959) was an account of a Quaker family. Parker was a drama critic for the weekly *Independent* and contributed to *Current Opinion* and *The Arts.*

ROLLO PETERS (1892–1967) Born in Paris, Peters started his career as a portrait painter after studying art in Europe. An actor, scene designer, and director with the Washington Square Players and the Provincetown Players, he co-founded the Theatre Guild in 1919. He appeared on Broadway with Ethel Barrymore, Ann Harding, Jane Cowl, Minnie Maddern Fiske, and Laurette Taylor; later became an assistant director in Hollywood. He died in Monterey, California.

DAVID PINSKI (1872–1959) Born in Magilov, Russia; as a young man in Warsaw, Pinski published in the Yiddish *Holiday Leaves*. He came to New York in 1899, edited numerous weeklies including the *Daily Socialist-Zionist,* founded a Zionist Labor Organization and became president of the Jewish National Workers Alliance 1920–1922. In 1920 the Theatre Guild produced his comedy, *The Treasure.* He continued to write plays, stories, and novels in Yiddish; many were translated. He was president of the Jewish Theatre Society of New York and the Jewish P.E.N. Club; he moved to Israel in 1950.

GRACE POTTER (1874–1947) Born in Syracuse, New York, Potter graduated from Syracuse University, spent two years in postgraduate medical work, and became an editor in New York. She journeyed to Europe, became a close friend of Sigmund and Anna Freud, and studied psychoanalysis with Ranke and Jung. Potter returned to New York about 1910 to practice, and to write for psychoanalytic journals. She also participated in the women's suffrage movement.

WILLIAM RAINEY (1894–1964) Rainey studied law at the University of California, then became interested in theatre and managed the Greek Theatre in Berkeley. After a World War I Army discharge, he "became an actor, director and man of all trades in theatrical productions wherever he could find them." In 1923, he founded the Cherry Lane Theatre. In 1928 he was chief of productions for the National Broadcasting Company. In 1954 he joined the Voice of America and retired in 1957.

IDA RAUH (1877–1970) Born in New York, Rauh was a founder of the Provincetown Players and an outspoken feminist who received a law degree from New York University in 1905, but never practiced. Known as "the Duse of Macdougal St." because of "the emotional exuberance of her acting," she married Max Eastman (q.v.), but "made it a point of honor to be known by her maiden name." Rauh directed the first production of O'Neill's *Where the Cross is Made.* In 1920, having been co-director (with James Light, q.v.) of the Provincetown Players, she "grew bored with the theatre," and began sculpting and painting.

NEIL REBER (1878–1951) Born in Fort Scott, Kansas, Reber grew up in Springfield, Missouri. After eighteen years as the Sherwin-Williams Paint Company's credit manager in Chicago, he moved to New York in 1918 and established the Handicraft Studio in Greenwich Village. He married Edna Kenton's sister, Mable Ruth.

JOHN SILAS REED (1887–1920) A versatile poet, reporter, and political agitator, Reed graduated from Harvard in 1910, and lived an adventurous life. He interviewed Pancho Villa; Lenin and Trotsky received him as a brother, and for a time he held the mythical post of Bolshevist Council in New York. One of the founders of the Communist Party of the United States, Reed made seditious statements and was arrested several times. His most famous book, *Ten Days That Shook the World,* is the best eyewitness account of the Russian revolution. Reed died of typhus in Moscow, and is buried under the Kremlin wall.

HENRIETTA RODMAN (1878–1923)   Born in New York City, Rodman was a dynamic and emancipated high school teacher. She founded the Feminist Alliance in 1914, urging a constitutional amendment so that "no civil or political right shall be denied to any person on account of sex." Rodman vigorously opposed the Wadleigh High School Board of Education's view that mothers cannot be teachers and, as a result of her agitation, New York City school systems allowed maternity leaves. When the Liberal Club split, she became the moving spirit at the new Macdougal Street headquarters.

ROBERT EMMONS ROGERS (1888–1941)   Born in Haddonfield, New Jersey, Rogers received a master's degree from Harvard and became an English instructor at Williams College. While lecturing at the M.I.T. University Extension, he became involved in a business venture with the Maude Adams Theatrical Company. He edited the *Technical Review* and *Creative Reading,* and wrote a column for the *Boston Evening American* as well as a play, *Behind A Watteau Picture.*

WILLIAM SAPHIER was a poet. His poems express the love, the sensations, and the value of working. Saphier edited a number of editions of *Others.* One of these contained Wallace Steven's poem "Thirteen Ways of Looking at a Blackbird." A play he wrote with Maxwell Bodenheim, *The Kitchen Absurd,* was also published in *Others.* His work appeared in numerous "little magazines" in the late 1910s and the early 1920s.

C. M. SAX (1885–1961)   After attending college Sax involved himself with art and theatre. In 1918 he started the Vagabond Theatre in Baltimore, later founded the Romany Theatre in Lexington, Kentucky. He taught art at the University of Kent (England), and at the University of Iowa, but kept returning to the stage. In 1929 he was a producer of an American Company in Paris, then became managing producer of the Manchester Repertory Theatre in England.

EDWIN D. SCHOONMAKER (1873–1940)   Born in Scranton, Pennsylvania, Schoonmaker taught in Kentucky, then began writing for socialist journals. A commentator on world affairs, he criticized the Soviet Government, denounced Hitler, and supported American neutrality in World War II. Schoonmaker wrote verse dramas (*The Saxons, The Americans*), books (*The World Storm and Beyond,* and *Our Genial Enemy: France*), essays and short stories. With his wife, Nancy (q.v.), he participated in the founding of the Provincetown Players.

NANCY M. SCHOONMAKER (1873–1965)   Born in Georgetown, Kentucky,

Schoonmaker studied at the Sorbonne and at Transylvania University in Kentucky. Active in politics, she campaigned for the League of Nations; later, on behalf of the League of Women Voters, she surveyed suffragist legislation in Europe. Schoonmaker served on the Democratic Committee of Connecticut and ran for Congress in 1937. She wrote *The Actual Government of Connecticut,* and articles for *Current History* and other journals. She married Edwin Schoonmaker (q.v.) and they had one son, Frank, a wine expert.

EVELYN SCOTT (1893–1963) A novelist and poet, Scott was born in Clarksville, Tennessee. At twenty, while a student at Tulane University, she eloped with C. Kay Scott to Brazil and lived for six years "in happiness, poverty and misery." Her autobiography, *Escapade* (1923), records her romance, and the hardships of pregnancy and poverty. Her play, *Love,* was produced by the Provincetown Players just before publication of her novel, *The Narrow House* (1921). She published poems and a book of poetry, *The Winter Alone* (1930).

FRANK SHAY (1888–1954) Born in East Orange, New Jersey, Shay worked as a lumberjack and a seaman, and began selling books and pulp magazines as a youth, traveling around the country. At one time or another he ran the Washington Square Book Shop, "Frank Shay's Book Shop," and published many new American plays, singly and in anthologies. He also became an authority on sea chanties.

HAROLD E. SIMMELKJAER (1890–1956) Born in the Virgin Islands, Simmelkjaer was a deputy clerk for the New York Supreme Court. He attended schools in New York City and studied at Cooper Union. In 1919 he played the title role of O'Neill's *The Dreamy Kid.* In 1921 he wrote *The Scientific Side of the Negro Problem.* Through various organizations, Simmelkjaer "was active in seeking equitable treatment for Negroes." He ran against Adam Clayton Powell in the Democratic primary of 1946.

JEAN PAUL SLUSSER (b. 1886) A painter and scene designer, Slusser studied at the University of Michigan and the University of Munich. With Charles Ellis (q.v.), Slusser made batik in a New York theatrical costume studio for John Murray Anderson's Greenwich Village Follies. He designed the set for Alfred Kreymborg's *Vote the New Moon* in 1920. In 1924 he settled in Ann Arbor and designed stylistic sets for an amateur group performing Restoration Comedy. Meanwhile Slusser exhibited on the East coast, did murals, published *Bernard Karfiol* (1931), then became professor (1944) and director (1947) of the Museum of Art at the University of Michigan.

WILBUR DANIEL STEELE (1886–1970) Born in Greensboro, North Carolina, Steele studied at the University of Denver and the Museum of Fine Arts in Boston. A writer who tells little in clear statement and much by implication, Steele won many prizes for short stories. His principal novels are *Storm, Land's End,* and *Shame Dance.*

FRANK TANNENBAUM (1893–1969)   Born in Austria and an immigrant to the United States in 1905, Tannenbaum was a social philosopher and professor of Latin American History. In 1914 he became a spokesman for the unemployed, homeless, and hungry in New York whom he led into churches, demanding housing and food from priests; he served a one-year prison sentence. Graduating from Columbia in 1921, he traveled through Mexico and South America as correspondent for *Survey* and the *Atlantic Monthly*. Receiving a doctorate in economics in 1927 from the Brookings Institution, Tannenbaum did a socio-economic survey of Mexico and taught criminology at Cornell and later at Columbia.

ORDWAY TEAD (1891–1973)   Born in Somerville, Massachusetts, Tead was an educator, editor, and author. He graduated from Amherst College and advocated women's rights. A lecturer at Columbia on personal administration from 1920, he was adjunct professor of industrial relations till 1956, and chairman of the Board of Higher Education from 1938 to 1953. Meanwhile, Tead served as director of business publications for McGraw Hill Book Company from 1920 to 1925, and as vice president and editor of social and economic books at Harper and Row from 1925 until his retirement in 1962. He also wrote books on economics, history, and education.

CLEON THROCKMORTON (1897–1965)   Born in Atlantic City, Throckmorton studied at the Carnegie Institute and became a scenic designer. Besides his work with the Provincetown Players, he designed for the Theatre Guild, the Neighborhood Playhouse, the Civic Repertory Theatre and the Group Theatre. In the thirties he owned a major scenic supply house, then served as technical director of the entire Federal Theatre Project.

EUNICE TIETJENS (1884–1944)   A poet, lecturer, and writer, Tietjens studied in Geneva, Paris, and Dresden, Germany. During World War I, she was correspondent for the *Chicago Daily News;* returning to the University of Geneva, she became instructor of poetry from 1933 to 1936. Her husband, Cloyd Head, was also a poet with whom she wrote *Arabesque* in 1925. A former associate of *Poetry Magazine,* she was noted for her *Profiles From China* (1917), and several other volumes on Japan and China, including children's books.

ALICE WOODS ULLMAN (1870–1959)   A novelist and magazine writer, Ullman was born in Goshen, Indiana. She moved to New York about 1900, did short stories and illustrations for *Smart Set* and other magazines. She married and divorced Eugene Ullman, an Impressionist artist. O'Neill encouraged her to turn her story, *The Devil's Claw*, into a play, later presented by the Players. Ullman wrote several novels including *Edges,* which was autobiographical, and *The Hairpin Duchess,* which was made into a film.

LAWRENCE VAIL (1891–1968)   Born in Paris, Vail grew up surrounded by his father's paintings, and attended Oxford University. He began writing for the

Dial, Smart Set, and *Transition.* His play, *What D' You Want?* performed by the Provincetown in 1920, was one of the earliest surrealist plays. He wrote three novels, of which *Murder Murder* brought him renown. In 1922 he married Peggy Guggenheim. Vail began painting in 1930, then switched to collage and sculpture. He exhibited in Paris, Rome, Milan, and London and is represented in the Museum of Modern Art.

MARY HEATON VORSE (O'BRIEN) (1881–1966)   A novelist and champion of labor, Vorse was born in New York. She studied art in Europe, and during World War I was a war correspondent. Her second marriage, to newspaperman Joseph O'Brien, stimulated her involvement with the labor movement. A resident of Provincetown since 1907, it was on her wharf that the Provincetown Players first held public performances in 1915. She wrote memoirs, novels, and hundreds of articles for the *Atlantic, Collier's, Harper's,* the *New Republic.*

MAX WEBER (1881–1961)   Born in Russia, Weber grew up in New York, studied art in Paris and was greatly influenced by Matisse and Rousseau. He joined Stieglitz at "291" and worked to bring acceptability to abstract and semiabstract painting. Between 1915 and 1923 he lived in virtual retirement, but in 1920 taught at the Art Students' League in New York.

HARRY WEINBERGER (1888–1938)   Born in New York, Weinberger served as a lawyer for Emma Goldman and Alexander Berkman whom he defended in their fight against deportation. He also represented O'Neill in a $2 million plagiarism suit, and acted as attorney for the Provincetown Players; he was instrumental in legitimizing use of the Provincetown name for the playhouse used by the Experimental Theatre, Inc. In 1923 Weinberger produced *The God of Vengeance* by Shalom Asch at the Apollo Theatre.

HELEN WESTLEY (1879–1942)   Born in Brooklyn, Westley attended the American Academy of Dramatic Arts in New York and made her debut in 1897 in *The Captain of the Nonsuch.* She helped organize the Washington Square Players; in 1919 she was a founder of the Theatre Guild. Westley continued to act, and is remembered especially for Zinida in *He Who Gets Slapped,* Mrs. Zero in *The Adding Machine,* Emma in *The Doctor's Dilemma.* She became the first of the Guild to enter Hollywood films and debuted in *Moulin Rouge.* She also appeared in *Bedtime Story, Rebecca of Sunnybrook Farm,* and *Heidi.*

PERCY WINNER (1899–1974)   Born in New York City, Winner was a foreign affairs specialist. After working for Paris editions of the New York *Herald* and the *Chicago Tribune,* he joined the Associated Press and later worked for Havas News Agency, the Columbia and National Broadcasting Systems, and the International News Service. Then he became assistant to the American Ambassador to Britain and deputy director of the Office of War Information in North Africa. In 1948 he was editor of the *New Republic.* At the time of his death Winner was director of foreign area studies at the American University in Washington, D.C.

HARRY WINSTON (1896–1978) Born in Manhattan, Winston was a gem dealer. He quit school at fifteen to work in his father's Los Angeles store and peddled "jewelry to oil prospectors in boomtown saloons." Returning to New York in 1916, he started his own Premier Diamond Company, and became famous for purchasing the world's largest diamonds. Paternal to his gems, Winston was responsible for the largest cutting in the United States.

LOUIS WOLHEIM (1881–1931) Born in New York City, Wolheim attended Cornell and taught mathematics until 1918, when Lionel Barrymore offered him a part in a motion picture. Wolheim then made a career as an actor. He played Yank in the Provincetown production of *The Hairy Ape,* later starred as Captain Flagg in *What Price Glory?* He had leading roles in *The Arabian Nights,* and *All Quiet On The Western Front.*

MARGARET WYCHERLEY (1884–1956) Born in London, Wycherley attended the American Academy of Dramatic Art, and made her first stage appearance in 1898 with Madame Janauschek. She played "stock" at the Alcazar Theatre in San Francisco, and acted Olivia in *Twelfth Night* with Ben Greet. She created Lydia in Shaw's *Cashel Byron's Profession* in Richard Mansfield's company. She played Claire in *The Verge* at the Provincetown in 1921. In 1922 Wycherley was in *Six Characters In Search Of An Author.* She also acted Rebecca West in *Rosmersholm* (1925), Mrs. Amos Evans in *Strange Interlude* (1929), and in 1946 she played Amanda in *The Glass Menagerie.*

HELEN ZAGAT (1893–1975) After graduating from Barnard College in 1915, Zagat became a leading modern dancer in the twenties and was later ordained a minister. Her book, *Faith and Works,* and articles were about the "new thought" of her practical Christian sect, an offshoot of Christian Science. Zagat was pastor of the Church of Divine Unity.

WILLIAM ZORACH (1887–1966) Born in Lithuania, Zorach immigrated with his family to America, where extreme poverty forced him to leave school at thirteen. He became a lithographer's apprentice, then educated himself at the Cleveland Institute of Art and the National Academy of Design in New York. In 1910 his future wife, Marguerite Thompson, introduced him to the Cubists and Fauvists in Paris. Together they participated in the founding of the Provincetown Players. Zorach painted until, in the 1920s, he began sculpting. His art had eloquence, power, and a stern pathos. In 1932 he was commissioned to do "The Spirit of Dance" for Radio City Music Hall, and in 1954 he sculpted four large figures for the Mayo Clinic.

The following personalities who participated in the history of the Provincetown Players to varying degrees were deemed too well known to require short biographical sketches: Charles Chaplin, Malcolm Cowley, Theodore Dreiser, Edna St. Vincent Millay, Eugene O'Neill, Paul Robeson, Wallace Stevens, William Carlos Williams.

Appendix C

Physical Structures

1. The Wharf　　No official records exist that might provide evidence on the physical aspects of the Lewis Wharf or the fishhouse on it. However, it is possible to arrive at a partial reconstruction on the basis of three sources: descriptions given by Mary Vorse, the wharf's owner in 1915; contemporary pictorial evidence including maps, photographs, and etchings; finally, estimates given by a Provincetown artist who had been involved in converting the fishhouse-theatre into a coffeehouse in 1919.

Mary Heaton Vorse twice described her wharf: in an account published twenty-five years after the Players' activity on it, and another twenty years later, in personal letters. According to Vorse:

> The Lewis Wharf . . . *pushed out to sea almost as far as Railroad Wharf*. On the end was a fishhouse and *so wide was the wharf* that there was another *sizable* building aside from *the fishhouse* which *was a large building*. Further down the wharf was another shed. The wharf and the buildings were gray and the door and the end of the smaller house were painted red, which time had mellowed and weathered. . . .
> . . . *The fishhouse was a hundred feet long and fifty feet wide*. It had a dark, weathered look, and around the piles the waves always lapped except at extreme low tide. There was a huge door on rollers at the side, and another at the end which made it possible to use the bay as a backdrop.[1]

> It was in 1916 that we really cleared the place out and returned boat anchors, etc., to their various owners. The stage was 10′ x 12′. The theatre held 90 people. The stage was in four sections so that it would get through the great

sliding doors. It made it possible to have sets on different levels. There were no dressing rooms. But in 1916 we had electric lights. . . . An oyster shell road led to *the wharf* which, I was told, *was the third largest in Provincetown.* Neither in pictures nor description does it give the effect of its length, nor does the wharf theatre give the effect of a building 50′ x 100′.[2]

The wharf was nine hundred feet long.[3]

Her description is a valuable source; many of these statements can be accepted. But Vorse's authority is weakened by errors that argue against a blanket acceptance of her testimony. She implies that Lewis Wharf was converted into a theatre as a community project when, in fact, hired carpenters did the job.[4] Further, she mentions a coffeehouse (the "Sixes and Sevens") as functioning simultaneously with the playhouse.[5] This establishment did not actually operate until nearly three years after the Players had abandoned their theatre, and it was to occupy the very same fishhouse on the wharf.[6]

It is Vorse's recollections of the size of the wharf and its buildings that need to be carefully examined. First, the Lewis Wharf could not have approximated the length of Railroad Wharf, which was 1200 feet. Whether it was the third longest in 1915 cannot be argued, but Vorse's assertion that extreme low tide left it without water negates her statement of length. On an 1880 map of Provincetown, Railroad Wharf is over three times as long as Lewis Wharf. Four others (Bowley's, Central, Cook's, and Bank) are also considerably longer.[7]

Vorse's overestimation of the size of the wharf leads to a corresponding expansion of its buildings. Her dimensions for the fishhouse (50 by 100 feet) are grandiose. It is inexplicable why, *if* this immense space were available, the Players would have confined their stage to the 10 by 12 foot area given by both Vorse and Susan Glaspell. Moreover, various accounts that mention "packed," "full," and "sold out" houses never refer to an audience in excess of ninety—a crowd remembered as having sat "close together." [8] A commercial theatre typically allows less than 4 square feet per spectator. Surely ninety people need not huddle in an auditorium of almost five thousand square feet.

It is possible to arrive at a more reasonable estimate by turning to the pictorial evidence. On the 1880 map already mentioned, Lewis Wharf is shown to be about 330 feet long; three photographs and an etching indicate that it was closer to 100 feet in length between 1915 and its destruction by fire in the spring of 1922.[9] The wharf's fishhouse must have been approximately 24–26 feet wide (it had the same height), and about 34–36 feet long. This estimate is based on clues given in the four pictures. A careful examination reveals the length of the fishhouse to be twelve times that of a door. It can be assumed that prefabricated doors and windows were purchased; such a door measures 2′8″ (3′ with trimmings); the length of the building was therefore 34–36 feet. By similar standards, the large upstairs window would be 8 feet wide; taken three times, it gives the total width of the building without corner posts. The front stairs rise at a 45 degree angle, with equal treads and risers, 8 inches each. They provide comparison with the doors and corroborate the width of the window.

Regarding other buildings on the wharf, Vorse rightly remembers two additional structures. One of these was destroyed by fire in the summer of 1916 and is therefore frequently forgotten. The Metropolitan photograph clearly shows three buildings: the fishhouse, a shed approximately one fourth the size of the fishhouse, and another shack about one half the shed's size. Vorse described the shed as "sizable," and called the shack "a large building." Remembering that the fishhouse was in all probability about 34–36 feet by 24–26 feet, these other two structures must actually have been quite small in comparison.

All these estimates can be judged against one final source of information. In 1919 a group of Provincetown artists transformed the wharf fishhouse-theatre into a coffeehouse. One of the artists was Courtney Allen, illustrator, builder of shipmodels, and woodcarver. Allen made two etchings of Lewis Wharf in 1921, and in 1962–63 he built its model for the Provincetown Museum of the Cape Cod Pilgrim Memorial Association.[10] His reconstruction was based on memories, etchings, and photographs. Even a person so intimately acquainted with the fishhouse stated its dimensions with slight variations on subsequent occasions: in one of Allen's sketches the wharf measures 48 by 36 feet, the fishhouse 28 by 22 feet; in the other, the wharf appears to be 50 by 42 feet and the fishhouse 30 by 20 feet.[11] In no case, however, did Allen's estimates approximate the great size that Vorse remembered.

On the basis of these three strains of evidence, then, it is possible to safely conclude that the total area of the fishhouse was between 600 and 900 square feet. It must have easily accommodated over one hundred spectators. It appears impossible to arrive at greater certainty regarding the size of the Provincetown Players' first theatre.

2. 139 Macdougal Street   The Provincetown Players' first New York headquarters was located just outside what is now the Greenwich Village Historic District. The first house south of the southwest corner of Washington Square, it sat on a lot 24 feet wide and 86 feet deep, on the west side of Macdougal Street. A four-story building with basement—almost certainly built with brick bearing walls and wood floor joists—covered approximately 48 feet of the front of the lot, a further 18 feet had two stories and basement, another 15 feet had a one-story extension; only the last 5 feet remained unimproved.[12]

According to Edna Kenton, "the parlour floor at 139 was twenty-five feet wide and three rooms deep; two rooms formed the auditorium, the third one became the stage, measuring 14 feet by 10'6", with 2'6" reserved in the back for storage of scenery." [13] Her account of general depth is corroborated in a review written shortly after the first season's opening, which states that the theatre was "the exact size of two parlours, dining room and butler's pantry." [14] It may be assumed that the parlors constituted the auditorium, the dining room served as the stage, and the pantry became the scene dock.

Deutsch and Hanau, having never seen the premises while in use by the Players, described the "entire theatre" as "fifteen feet wide and forty-four feet deep." [15] They also reported a seating capacity of one hundred and fifty.

Both sets of dimensions are in part misleading, yet they allow one to surmise the truth. Had the "entire" length of 44 feet contained the stage, one hundred and fifty seats could not have been accommodated—taking into account a narrow aisle and a standard $3\frac{1}{2}$ square feet per spectator. The 25 feet width given by Kenton, on the other hand, would have provided sufficient space for an audience of almost three hundred. Most Greenwich Village brownstones, however, had a lengthwise hallway that might have taken up as much as ten feet. Thus Kenton probably refers to the building's entire width (she only errs one foot), whereas Deutsch and Hanau give the width of the auditorium. One may, then, accept Kenton's account of general depth as well as her dimensions of the stage, and apply Deutsch and Hanau's 44 by 15 feet to the auditorium alone—thus arriving at a reasonable space in which to locate one hundred and fifty spectators.

To turn these rooms into a theatre, a partition (containing a set of double doors) had to be removed "between the front and back parlors," and a steel girder installed. Though this alteration was "done quietly on a Sunday and the debris surreptitiously carted away . . . in the dead of night," [16] it occasioned the group's first encounter with the law. The inspection before the season began, described by Glaspell as having ended in a friendly drink, was not the end of the story. According to Vorse, the group was "having trouble with the tenement-house commission," while preparing for the season's fourth bill.[17]

As in Provincetown, space was too cramped for an adjacent dressing room. It was arranged "on the floor above, so that the actors reached the stage by tiptoeing down the stairs and sneaking artfully through the side hall when the audience was not looking." [18]

3. 133 Macdougal Street   Three doors further south on the same side of the street, the Players' second theatre was bigger, and better equipped, than the first. Of the 24'6" wide and 89'9" deep lot, a four-story building with basement occupied about 48 feet toward the front, a one-story extension covered the rest.[19]

In this "pre-Victorian" structure which "had been successively a storehouse, a bottling works and a stable," [20] an ambitious construction project was set in motion: bills from the plumber ($350) and the electrician ($230) were depleting the budget by late October 1918.[21] The basement was turned "into workshop and storeroom; one corner, directly under the stage, was walled off for the use of the actors, forming the first real dressing rooms." [22] On the ground floor carpenters were putting up an office partition[23] while on the upper floor which "still retained the charm of high ceilings, dignified mantels and finely wrought lintels and door-posts," [24] Christine Ell and Neil Reber had begun setting up the restaurant.

Overall interior dimensions are unavailable. The most complete physical description, part of the Federal Theatre Technical Survey, derives from May 1937. It contradicts in part Kenton's set of dimensions for the stage ("it was twelve feet by twenty-six") [25] and suggests that either there was no hallway when the Provincetowners moved in, or its constituent wall was removed before or during installation of the dome in 1920. For according to both diagram and data sheet, the stage was 22'10" wide and 22' deep—to the plaster dome, not counting a "small passage way" behind it, nor a 3'9½" apron in front of the curtain line.[26]

All sources agree that an inclined floor was built in the auditorium.[27] The fall circular proudly announced that the "new seats with cushions and solid backs have six inches more space from back to back," [28] but the arrangement was less than satisfactory. According to Kenton, "The front rows, because the stage was so close and so low,[29] were placed on the shortest legs possible, at kindergarten distance from the floor—eight, twelve, sixteen inches." [30] Capacity, according to a ground plan from the time of The Experimental Theatre, Inc., was two hundred and two,[31] the Federal Theatre Technical Survey, however, shows only one hundred and eighty-four seats.

This auditorium, too, was painted dark: "the walls a rich tawny orange brown, . . . the ceiling deep indigo and the plain proscenium rectangle . . . neutral grey." [32] Houselights were provided with shades, and a dimmer and a smoothly running curtain were also installed.[33]

A single reminder of the building's past as a stable "was left undisturbed— a hitching ring firmly embedded in the right wall of the auditorium." It was eventually inscribed, "Here Pegasus Was Hitched." [34]

4. The Dome   Jig Cook's dome was both a real physical object and an unrealized concept; the Macdougal Street structure merely prefigured the Ideal. Only a partial knowledge of the Players' new scenic device—its shape, size, and basic functions—can be gleaned from the meager available evidence. Even less well documented is the significant theory behind the construction, Cook's "pure space" idea. Although it is possible to augment Cook's fervid notes with his daughter Nilla's practical application of the theory, the vision remains elusive.

According to James Light, the completed dome in The Playwright's Theatre consumed 8 feet of the shallow stage's precious depth, and was 28 feet wide. A data sheet in the Federal Theatre Project's technical survey delineates the dimensions as 12 by 30 feet.[35] Because the same survey shows the entire width of the stage as only 22'10", the dome itself could not have been either 28 or 30 feet "wide." These dimensions become understandable upon analysis of the dome's actual shape and size. If 22 feet is accepted as the length of the major axis for half an ellipse, a dome constructed on that ground plan would have a circumference of about 29 feet (the horizontal measurement varies with the height at which it is taken, because the cross section is also a curve). Half the minor axis of such an ellipse will be about 8 feet—the dome's depth according to Light. Rotated around its major axis, the ellipse describes a circle, a quarter segment of which equals the dome's cross section: the length of that curve is the "height" as given by the F.T.P. survey. If "twelve feet" is taken to mean actual height (i.e., minor axis), a ground plan too close to a circle results.

The Macdougal Street dome was constructed of a series of uprights that were covered with a network of iron rods. Over this framework, plaster was applied and the surface completed with an application of sand. Ice was rubbed onto the final finish in order to remove any particles from the sand crystals' reflecting surfaces. Once lighted, the dome's curved and polished face functioned in two ways: it gave an illusion of great depth through control of the intensity of reflected light; it turned into a "mixing bowl of colors" by having its opposite sides illuminated in different hues. These two effects, Light explained, were connected: "Every light ray, as it strikes the small particles of sand finish, casts its shadow as a complementary color. The mingling of colored light with its complementary shadow produces, with the constant curve of the surface, the effect of distance, and makes the dome appear what in reality it is—a source of light." [36]

An examination of Cook's notes on his projected theatre of "pure space" reveals that the plaster dome as actually constructed was but a small part of a grand vision. In the wake of the dizzying success of *The Emperor Jones'* production with its experimental scenic device, Cook contemplated a "new" dome

used in connection with an invention which makes it possible to raise the curtain and play your play in pure space. Nothing there but infinity and the stage, and the stage broken up into big plastic elements with which you may compose.

The four sections combine into one deep stage; they separate into main and inner stages, to be used in swift succession of changing scenes—so restoring to drama its Elizabethan power of story telling.

Behind, around, above this trinity of stages there is nothing to mask—a pleasant symbol of artistic sincerity.

Permitting the swift handling of bulky scenery, this playing space does not compel the use of a single inch of scenery. The artist of the theatre shall at last be free to let his human figures and chosen objects receive mystically deep significance from their background of infinity.[37]

Torn from their context, some expressions seem obscure, others contradictory. One best approaches this dream theatre by imagining it as a cluster of domes with no straight walls at all: by the "big plastic elements" of the stage Cook perhaps meant various kinds of domes, or dome segments; his "four sections" recall the tiny stage on the wharf, four segments of which could be arranged at will.[38] Whether the "trinity of stages" refers to the shapes ("deep," "main," and "inner") into which "you may compose" the four sections or to something entirely different, is unclear. Cook's last paragraph gains a little in clarity from a passing reference to a "flygallery and pushbuttons" in Kenton's discussion of the imagined theatre structure.[39]

In related notes, Cook sketched ideas for appropriate audience space in his theatre. To achieve "unison between audience and players," all spectators were to sit facing "straight front, no one looking at the play from a limited angle"—an idea that echoes Richard Wagner's demands for the *Festspielhaus* seating. For members and friends, a club room was planned with a glass dome, the amount of entering light controlled by "big awnings . . . that swing open like a greenhouse." Cook also included a secret chamber for the director of the dream theatre. This private room, located behind a central dome, would ensure the creative artist freedom from interruptions.

Although Jig Cook had no opportunity to convert this vision into a structure, his teenage daughter, Nilla, saw realization of the "theatre of many domes, of lights and dancers" her father talked of as "the goal of my life." She later caused construction of a dome made of "khaki" ("the heaviest hand-spun cotton") hung on a "heavy wire frame" and held up "with light wires from above" in the Shivananda Theatre, Bangalore. It followed "a drawing of the dome as I remembered it in the Provincetown Playhouse." Back in the States a few years later, Nilla "went to General Electric with my drawings for the Tent of Domes. It was not only an exciting and beautiful drawing for a portable theatre, they said there, but it could also be air-conditioned." [40] She returned to India, and not until after World War II did she adapt "to a cluster of traditional Persian tents with umbrella domes the dream of the theatre of domes" for the Iranian National Ballet, which she organized.[41]

Notes

Chapter 1

1 Sydney Smith, review of *Statistical Annals of the United States of America* by Adam Seybert, *Edinburgh Review* 33, no. 65 (January, 1820): 79.

2 Henry F. May, *The End of American Innocence: A Study of the First Years of Our Own Time, 1912–1917* (New York, 1959), eloquently analyzes this otherwise quite neglected period. Key terms as well as key personalities referred to in this and subsequent paragraphs are derived from his work.

3 Malcolm Cowley, *Exile's Return* (New York, 1951), pp. 67–73.

4 Thomas H. Dickinson, *The Insurgent Theatre* (New York, 1917), p. 75.

5 Ibid., pp. 76–80.

6 Kenneth Macgowan, *Footlights Across America* (New York, 1929), p. 52. During the nineteenth century this function of theatre was greatly emphasized in countries vigorously asserting their incipient nationhood: Germany as well as most Scandinavian, southern and eastern European countries (including Russia).

7 Edward Gordon Craig's demand for a single Artist of the Theatre is a notable exception; see chap. three, below.

8 The Players are regularly mentioned as one of two or three most important forces in American theatre. See Ludwig Lewisohn, "Harvest," *Nation,* May 17, 1922, p. 604; Sheldon Cheney, *The Art Theatre* (New York, 1925), p. 68; Conrad Aiken, Barrett H. Clark, Arthur Hobson Quinn, James Weldon Johnson cited, "The Provincetown Playhouse In the Garrick Theatre" (New York, 1929); Margarete Berthold, *Weltgeschichte des Theaters* (Stuttgart, 1968), p. 478; Stuart W. Little, *Off Broadway, The Prophetic Theatre* (New York, 1972), pp. 30–35; O. G. Brockett, *History of the Theatre,* 3d ed. (Boston, 1977), p. 536.

9   Cowley, *Exile's Return,* p. 71.

10   Oliver Sayler, *Our American Theatre* (New York, 1923), p. 92.

Chapter 2

1   Mary Heaton Vorse, *Footnote to Folly* (New York, 1935), p. 129.

2   Some documents relating to the pageant were published in Brooks Mc-Namara, "Documents on the Pageant," *Drama Review* 15 (Summer 1971): 60–71.

3   Susan Glaspell, *The Road to the Temple* (New York, 1927), p. 248.

4   Bernard Frank Dukore, "Maurice Browne and the Chicago Little Theatre" (Diss., University of Illinois, 1957), p. 12.

5   Maurice Browne, *Too Late to Lament: An Autobiography* (Bloomington, 1956), p. 202.

6   Browne, *Too Late to Lament,* p. 202.

7   Dukore, "Maurice Browne," p. 17.

8   Browne, *Too Late to Lament,* pp. 200, 201.

9   Emily Hahn, *Romantic Rebels* (Boston, 1967), p. 77.

10   Floyd Dell, *Love in Greenwich Village* (New York, 1926), pp. 29–32. My emphases.

11   Lawrence Langner, *The Magic Curtain* (New York, 1951), p. 76.

12   Max Eastman, *Enjoyment of Living* (New York, 1948), pp. 250–51. Langner confirms that account, then adds: "After the second bill, Ida Rauh resigned from the Washington Square Players, not caring for the parts that were offered to her" (*Magic Curtain,* pp. 92, 99).

13   Cook to Glaspell, January 26, 1915, writes that he was "asked to take a part in a play of the Washington Square Players.... I said yes. You know I harbor a belief that maybe I can act" (Cook Papers, Berg Collection, New York Public Library).

14   Harry Kemp, "A Few Words Beforehand," *Bocaccio's Untold Tale* (New York, 1924), p. 2.

15   Marsden Hartley, "Farewell, Charles," *The New Caravan* (New York, 1936), pp. 556–57.

16   Hutchins Hapgood, *A Victorian in the Modern World* (New York, 1939), pp. 391–94. My emphases.

17   "Many Literary Lights Among Provincetown Players," *Boston* (Sunday) *Post,* September 10, 1916, p. 44; Edna Kenton, "Provincetown and Macdougal Street," in George Cram Cook, *Greek Coins* (New York, 1925), p. 20; Mary Heaton Vorse, *Time and the Town, A Provincetown Chronicle* (New York, 1942), p. 117.

18   Louis Sheaffer, *O'Neill, Son and Playwright* (Boston, 1968), pp. 343, 498 n, refers to a letter from Neith Boyce that gives the date as July 15.

19   Hapgood Papers, Yale Collection of American Literature, Beinecke Library.

20   Mary Heaton Vorse to Catharine S. Huntington, January 23, 1962. Courtesy of Miss Huntington.

21   Vorse, *Time and the Town,* p. 117.

22   Ibid.; Glaspell, *Road to the Temple,* p. 250. Script in Susan Glaspell, *Plays* (Boston, 1920).

23   Cook to Glaspell, September 12, 1916, Cook Papers, Berg Collection, New York Public Library.

24   Cited without attribution, Helen Deutsch and Stella Hanau, *The Provincetown, A Story of the Theatre* (New York, 1931), p. 7. The photograph is discussed in chap. two, sec. 4.

25   See Appendix C for detailed description and discussion of history.

26   Vorse, *Time and the Town,* p. 110.

27   Vorse to Huntington, March 27, 1962. Courtesy of Miss Huntington.

28   Vorse, *Time and the Town,* p. 118.

29   See Appendix C for estimates of size and capacity.

30   Vorse, *Time and the Town,* p. 118; Glaspell, *Road to the Temple,* p. 253. Instead, there was a thunderstorm opening night; some spectators lost their tightly rolled umbrellas through knot-holes in the floor. The fire came the following year, but not during a performance (see below).

31   Date in typescript of *Change Your Style,* among O'Neill Papers, Alderman Library, University of Virginia.

32   Vorse, *Time and the Town,* pp. 118–19. A Provincetown grocer, John Francis was landlord to numerous artists and writers, including Eugene O'Neill.

33   Wilbur Daniel Steele Papers, Stanford University Library.

34   Deutsch and Hanau, *The Provincetown,* p. 8.

35   According to Mary Heaton Vorse, interview, June 27, 1962, Provincetown, Mass. But Ida Rauh (interview, June 26, 1962, Provincetown) claimed to have played the twelve-year-old son, costumed in a bathrobe. Vorse and Rauh may, of course, recall different performances.

36   Glaspell, *Road to the Temple,* p. 251.

37   Cook, cited by Glaspell, ibid., pp. 251–52. My emphasis.

38   Cook Papers, Berg Collection, New York Public Library.

39   Printed announcement of the Liberal Club performance, dated March 5, 1916, Cook Papers, Berg Collection, New York Public Library. Reprise at Remsen's given by Edna Kenton, untitled manuscript history of the Provincetown Players, p. 7, Fales Collection, New York University. (Subsequently referred to as "His-

tory.") Sheaffer mistakenly dates the Liberal Club performance a year earlier (*Playwright,* p. 343).

40 Kenton, "History," p. 7.

41 *Provincetown Advocate,* June 8, 1916, p. 2. Versions of the myth are told by Vorse, *Time and the Town,* p. 118; Glaspell, *Road to the Temple,* p. 253; Vorse to Huntington, March 27, 1962.

42 A printed card in the Museum of the City of New York reads:

The Provincetown Players

Open their season, Thursday, July 13th, 1916

at Mrs. O'Brien's wharf

with two new one-act plays:

Neith Boyce's "Winter Night"

and Jack Reed's "Freedom"

Ticket prices, and the success of the sale are given in Deutsch and Hanau, *The Provincetown,* p. 11. It appears that *Suppressed Desires* was added to the program later.

43 "Many Literary Lights." The article is headed by a two-column photograph of the burning wharf.

44 Published in Frank Shay, ed., *Fifty More Contemporary One-Act Plays* (New York, 1928).

45 Interview, June 27, 1962, Provincetown. Cast in "Many Literary Lights."

46 Arthur Gelb and Barbara Gelb, *O'Neill,* 2d ed. (New York, 1974), p. 308; interview with Dell, July 24, 1963, Washington, D.C.

47 Deutsch and Hanau, *The Provincetown,* p. 11.

48 John Reed, *Freedom,* in *The Provincetown Plays, Second Series,* ed. Frank Shay (New York, 1916), pp. 72, 93.

49 Glaspell's account, *Road to the Temple,* pp. 253–54, is embellished by Deutsch and Hanau, *The Provincetown,* pp. 11–12, and Vorse, *Time and the Town,* pp. 20–23. Other accounts of this historic event are based on these three.

50 Harry Kemp, "Out of Provincetown," *Theatre Magazine,* April 1930, p. 22.

51 Sheaffer, *Playwright,* pp. 348, 498 n. 2, asserts on the basis of a letter from Wilbur Daniel Steele that the date was July 28. Sheaffer gives the exact dates of several performances for which I offer only approximate ones, but his references are casual; not all dates, addresses, or whereabouts of letters are clearly given. As for the "all-important" date of the O'Neill world premiere, I have (based on specified documents for the certain dates) calculated a four-day time span within which it most likely occurred (see my "Wharf and Dome: Materials for the History of the Provincetown Players," *Theatre Research/Recherches Théâtrales* 10, 3 [1970]). Sheaffer's date falls within that frame.

52 Glaspell, *Road to the Temple,* p. 255; Deutsch and Hanau, *The Province-town,* p. 11; Kenton, "History," p. 9. The number of subscribers is uncertain. Kenton mentions eighty-seven, each of whom paid $2.50 for a pair of tickets to each planned bill (i.e., one hundred and seventy-four spectators per performance!); the "first subscription list" reproduced by Deutsch and Hanau, opp. p. 29, records only twenty-nine associate members (each contributing $2), eighteen active members (who paid $5), and two honorary ones, one of them O'Neill. If Cook offered three bills for a dollar per subscriber, then each $2 subscription equals two associate members, i.e., altogether fifty-eight spectators. Adding the eighteen active members produces a grand total of seventy-six paying members. If active memberships are also assumed to cover two members each, the total climbs to ninety-four excluding honorary members. Nor does any arithmetic resolve contradicting prices. See sec. 5 and n. 85 below.

53 Glaspell, *Road to the Temple,* p. 253–54.

54 The first and third pictures are in the Yale Collection of American Literature, Beinecke Library, the second is in the Museum of the City of New York. The first of these is inscribed in O'Neill's hand on the back: "Original production in July, 1916 in the Provincetown Players' first home in an old boat house at the end of a wharf, Provincetown, Mass."

55 Eugene O'Neill, *Bound East for Cardiff,* in *The Plays of Eugene O'Neill* (New York, 1955), p. 481.

56 Deutsch and Hanau, *The Provincetown,* p. 12.

57 O'Neill, *Bound East,* p. 484. The actors are named on the back of the photograph.

58 Letter to the author, January 24, 1964.

59 "Original Director for O'Neil [sic] Tells of First Night," *New York Herald Tribune,* January 6, 1929, sec. 7, p. 5.

60 Gelb and Gelb, *O'Neill,* p. 310, mentions Kemp in the cast. The eyewitnesses were Alice Hall and her daughter, Julia Ward Stickley; the first in an interview (June 27, 1963, Newport R. I.), the second in a letter (July 23, 1963).

61 Published in Frank Shay, ed., *The Provincetown Plays, First Series,* (New York, 1916).

62 "Many Literary Lights"; corroborated in an interview with Marguerite and William Zorach, March 16, 1962, New York City.

63 Photographs courtesy of the Zorachs and of Peter A. Juley and Sons, photographers.

64 Published in Cook and Shay, *The Provincetown Plays.*

65 Date in Glaspell, *Plays,* p. 2.

66 Granville Hicks, *John Reed, The Making of a Revolutionary* (New York, 1936), p. 221.

67 John Reed, *The Eternal Quadrangle,* unnumbered page preceding p. 1 (Reed Papers, Houghton Library, Harvard University).

68 Cast in part from typescript, in part from Hapgood, *Victorian,* p. 354. Mary Heaton Vorse and Ida Rauh remembered the rollerskating, but not the skater or the play. Separate interviews, June 1962.

69 Glaspell, *Road to the Temple,* pp. 255–56.

70 Cast in Glaspell, *Plays,* p. 2.

71 "Many Literary Lights."

72 Hapgood, *Victorian,* p. 395.

73 Hapgood Papers, Yale Collection of American Literature, Beinecke Library.

74 Julia Ward Stickley (letter to the author July 23, 1963) claims that part of the purpose behind the enterprise was to keep the children out of the adults' hair. Nilla Cram Cook (December 18, 1963) contradicts her, saying the project created more rather than less havoc. They both comment on the dichotomy between bohemian parents' liberal posture toward adult rights and their strict principles of child-rearing.

75 *Time and the Town,* p. 124.

76 Julia Ward Stickley to the author, July 23, 1963.

77 Interview, June 23, 1963, Winchester, N. H.

78 Stickley to the author.

79 Alice Hall, interview, June 27, 1963.

80 Stickley to the author.

81 Nilla Cram Cook to the author, December 18, 1963.

82 Cook to Glaspell, September 13, 1916. Cook Papers, Berg Collection, New York Public Library.

83 Kenton, "Provincetown and Macdougal Street," p. 17; "History," p. 14.

84 Glaspell, *Road to the Temple,* p. 255.

85 The hallowed—and scrawled—"first subscription list" is reproduced by Deutsch and Hanau, *The Provincetown,* opp. p. 29. It records the names of only *eighteen* active members (who, the constitution was to specify, participate in play production and contribute $5), *twenty-nine* associate members (getting two tickets to each performance for a $2 contribution), and *two* honorary ones: one Robert Conville, and Eugene O'Neill. The presence of the dramatist's name on the list supports dating it after the acceptance of *Bound East* for production. Counting two associate members for each $2 donation brings that number to *fifty-eight,* adding up to a grand total of (18 + 2 + 58) *seventy-eight.* Doubling the actives would result in a count of *ninety-four,* excluding honorary members. But some couples paid for two memberships. How Kenton arrived at *eighty-seven* (a figure both the Gelbs and Sheaffer adopt), is not clear. Unless, by mistake, she added twenty-nine (instead of eighteen) to fifty-eight. See Kenton, "History," p. 9; Gelb and Gelb,

O'Neill, p. 308; Sheaffer, *O'Neill, Son and Artist* (Boston, 1973), p. 345; and note 52, above.

86   "Minutes of the Provincetown Players" handwritten in a hardbound volume, Theatre Collection, New York Public Library, Lincoln Center. All deliberations here referred to are recorded on pp. 4–5. (Subsequently referred to as "Minutes.")

87   "Minutes," p. 6. For a detailed discussion, see chapter 4.

88   Huffaker to Goodman, undated letter, Theatre Collection, New York Public Library, Lincoln Center.

Chapter 3

1   Barret H. Clark, *Eugene O'Neill* (New York, 1947); Gelb and Gelb, *O'Neill;* Travis Bogard, *Contour in Time* (New York, 1972); Sheaffer, *Playwright;* Sheaffer, *Artist.*

2   Michael Gold cited, "The Provincetown Playhouse in the Garrick Theatre" (New York, 1929).

3   Floyd Dell, *Homecoming, An Autobiography* (New York, 1933), p. 204.

4   Repeatedly described by Glaspell, *Road to the Temple,* pp. 90–96, 251, 307.

5   Margaret Anderson, "Art and Anarchism," *Little Review,* March 1916, p. 3.

6   Marsden Hartley, *Adventures in the Arts* (1921; reprint ed., New York, 1972), p. 27.

7   Edward Gordon Craig, *On the Art of the Theatre* (London, 1905), pp. 99, 156–57.

8   Cook cited by Glaspell, *Road to the Temple,* pp. 252–53.

9   Ibid., p. 245.

10   Nilla Cram Cook to the author, November 24, 1975, citing an often used phrase of her father's, also included in his poem, "Nilla Dear" (Cook, *Greek Coins,* p. 111).

11   Shank, "Collective Creation," the *Drama Review* 16, 2 (June 1972): 3.

12   Paul Emanuel Johnson, *Psychology of Religion* (New York, 1959), p. 43, mentions Robert McDougal as the first user of the term "interpersonal relations," in discussing the kinship of Moreno's *Einladung zu einer Begegnung* (1914) and Buber's *Ich und Du* (first draft, 1916; published, 1923).

13   There are few unbiased treatments of Moreno, but Kurt W. Back, *Beyond Words: The Story of Sensitivity Training and the Encounter Movement,* 2d. ed. (New York, 1974), gives this self-proclaimed prophet due recognition. Moreno

tells the history of his own work in the introduction to *Who Shall Survive?*, 2d. ed. (New York, 1953).

14 Dickran Tashjian, *Skyscraper Primitives; Dada and the American Avant-Garde 1910–1925* (Middletown, Conn., 1974), p. x.

15 Back, *Beyond Words,* Preface to the Pelican Edition, p. xiv.

16 These connections can be indicated here sketchily; they would provide sufficient material for a book dealing with the history of ideas. First, Moreno (whose works in Vienna were published with his original name, Jakob Moreno Levy) began publishing *Der Daimon* in 1918. This periodical (the title changed to *Der Neue Daimon* in 1919, and to *Die Gefaehrten* in 1920) provided an outlet for expressionists, mystics, and existentialists (Yvan Göll, Paul Kornfeld, Georg Kaiser, Franz Werfel, Paul Claudel, Max Brod, Jakob Wassermann, Franz Blei, and others). The only known public performance of his Impromptu Theatre took place at the Guild Theatre, home of the Theatre Guild's Studio, from which the Group Theatre evolved. Simultaneously, in 1931 Moreno published *Impromptu,* the only two issues of which contain contributions from psychotherapists and from Hans (for Franz?) Kafka, and Theodore (for Adolph?) Appia, among others. Second, Viola Spolin, whose "Seven Aspects of Spontaneity" (in *Improvisation for the Theatre,* Evanston, 1963) closely parallel both Cook's and Moreno's thought, had once been Neva Boyd's pupil, but developed her game techniques for actors independently. Inspiration for her influential book derived from the renewed interest in improvisation, largely as a result of her son's success. Third, that Maria Montessori had embraced Theosophy after a sojourn in India, as some Village bohemians and German Expressionists did without such a voyage, tallies with current mingling of play and meditation, whether at Esalen or in alternative theatre groups.

17 Ross Wetzsteon, "Chaikin and O'Horgan Survive the '60s," *Village Voice,* November 3, 1975, p. 81.

18 Calvin Tomkins, "Time to Think" [a profile of Robert Wilson], *New Yorker,* January 13, 1975, pp. 43, 51.

19 This passage is based on an unpublished manuscript, written with Douglas McDermott.

20 Cook's unpublished notes, cited by Glaspell, *Road to the Temple,* p. 245.

21 Hans Richter, *Dada: Art and Anti-Art* (New York, 1966), p. 12, cited by Tashjian, *Skyscraper,* p. 8. Richter's description of the Zurich dada group fits the Provincetown Players to a "T".

22 Hutchins Hapgood, "The Provincetown Players," p. 10 (Hapgood Papers, Yale Collection of American Literature, Beinecke Library).

23 Cook cited by Glaspell, *Road to the Temple,* pp. 252–53.

24 Concepts and terminology relating to "accusing" versus "established" use of ideas derive from Paul P. Krueger, "Theology and Literary Criticism: An At-

tempt at Common Categories" (Master's thesis, Pacific Lutheran Theological Seminary, 1976), esp. subsections "Law as Accuser," and "Law as Structure," in chap. one.

25 Cf. Carl Jaspers, *Tragedy is Not Enough* (London, 1953), p. 49.

26 All quotations in this paragraph: Nilla Cram Cook to the author, December 17, 1975.

27 Kenton, "History," pp. 20–21.

28 According to Dell, *Homecoming,* p. 149, in 1906 he and Cook participated in founding a "society of free thinkers" at Davenport, Iowa, the Monist Society. Cook then joined the Contemporary Club, the Chicago Little Theatre, and, presumably, the Socialist Party prior to moving to New York. There he became a member of the Liberal Club and the Washington Square Players before forming the Provincetown Players.

29 Hapgood, *Victorian,* p. 394; May, *End of American Innocence,* pp. 280–81.

30 Vorse, *Footnote,* p. 129. I have summarized main events of the Provincetown summers of 1915 and 1916 in the previous chapter; here my concern is with mental processes and concepts.

31 Hapgood, *Victorian,* pp. 391, 392–93. My emphases.

32 Marsden Hartley, "The Great Provincetown Summer," Yale Collection of American Literature, Beinecke Library.

33 Cook, cited by Glaspell, *Road to the Temple,* pp. 256, 260.

34 Hapgood, *Victorian,* p. 394.

35 Cook, cited by Deutsch and Hanau, *The Provincetown,* p. 26.

36 Hapgood, *Victorian,* p. 394.

37 Glaspell, *Road to the Temple,* p. 236.

38 Hapgood, *Victorian,* p. 394.

39 Dell, *Homecoming,* p. 266.

40 Hapgood, "The Provincetown Players," pp. 5, 10.

41 Eugene O'Neill, *The Great God Brown,* act 4, sc. 1.

42 Eunice Tietjens, *The World at My Shoulder* (New York, 1938), pp. 18–19.

43 Glaspell, *Road to the Temple,* pp. 255–56.

44 Cited by Deutsch and Hanau, *The Provincetown,* pp. 41–42.

45 Nilla Cram Cook, *My Road To India* (New York, 1939), pp, 448–49; amplified in letters to the author, 1974–75.

46 Kenton, documents this throughout "History."

47 Dell, *Homecoming,* pp. 263–64, 265, 266, 267, 368.

48 Hutchins Hapgood, "The Instinct to Conform," *New Republic,* November 29, 1933, p. 80.

49   Hapgood, *Victorian,* pp. 374–75.

50   Eastman, *Enjoyment,* p. 566.

51   Kenton, "Provincetown and Macdougal Street," pp. 22, 20–21.

52   Glaspell, *Road to the Temple,* p. viii.

53   Dell, *Homecoming,* p. 266.

54   Cook, cited by Kenton, "Provincetown and Macdougal Street," p. 30, and by Glaspell, *Road to the Temple,* p. 310.

55   Statements of esthetic and philosophical intent in those circulars, when not otherwise accounted for are assumed to have been written by Cook.

56   Eric Bentley, *The Life of the Drama* (New York, 1964), p. 64.

57   J. L. Moreno, *Who Shall Survive,* 2d ed. (New York, 1953), pp. xix ff.

58   *Das Stegreiftheater* (Potsdam, 1923), p. 12; and plate 1. Compare with photograph of a model in *Psychodrama I,* 2d rev. ed. (New York, 1946), fig. 1.

59   Cook's notes cited by Glaspell, *Road to the Temple,* pp. 292–96.

60   Moreno, *Who Shall Survive,* pp. xv, xxvii.

61   Zerka Moreno to the author, September 22, 1978.

62   Eric Bentley, *Theatre of War* (New York, 1972), p. 395.

63   Gerald F. Else, *Aristotle's Poetics: The Argument* (Cambridge, Mass. 1957), pp. 224–32, 423–50.

64   Ibid., p. 441.

65   "The pain of pity and fear gives rise to pleasure" and "the pleasure that springs from the tragic emotion is the task of construction" (ibid., pp. 448, 449).

66   Senator Daniel Patrick Moynihan.

67   Kenton to Cook and Glaspell, October 21, 1923, Harvard Theatre Collection.

Chapter 4

1   Deutsch and Hanau, *The Provincetown,* p. 26.

2   "First subscription list" reproduced in ibid., opposite p. 29.

3   Ibid., p. 7. A photograph of a scene from *Enemies* (see above, chap. two), is described by Cook to have been more like that of the first play ever done by the group—and the two cushions on the sofa are only a small part of set, which also contained a table and two chairs.

4   *New York Herald Tribune,* January 6, 1929.

5   Letter to the author, December 18, 1963.

6   "Minutes," p. 5.

7   "Minutes," pp. 6, 11–13.

8   "Minutes," pp. 7–9.

9   Greenwich Village topographical information was gathered from published memoirs, guide books, area maps, letters, and field trips. The most useful sources were Egmont Arens, *The Little Book of Greenwich Village,* 3d ed. (New York, 1919); Agnes Boulton, *Part of a Long Story* (Garden City, N.Y., 1958), pp. 12, 25–27; Anna Alice Chapin, *Greenwich Village* (New York, 1917), pp. 222–38; Gorham B. Munson, "Greenwich Village That Was—Seedbed of the Nineteen Twenties," *Literary Review* 5, no. 3 (Spring 1962), pp. 313–35; Federal Writers' Project, *New York City Guide* (New York, 1939), pp. 126–43; *The Village Voice Map of Greenwich Village* (New York, 1973); Caroline F. Ware, *Greenwich Village 1920–1930* (Boston, 1935), pp. 43–44, 53–54, 63–64, 241–63, and appendix G.

10   Malcolm Cowley to the author, May 11, 1978, and Boulton, *Long Story,* p. 12.

11   Boulton, *Long Story,* p. 12.

12   Deutsch and Hanau, *The Provincetown,* p. 34.

13   "Minutes," pp. 15–16.

14   Louise Bryant to Reed, November-December 1916, Reed Papers, Houghton Library, Harvard University.

15   Cook to Glaspell, September 13 and 19, 1916, Cook Papers, Berg Collection, New York Public Library.

16   Descriptions of the Players' first New York theatre at 139 Macdougal Street are either unclear or conflicting, or both. For this study, older accounts were checked and further information obtained by correspondence with various individuals and organizations, including Sidney Bernard, Harmon H. Goldstone of Goldstone and Hinz, Architects, Geraldine Lust, Dr. James M. Sacks, Native New Yorkers' Historical Association, and The New York Historical Society. In addition, Stella Bloch Hanau helped clarify problems of the building's interior layout (letter to the author, February 29, 1964); and Mrs. Lee Roberts kindly provided specifications from Manhattan Building Department files, New York City Tax Assessment Records, the Perris and Brown Atlas, and the Bromley & Company Manhattan Land Book (letters to the author, October 31 and December 18, 1979).

17   "No Mark of 'Sacred Cod,' " *New York Herald,* December 3, 1916.

18   Kenton, "History," p. 22.

19   Deutsch and Hanau, *The Provincetown,* p. 19.

20   Glaspell, *Road to the Temple,* p. 260.

21   Kenton, "History," p. 22.

22   Hanau to the author, April 11, 1964.

23   Deutsch and Hanau, *The Provincetown,* p. 18.

24   Sheaffer, *Playwright,* p. 362.

25   Kenton, "History," p. 27a.

26 Ibid., and Sheaffer, *Playwright,* p. 362.

27 "First Circular," October 1916, Harvard Theatre Collection.

28 "Minutes," p. 14.

29 Macgowan, *Footlights,* pp. 54–55.

30 Kenton, "History," pp. 61, 94-b.

31 Deutsch and Hanau, *The Provincetown,* p. 20.

32 Photographs of the Provincetown performance are in O'Neill's scrapbooks in the Yale Collection of American literature; a snapshot of the set used in
New York is in the author's possession; another, showing O'Neill at work on the
set is reproduced by Gelb and Gelb, *O'Neill,* opposite p. 554.

33 First Playbill of the Provincetown Players (New York, 1916), Yale Collection of American Literature, Beinecke Library.

34 Floyd Dell, *King Arthur's Socks and Other Village Plays* (New York,
1922).

35 Second Playbill, Yale Collection of American Literature, Beinecke Library.

36 Gelb and Gelb, *O'Neill,* pp. 322–23. O'Neill's comment is in a letter
which forms the appendix of "James O'Neill," *San Francisco Theatre Research,* ed.
Lawrence Estevan (San Francisco, 1942), 20: 119.

37 Alfred Kreymborg, *Troubadour* (New York, 1925), pp. 308, 309.

38 Kenton, "History," p. 40.

39 "Minutes," pp. 19–22; Kenton, "History," p. 23; Hapgood, "The Provincetown Players," p. 5.

40 Kenton, "History," p. 45.

41 Cook to Glaspell, December 11, 1916; Cook Papers, Berg Collection,
New York Public Library.

42 Bryant to Reed, December 2, 1916; Reed Papers, Houghton Library,
Harvard University.

43 Dell, *Homecoming,* p. 266.

44 Moise to Kenton, October 16, 1933; in Kenton's scrapbook, Fales Collection, New York University.

45 "Minutes," p. 28.

46 Ibid., p. 29.

47 Kenton, "History," pp. 53, 55.

48 Heywood Broun, *New York Tribune,* March 18, 1917, sec. 4, p. 3. His
review of scripts had appeared on January 30, 1917, p. 9.

49 Jacques Copeau, *Registres I: Appels,* ed. Marie-Helene Dasté and Suzanne
Maistre Saint-Denis (Paris: Gallimard, 1974), p. 146; see also Norman H. Paul,
"Copeau Looks at the American Stage," *Educational Theatre Journal,* March 1977,
pp. 67–68.

50 "Minutes," p. 23.

Chapter 5

1 Kenton, "History," p. 140.

2 "Minutes," p. 15.

3 Kenton, "History," p. 61.

4 "Minutes," p. 23.

5 Circular for the season of 1917–18, Yale Collection of American Literature, Beinecke Library. Its first sentence, "The Provincetown Players are making their plans for next season," dates this circular.

6 Fall circular begins, "The Provincetown Players open their second New York season Friday, November second." Cook's copy (Berg Collection, New York Public Library) carries the note: "best circular." Kenton, "History," p. 66, concurs with that judgement.

7 "Minutes" and "History" document this, and interviews and circulars bear it out, for they promise plays by Lincoln Steffens (Fall 1917); George Cronyn, Bobbie Edwards, Peggy Baird, and Witter Bynner (Fall 1918).

8 Subscription form, Performing Arts Collection, Shields Library, University of California, Davis.

9 Balance sheet, 1917–18, Weinberger Papers, Yale University Library.

10 "History," p. 66.

11 Kreymborg, *Troubadour,* p. 318.

12 Mary Jane Matz, *The Many Lives of Otto Kahn* (New York, 1963), pp. 134–35.

13 Cook to Glaspell, March 24, 1918, Cook Papers, Berg Collection, New York Public Library.

14 Phillip MacKenzie to Robert Elliott, March 18, 1776, cited in W. E. Woodward, *The Way Our People Lived* (New York: Dutton, 1945), p. 142.

15 The recipe is given by Kenton, "History," p. 45. Personal experience confirms both the smoothness and the potency of the potion. It is also very expensive.

16 *New York Times,* November 4, 1917, sec. 8, p. 7.

17 In *"The Moon of the Caribbees" and Six Other Plays of the Sea* (New York, 1923), p. 57.

18 *Troubadour,* pp. 305–6.

19 Yale Collection of American Literature, Beinecke Library.

20 Cook's family background in Glaspell, *Road to the Temple,* p. 13. Deutsch and Hanau, *The Provincetown,* p. 24, explicate the connection.

21 Gelb and Gelb, *O'Neill,* p. 343; interview with Light, July 19, 1962.

22 In Cook and Shay, *Provincetown Plays,* p. 116.

23 *New York Times,* November 11, 1917, sec. 8, p. 6.

24 *New York Tribune,* November 3, 1917, p. 13.

25 Cook and Shay, *Provincetown Plays,* p. 96.

26 Kreymborg, *Troubadour,* p. 312.

27 Unpublished typescript, Theatre Collection, New York Public Library, Lincoln Center.

28 Interview, November 8, 1963, Los Angeles.

29 Boulton, *Long Story,* p. 27.

30 In *Drama Magazine,* January 1920, pp. 132–33.

31 In Margaret G. Mayorga, ed. *Representative One-Act Plays by American Authors* (Boston, 1922).

32 Interview, February 3, 1964, Oakland, Ca.

33 Dell, *Homecoming,* p. 299.

34 In *King Arthur's Socks,* p. 50.

35 *Homecoming,* p. 299.

36 Interview, July 24, 1963, Washington, D.C.

37 Corroborated by Nina Moise, interview, November 8, 1963, Los Angeles.

38 In Glaspell, *Plays,* p. 107.

39 In the *Flying Stag Plays,* no. 6 (New York, 1918).

40 Photograph in Deutsch and Hanau, *The Provincetown,* opposite p. 28; Kreymborg is credited both on the playbill and the frontispiece of the published play.

41 Playbill in Yale Collection of American Literature, Beinecke Library. James Light, interview, July 18, 1963.

42 Dell, *Homecoming,* pp. 284, 299.

43 Deutsch and Hanau, *The Provincetown,* p. 30.

44 George Cram Cook, *The Athenian Women* (Athens, 1926), p. 4. In addition to the original text and a modern Greek translation, this volume contains a preface by the author. The exact date of opening could not be determined; but it antedated Broun's review, see below.

45 The first of these photographs is in the Theatre Collection, New York Public Library, Lincoln Center, the second is pasted in Edna Kenton's Scrapbook, Fales Collection, New York University; the third is reproduced in Deutsch and Hanau, *The Provincetown,* opposite p. 48. Broun's comment in *New York Tribune,* March 4, 1918, p. 9.

46 Kreymborg, *Troubadour,* pp. 312, 313.

47 Alfred Kreymborg, *Manikin and Minikin* in *A Treasury of Plays for Women,* ed. Frank Shay (Boston, 1922), p. 203.

48 Kreymborg, *Troubadour,* p. 316.

49 Letter to the author, September 6, 1965.

50 Allan Ross Macdougall, ed., *Letters of Edna St. Vincent Millay* (New York, 1952), p. 337. The script is in Millay's *Three Plays* (New York, 1926).

51 Kreymborg, *Troubadour,* pp. 314, 316.

52 Ibid., p. 318.

53 See chap. seven, below.

54 *New York Tribune*, March 31, 1918, sec. 4, p. 4.

55 Playbill, Yale Collection of American Literature, Beinecke Library; Gelb and Gelb, *O'Neill*, p. 371.

56 Typescript, Copyright Office, Library of Congress.

57 Typescript, Yale University Library; Samuel A. Eliot to the author, March 30, 1964.

58 *The Hermit and His Messiah*, p. 3.

59 Yale Collection of American Literature, Beinecke Library. First letter, April 9, 1918; second refers to wedding with Agnes Boulton "two evenings ago," dating it April 14.

60 Interviews with Moise, November 8, 1963 and with Ellis, July 10, 1963.

61 Glaspell, *Plays*, p. 156.

62 Pasted in Edna Kenton's Scrapbook, Fales Collection, New York University.

63 "Minutes," pp. 46–47.

64 Balance sheet, 1917–18, Weinberger Papers, Yale University Library.

65 Cook to Glaspell, October 24, 1918, Cook Papers, Berg Collection, New York Public Library.

66 *New York Times*, May 19, 1918, sec. 4, p. 8.

67 *New York Times*, May 26, 1918, sec. 4, p. 7.

68 "Unorganized, Amateur, Purely Experimental," *Boston Evening Transcript*, April 27, 1918, sec. 2, pp. 8, 9.

69 Cook to Glaspell, March 24, 1918, Cook Papers, Berg Collection, New York Public Library. Either the letter is misdated, or Jig saw the article (see previous note) in manuscript.

70 Circular for third New York Season, issued Spring 1918 (still from 139 Macdougal Street), Yale Collection of American Literature, Beinecke Library.

71 Kenton, "History," p. 94b corrects the number of first year's subscribers from 550 (a printing error) to 450.

72 "Minutes," p. 49; Deutsch and Hanau, *The Provincetown*, p. 43.

73 *New York Sun*, May 17, 1918, p. 9.

74 See chap. six, note 11, below.

75 Kenton, "History," p. 118.

76 *Dramatic Mirror*, November 29, 1918; *New York Tribune*, November 25, 1918, p. 9.

77 Typescript, Copyright Office, Library of Congress.

78 In *"Moon of the Caribbees,"* p. 147.

79 Boulton, *Long Story*, pp. 236, 246.

80 Kenton, "History," p. 113.

81 In *Liberator,* March 1919, p. 25.

82 James Light, interview, July 19, 1963.

83 In Glaspell, *Plays.*

84 John Corbin, "Seraphim and Cats," *New York Times,* March 30, 1919, sec. 4, p. 2.

85 In *Plays of the Harvard Dramatic Club, First Series,* ed. George P. Baker (New York, 1918).

86 *New York Tribune,* December 23, 1918, p. 9.

87 In Cook and Shay, *The Provincetown Plays.*

88 In Ibid.

89 *New York Tribune,* January 23, 1919, p. 9.

90 In Frank Shay and Pierre Loving, eds., *Fifty Contemporary One-Act Plays* (New York, 1920).

91 Typescript, Copyright Office, Library of Congress.

92 Clark, *Eugene O'Neill,* pp. 58–59.

93 O'Neill to Moise, January 17, 1919, Yale Collection of American Literature, Beinecke Library.

94 Macdougal, *Letters,* p. 117; corroborated by Norma Millay, interview, July 10, 1963.

95 Typescript, Bancroft Library, University of California, Berkeley.

96 Interview, July 10, 1963.

97 Kenton, "History," p. 126.

98 Printed in Glaspell, *Plays.* Personal background explained, *Road to the Temple,* pp. 278–81.

99 Kenton, "History," pp. 116–18.

100 Ida Rauh, cited by Barry O'Rourke, "At the Sign of the Sock and Buskin," *Morning Telegraph,* February 16, 1919.

Chapter 6

1 Kenton, "History," p. 140.

2 "Many Literary Lights." The headline of a brief article in the *Survey* (October 28, 1916), p. 78, "On the Road from Cape Cod to Broadway," carries the same implication.

3 Allen Churchill, *The Improper Bohemians* (New York, 1958), p. 212. During an interview in June 1962, Ida Rauh reiterated the validity of principle. So did Nilla Cook in a series of letters.

4 This paragraph sums up a consensus of erstwhile Provincetown Players in the course of interviews and correspondence, including William Zorach, James Light, Norma Millay, Charles Ellis, Jasper Deeter, Nina Moise, Michael Gold, and Susan Jenkins Brown.

5   This statement was made in a letter, with the request that it not be attributed. In *Road to the Temple,* pp. 277–79, Glaspell essentially acknowledges its verity.

6   Drinking bouts and Indian wrestling have been recounted by Deeter, Dell, Ellis, Moise, and others. Similar anecdotes appear in print.

7   Glaspell, *Road to the Temple,* pp. 276–77.

8   Deutsch and Hanau, *The Provincetown,* pp. 54–55.

9   Glaspell, *Road to the Temple,* p. 278; circumstances more explicitly stated in a letter to the author from Susan Jenkins Brown, February 17, 1965.

10   Glaspell, *Road to the Temple,* pp. 278, 286.

11   The most noteworthy scripts of the season, according to Broun's regular reviews in the *Tribune,* and Corbin's in the *Times,* were O'Neill's *Where the Cross Is Made,* and *The Moon of the Caribbees;* Cook and Glaspell's *Tickless Time;* Alice Rostetter's *The Widow's Veil;* and Glaspell's first full-length play, *Bernice.* The acting of Rostetter, Glaspell, and Rauh was praised especially by Broun (see n. 14, below); whereas Rebecca Drucker (*Tribune,* April 20, 1919, sec. 4, p. 2), and even otherwise antagonistic critics in the *Morning Telegraph* (November 23, 1918), and the *Herald* (March 24, 1919) praised the effective staging.

12   First Bill, Sixth Season (November 1–13, 1919), Yale Collection of American Literature, Beinecke Library; Kenton, "History," pp. 146–47.

13   May 3, 1919, pp. 702–3; my emphasis. The article is signed, T. H. (Theresa Helburn, a member of the Theatre Guild's Board of Directors was a regular contributor).

14   April 13, 1919, sec. 4, p. 1.

15   Letter to the author, with the request that this statement not be attributed.

16   Light's qualifications are assessed on the basis of a resumé his agent distributed some time after 1950, on a letter from Susan Jenkins Brown (February 17, 1965), and on interviews with Light. During one of these (July 19, 1962), he made a vehement gesture as if throwing something into the air with his right hand and said: "We did it all like . . . *this!*"

17   Deutsch and Hanau, *The Provincetown,* p. 55; Susan Jenkins Brown to the author, February 17, 1965.

18   *New York Times,* November 9, 1919, sec. 8, p. 2.

19   *Getting Unmarried,* in *Smart Set,* April 1918, p. 98.

20   *New York Globe,* November 3, 1919.

21   *Three from the Earth,* in Djuna Barnes, *A Book* (New York, 1930), pp. 15, 30.

22   *New York Tribune,* November 16, 1919, sec. 4, p. 7.

23   *New York Times,* November 9, 1919, sec. 8, p. 2.

24   Edna St. Vincent Millay's *The Princess Marries the Page* had been the first. Harold Chapin, *The Philosopher of Butterbiggins* (London, 1921).

25 Kenton, "History," p. 145.

26 *New York Times,* November 9, 1919, sec. 8, p. 2.

27 *New York Tribune,* November 16, 1919, sec. 4, p. 7.

28 Ibid.

29 *New York Globe,* November 3, 1919.

30 In Frank Shay and Pierre Loving, eds. *Fifty Contemporary One Act Plays.*

31 Edna St. Vincent Millay, *Aria da Capo* (New York, 1920), p. 39. The photograph is reproduced by Deutsch and Hanau.

32 Interview, July 10, 1963, Steepletop, Austerlitz, N.Y.

33 In Barrett H. Clark and Kenyon Nicholson, eds. *The American Scene* (New York, 1930). According to Kenton, "History," p. 145, an adaptation of the story by someone other than the author was scheduled for the previous bill; it was withdrawn due to Ferber's insistence that her version be substituted.

34 In *Playboy,* no. 7 (1921), pp. 3–5.

35 Michael Gold, *Money,* in Clark and Nicholson, *The American Scene.*

36 In Alfred Kreymborg, *Plays for Merry Andrews* (New York, 1920).

37 Jean Paul Slusser to the author, May 27, 1965. All quotations in this paragraph are from that letter, interwoven with information from an interview with Norma Millay and Charles Ellis, July 10, 1963, Steepletop, Austerlitz, N.Y.; and one with Jasper Deeter, July 25, 1963, Media, Pa.

38 Wallace Stevens, *Three Travelers Watch a Sunrise,* in Shay and Loving, eds., *Fifty Contemporary One-Act Plays,* p. 496.

39 In Lawrence Langner, *Five One-Act Comedies* (Cincinnati, 1922).

40 Kenton, "History," p. 155, in combination with a clipping in "Provincetown Players' Scrapbook, 1916–1920," Harvard Theatre Collection, which is dated February 27, but lacks identification as to year and newspaper.

41 Part of Schnitzler's loose cycle of plays, *Living Hours,* and published in Arthur Schnitzler, *Anatol, Living Hours, The Green Cockatoo,* trans. Grace Isabel Colborn (New York, 1917).

42 Djuna Barnes, *Kurzy of the Sea,* TS, Copyright Office, Library of Congress, p. 13.

43 *New York Times,* April 4, 1920, sec. 6, p. 6.

44 Arthur G. Hays, letter to Commissioner of Internal Revenue, May 6, 1919, Weinberger Papers, Yale University Library.

45 Treasury Department "Claim for Refund," filed for the Provincetown Players by M. Eleanor Fitzgerald, March 11, 1921, Weinberger Papers, Yale University Library.

46 List of checks made on Corn Exchange Bank, submitted to Internal Revenue Service by Provincetown Players, January 22, 1921, Weinberger Papers, Yale University Library.

47 *New York Clipper,* March 24, 1920.

48 Kenton, "History," p. 158, uses the figure $2,100 without making clear whether this was the total payment finally made to the government, or the amount contributed by subscribers, or the difference between the payment to Internal Revenue and the amount raised, i.e., money to be paid from "cash-on-hand."

49 Statement submitted to Internal Revenue Service by M. Eleanor Fitzgerald showing all taxes paid, August 22, 1921; Internal Revenue Service to Provincetown Players, October 17, 1921 and "Offer of Compromise" submitted to Internal Revenue by Provincetown Players, October 31, 1923, Weinberger Papers, Yale University Library.

50 Arthur G. Hays, letter to Commissioner of Internal Revenue, May 6, 1919, Weinberger Papers, Yale University Library.

51 Balance Sheet, 1917–18, Weinberger Papers, Yale University Library.

52 Provincetown Players Subscription Form, 1917–1918 Season, Performing Arts Collection, Department of Special Collections, Shields Library, University of California at Davis.

53 Balance sheet pasted in Edna Kenton's Scrapbook, Fales Collection, New York University.

54 "History," p. 118, explains this action as a response to demands that the box-office be kept open at regular hours.

55 Interview, July 25, 1963, Media, Pa.

56 "History," p. 97.

57 Interview, July 10, 1963.

58 Interview, July 25, 1963.

59 Same interview.

60 *New York Times,* January 22, 1920, p. 22, mentions her in the cast of the Tolstoy play. Provincetown playbills give credit for her directing; both Light and Deeter recalled working with her.

61 The *Times* (see preceding note) lists her as well.

62 Several of the interviewed Players laid stress on the close connection between Jig and Ida, including Norma Millay who said "Jig and Ida *were* the Provincetown Players," and Susan Jenkins Brown who expressed it in more rational terms. Occasional innuendos suggested that this intimacy was an important reason behind Glaspell's willingness to encourage Cook to leave New York for the 1919–20 season.

63 It is remarkable that Kenton, who often provides insight into motivation behind facts recorded by others, makes no comment on Rauh's departure beyond stating the fact ("History," p. 155).

64 "The First Bill—Seventh Season, December 6 to 18, inclusive." Yale Collection of American Literature (see chap. seven, nn. 29, 30 for different versions of this program).

Chapter 7

1 Kenton, "Provincetown and Macdougal Street," p. 24.

2 Hartley, "The Great Provincetown Summer," Yale Collection of American Literature, Beinecke Library.

3 William Zorach, interview, March 16, 1962, New York City.

4 Glaspell, *Road to the Temple,* pp. 286, 287.

5 Susan Jenkins Brown to the author, February 17, 1965. This entire paragraph combines views expressed in her letter and in interviews with Jasper Deeter, Norma Millay, Charles Ellis, and James Light.

6 Nilla Cram Cook cites O'Neill's response to an attack from her father "for sticking to the conventional, after the Emperor, which opened the way to new forms" as follows: "Gene turned on Jig and said, 'well, *you* did it, and look at the result! Your *Spring* as a play is not what it was on the dunes when you *told* it to us!' " On the dunes, Nilla Cook explains, "it had been in the idealized American Indian tradition. . . . a new dance-play form in which 'theatre is *faith,* not entertainment.' " Letter to the author, February 5, 1975.

7 Kenton, cited by Gelb and Gelb, *O'Neill,* p. 444.

8 Deutsch and Hanau, *The Provincetown,* p. 60, mention "three hundred and sixty dollars in the treasury"; Glaspell, *Road to the Temple,* p. 289, writes the "dome took five hundred of" the "five hundred and thirty dollars in the treasury"; Kenton, "History," p. 165, adopts Glaspell's figures. The 1919–20 season closed with a balance of over $1,600. Objections to the dome's possible effect on staging were summarized by Deeter and Throckmorton in separate interviews, July 25, 1963, Media, Pa., and July 27, 1963, Atlantic City, N.J.

9 Kenton, "History," p. 166.

10 Kenton, "Provincetown and Macdougal Street," pp. 26, 25, 26, and "History," p. 167.

11 Of this article's two versions, one (typescript, dated November 11, 1920) is in Edna Kenton's Scrapbook (Fales Collection, New York University); the other is reproduced by Deutsch and Hanau, *The Provincetown,* pp. 61–62. Much information was corroborated and supplemented in interviews with Light, July 19 and August 9, 1962, and July 13, 1963, New York City.

12 Deutsch and Hanau, *The Provincetown,* pp. 60–61. Kenton mentions neither Corley nor Light; Light made no reference to Corley; Nilla Cram Cook asserts Corley, but not Light, was involved.

13 For technical details and their documentation, see Appendix C, on Structures.

14 See Appendix B.

15 Kenneth Macgowan, Introduction to Deutsch and Hanau, *The Provincetown,* p. ix. President Harding was elected the day after *The Emperor* opened, keeping newspapermen busy.

16 *New York Tribune,* November 4, 1920, p. 8.

17 *New York Call,* November 10, 1920.

18 *New York Sun,* November 6, 1920.

19 *New York Times,* November 7, 1920, p. 8.

20 Kenton, "History," p. 168.

21 The *New York Tribune* announced one-week extensions on November 11 (p. 10) and November 18 (p. 10); the bill was "extended through December, playing every night," as of December 3 (p. 10).

22 Kenton, "History," p. 174.

23 Although Kenton does not identify herself as the sole opponent in "History," she does in a letter to Cook and Glaspell, July 14, 1922, Harvard Theatre Collection.

24 Cited by Glaspell, *Road to the Temple,* pp. 304–5.

25 Cook to Glaspell, August 27, 1921, Cook Papers, Berg Collection, New York Public Library. Agreement, dated Aug. 26, 1921, between F. Ray Comstock and Provincetown Players (signed by Cook and Fitzgerald) in Weinberger Papers, Yale University Library.

26 This letter is further cited in chap. eight, n. 16.

27 Often repeated phrases of Cook's, which appear in his poem "Nilla Dear" (Cook, *Greek Coins,* p. 111).

28 Cook cited by Glaspell, *Road to the Temple,* p. xii.

29 "The First Bill—Seventh Season" has at least two versions; the first is dated "November 1 through 14, inclusive," and gives no directorial credit. Yale Collection of American Literature, Beinecke Library.

30 This version of "The First Bill—Seventh Season" is dated "December 6 to 18, inclusive." Yale Collection of American Literature. I have not found versions covering the period between November 14 and December 6. (Most interviews with erstwhile Players have called Jig's directorial responsibilities into question.)

31 For a summary history of this phrase, see chaps. five and six, above.

32 Kemp, "Out of Provincetown," p. 22.

33 Deutsch and Hanau, *The Provincetown,* p. 55, mention the incident without naming "one of the younger men," and date it so early (upon Cook's return from his year's leave) as to make its connection with Deeter improbable. Deeter thought it happened just prior to Jig and Susan's departure for Greece (March 1, 1922), and recalled having shrugged off the gesture as condescending (Interview, July 25, 1963, Media, Pa.). Had the designee been Light, the incident would have to have occurred on Cook's return for *The Emperor;* it would then strengthen Light's account of the cooperation on the dome, and make later events (see chap. eight) more easily understood. But Light did not mention it.

34 Gelb and Gelb, *O'Neill,* p. 445, and Sheaffer, *Artist,* p. 32, both conclude that it was thought that Ellis might play Brutus Jones in blackface, until Ida Rauh

and/or Jasper Deeter prevailed that a black actor was needed. Deeter told me that Robeson was approached but would not hear of it. It was after that that the choice fell on Gilpin, he said. Paul Robeson became identified with the role in the Experimental Theatre, Inc.'s, revival of the play in 1924. He also played it in Louis Gruenberg's opera based on the play, and in a motion picture adaptation (1933).

35 Interview, July 25, 1963.

36 Dismissal mentioned in interview; Spring Season announcement in *New York Tribune,* May 22, 1921, sec. 3, p. 5. *Inheritors* was Deeter's favorite; it was kept in the repertory at his Hedgerow Theatre every year, 1923–1941, then again in 1946–1948 and 1954.

37 Choice reported in *New York Tribune,* December 17, 1920, p. 12. Circumstances illuminated in interviews with Norma Millay, Charles Ellis, James Light, and Jasper Deeter.

38 O'Neill to Tyler, December 15, 1920, Manuscript Collection, Princeton University Library.

39 Deutsch and Hanau, *The Provincetown,* p. 67.

40 Interview, July 10, 1962, Steepletop, Austerlitz, N.Y. See also Gelb and Gelb, *O'Neill,* p. 447.

41 Playbill, second version (i.e., "December 6 to 18, inclusive").

42 Glaspell, *Road to the Temple,* p. 298.

43 Kenton to Cook, May 8, 1921, Harvard Theatre Collection.

44 Cook's letter cited, *Road to the Temple,* pp. 304–5, above, n. 24.

45 Cook to Glaspell, August 23, 1921, Cook Papers, Berg Collection, New York Public Library.

46 Cook cited by Deutsch and Hanau, *The Provincetown,* pp. 83–84, as "published in the *Globe.*" Notes, letters, and the draft of an appeal are in the Weinberger Papers, Yale University Library. They suggest that Cook had several buildings and major reconstructions in mind—with totally unrealistic budgetary implications.

47 Playbill, Second Bill, Seventh Season (December 27, 1920 – January 9, 1921), Yale Collection of American Literature.

48 The late Lawrence Vail kindly permitted me to make a copy of his typescript.

Chapter 8

1 *New York Tribune,* January 11, 1922, p. 6; *New York Times,* January 31, 1922, p. 11.

2 "Minutes," p. 51. According to Susan Jenkins Brown, *Robber Rocks* (Middletown, Conn., 1969), p. 12, she had "started the slow process of a divorce"

from Light when he had decided, early in 1922 "to go to France, for an indefinite stay."

3 Kenton, "History," p. 191.

4 Burns Mantle, *Best Plays 1921–22* (Boston, 1922), p. 11.

5 O'Neill to Nathan, January 2, 1922, cited in Gelb and Gelb, *O'Neill,* p. 492.

6 O'Neill to Macgowan, January 22, 1922, cited in ibid.

7 Accounts by Deutsch and Hanau, *The Provincetown,* p. 86; Gelb and Gelb, *O'Neill,* pp. 492–94; and Sheaffer, *Artist,* pp. 77–79, refer to collaborative arrangements with Hopkins, involving Kennedy, Wohlheim, Jones, Throckmorton, Light, and Cook to varying degrees.

8 *New York Tribune,* February 5, 1922, sec. 4, p. 1; February 12, 1922, sec. 4, p. 1; February 26, 1922, sec. 4, p. 1.

9 Playbill, Fifth Bill, Eighth Season (March 9, 1922), Yale Collection of American Literature, Beinecke Library.

10 Interview with the author, July 18, 1963, New York City.

11 Glaspell, *Road to the Temple,* p. 311.

12 Date of departure in ibid., p. 315.

13 Eugene O'Neill to M. Eleanor Fitzgerald, in a typed, signed letter written (according to internal evidence) between March 1 and July 10, 1922. Courtesy of Susan Jenkins Brown.

14 Date of uptown opening from playbill, though Deutsch and Hanau give April 17 (*The Provincetown,* p. 88).

15 Harry Weinberger first makes the claim in a letter to Arthur Hopkins, June 26, 1922; a payment of $500 is made over a year later, but no resolution of the issue is evident from the Weinberger Papers in the Yale University Library.

16 Written in Delphi, spring or early summer 1922, collated from Kenton, "Provincetown and Macdougal Street," pp. 29–30, and Glaspell, *Road to the Temple,* pp. 309–10.

17 "Minutes," p. 53; my emphasis.

18 Throckmorton was the sixth, according to "Minutes," p. 53.

19 Provincetown valedictory: "The Provincetown Players Announce an Interim for the Season 1922–1923," Yale Collection of American Literature.

20 Kenton to Cook and Glaspell, July 14, 1922, Harvard Theatre Collection.

21 Harvard Theatre Collection.

22 Kenton to Cook and Glaspell, October 21, 1923, Harvard Theatre Collection.

23 Departure date in Glaspell, *Road to the Temple,* p. 315; Light's announcement in Kenton to Cook and Glaspell, May 5, 1922, Harvard Theatre Collection.

24 Sayler, *Our American Theatre,* p. 89.

25 Kenton to Cook and Glaspell, June 2, 1922, Harvard Theatre Collection.

26 Gelb and Gelb, *O'Neill,* p. 515, citing O'Neill's undated letter to "Fitzie."

27 Kenton to Cook and Glaspell, May 5, 1922, Harvard Theatre Collection.

28 O'Neill to Fitzi, see n. 13, above.

29 Statements to that effect recur in almost every letter.

30 To Cook and Glaspell, May 5, 1922.

31 June 16, 1922, p. 10.

32 Agreement June 30, 1922, and indenture, July 10, 1922, in Harry Weinberger Papers, Yale University Library. Kenton to Cook and Glaspell, July 14, 1922, Harvard Theatre Collection.

33 O'Neill to Fitzi, see n. 13, above.

34 Cook to Kenton, July 10–23, 1922, from Parnassos. Cook Papers, Berg Collection, New York Public Library.

35 Kenton to Cook and Glaspell, September 24, 1923, Harvard Theatre Collection.

36 Glaspell to Kenton, October 29, 1923, Harvard Theatre Collection.

37 Kenton to Cook and Glaspell, October 29, 1923, Harvard Theatre Collection.

38 Gelb and Gelb, *O'Neill,* p. 525, citing Macgowan.

39 Weinberger to O'Neill, October 3, 1923, Weinberger Papers, Yale University Library.

40 Weinberger to Fitzgerald, October 5, 1923, Weinberger Papers, Yale University Library.

41 O'Neill to Weinberger, October 3, 1923, Weinberger Papers, Yale University Library.

42 Kenton to Cook and Glaspell, November 17, 1923, Harvard Theatre Collection.

43 Kenton to Glaspell, May 23, 1924, Harvard Theatre Collection.

44 Glaspell to "Fitzie, though not to Fitzie alone, but to all those new members of the Provincetown Players," May 23, 1924, Harvard Theatre Collection.

45 Glaspell to Fitzgerald, May 31, 1924, Weinberger Papers, Yale University Library.

Chapter 9

1 Lewisohn, "Harvest," *Nation,* May 17, 1922, p. 604.

2 Provincetown Players' Circular, Fall 1917, Yale Collection of American Literature, Beinecke Library.

3 Provincetown Players' Circular, Fall, 1918, Yale Collection of American Literature, Beinecke Library.

4   Ida Rauh interviewed, Barry O'Rourke, "At the Sign of the Sock and Buskin," *Morning Telegraph* (N.Y.), February 16, 1919.

5   Dickinson's criteria for identifying little theatres were cited in chap. one, above.

6   A position consistently taken in published accounts, and confirmed in letters to the author by Susan Jenkins Brown, Nilla Cram Cook, and most recently, Malcolm Cowley.

7   The cited phrase is from "a copy of my semi-drunken letter to Fitzie" that Cook sent Kenton from Delphi, June 8, 1922. The assessment of Eleanor Fitzgerald as a warm-hearted but uncritical friend emerges indisputably from Kenton's correspondence with Cook and Glaspell, Harvard Theatre Collection. It is rarely contradicted by anyone.

8   The Players' subscription to Romeike's clipping service is mentioned in passing by Kenton, "History," p. 118.

9   According to "Minutes," pp. 11–13, Reed's original resolutions stipulated "a new bill every two weeks." On October 22, 1916, it was decided to play each bill for five nights, Friday to Tuesday ("Minutes," p. 18). According to playbills, the first seven bills of the 1916–17 season observed both those rules; the eighth and ninth bill each ran six nights. During the 1917–18 season, bills followed at four week intervals; the length of the run had increased from five to seven nights. The 1918–19 season continued that practice; "the need to double playing time" (Kenton, "History," p. 139) was satisfied by running each bill of the "Season of Youth" for two entire weeks, and reducing the interval between them to three weeks.

10   Macgowan, *Footlights*, p. 212.

11   Cited, "The Provincetown Playhouse in the Garrick Theatre" (New York, 1929).

12   This statement is based on an unpublished seminar paper by Rakesh H. Solomon, who examined *Paradise Now* notebooks in the Performing Arts Collection, Shields Library, University of California, Davis, and concluded that the Becks' notes reveal their dominant role in the creative process.

13   Holden, "Collective Playmaking: the Why and the How," *Theatre Quarterly* (June–August 1975). On the other hand, William Kleb, "*Hotel Universe*, Playwriting and the San Francisco Mime Troupe," *Theatre* 9, 2 (Spring 1978), concludes that the Troupe was always primarily a writers' theatre—the parallel with the Provincetown Players thus comes full circle.

Appendix A. Chronology

1   See chap. 2, n. 18.

2   It is called "Mrs. O'Brien's wharf" on a card of invitation (see chap. 2,

n. 42) and "The Modern Art School Wharf" on the playbill for the Special Bill on Sept. 1, 2, 1916.

3   Unless otherwise noted, all further performances of this Spring–Summer 1916 season were at Lewis Wharf.

4   See chap. 2, n. 51.

5   See my "Wharf and Dome," *Theatre Research/Recherches Théâtrales,* p. 172, n. 34.

6   Unless otherwise noted, all further performances were hereafter at The Playwright's Theatre, which moved in 1918 to 133 Macdougal Street.

7   Granich adopted the pen name Mike Gold after his three plays were produced by the Provincetown Players, but before he published *Money.*

8   I have not been able to find a playbill that verifies this ending date or that of the thirty-two-day run of the second bill.

Appendix C. Physical Structures

1   Vorse, *Time and the Town,* pp. 110, 118.

2   Vorse to Huntington, March 27, 1962. Courtesy of Miss Huntington.

3   Vorse in an interview, June 27, 1962, Provincetown, Massachusetts.

4   *Provincetown Advocate,* June 8, 1916, p. 2.

5   Vorse, *Time and the Town,* p. 114.

6   Courtney Allen to the author, July 21, 1962, and March 4, 1966.

7   *Atlas of Barnstable County,* p. 80.

8   "Many Literary Lights"; Vorse, *Time and the Town,* pp. 118–19; Glaspell, *Road to the Temple,* p. 253; Deutsch and Hanau, *The Provincetown,* p. 11—among many others.

9   See figure 1 for photo.

10   Dedication ceremony described with some background by Arthur Gelb, "Wharf-Theatre Era Takes Curtain Call," *New York Times,* July 24, 1963, p. 25; cols. 3–6. See figure 4 for photograph of model. For additional photos, a copy of an etching, and sketches, see my "Wharf and Dome," plates 1–7.

11   Sketches were enclosed with letters of Courtney Allen to the author, July 21, 1962, and March 4, 1966, respectively.

12   Bromley & Company Manhattan Land Book, 1934, cited by Harmon H. Goldstone in a letter to the author, October 4, 1979.

13   Kenton, "History," p. 22.

14   "No Mark of 'Sacred Cod,'" *New York Herald,* December 3, 1916.

15   Deutsch and Hanau, *The Provincetown,* pp. 18–19.

16   Ibid.

17 Mary Heaton Vorse to John Reed, December 2, 1916, Houghton Library, Harvard.

18 Deutsch and Hanau, *The Provincetown*, p. 19.

19 Bromley & Company Manhattan Land Book, 1934, cited by Harmon H. Goldstone in a letter to the author, October 4, 1979.

20 Deutsch and Hanau, *The Provincetown*, p. 45.

21 Cook to Glaspell, October 24, 1918, Berg Collection, New York Public Library.

22 Deutsch and Hanau, *The Provincetown*, p. 45.

23 Cook to Glaspell, October 24, 1918, Berg Collection, New York Public Library.

24 Deutsch and Hanau, *The Provincetown*, p. 45.

25 Kenton, "History," p. 110.

26 "Provincetown" folder, Federal Theatre Technical Survey. Production File, The Play Bureau, F.T.P., W.P.A. (May 1937), unnumbered pages 2–4. Research Center for the Federal Theatre Project, George Mason University, Fairfax, Va.

27 Kenton, "History," p. 109; Deutsch and Hanau, *The Provincetown*, p. 45; Boulton, *Part of A Long Story*, pp. 240–41.

28 Provincetown Players' Circular, Fall 1918, Yale Collection of American Literature, Beinecke Library.

29 Height of the stage is given as 2′4″ in the Federal Theatre Technical Survey, unnumbered p. 4.

30 Kenton, "History," p. 109.

31 Undated "Seat Diagram Provincetown Play House," Kenneth Macgowan Papers, Special Collections, U.C.L.A.

32 Kenton, "History," p. 110.

33 Neither Kenton ("History," p. 113) nor Boulton—who calls it a "switchboard" (*Part of A Long Story*, p. 241)—makes clear whether the dimmer served stage, auditorium, or both.

34 Deutsch and Hanau, *The Provincetown*, p. 45.

35 "Provincetown" folder, Federal Theatre Technical Survey.

36 Of this article's two versions, one (typescript, dated November 11, 1920) is in Edna Kenton's Scrapbook (Fales Collection, New York University); the other is reproduced by Deutsch and Hanau, *The Provincetown*, pp. 61–62. Much information was corroborated and supplemented in interviews with Light, July 19 and August 9, 1962, and July 13, 1963, New York City.

37 Cook's notes are excerpted and in part cited by Glaspell. Plans she refers to are presumably lost (Nilla Cram Cook to the author, February 5, 1975), though Sheaffer, *Artist*, p. 51 (p. 690n), claims to have seen relevant "plans and a pam-

phlet'' at the University of Virginia, which librarians there have been unable to locate.

38 Vorse, *Time and the Town,* p. 118; Glaspell, *Road to the Temple,* p. 253.

39 Kenton, "History," p. 189.

40 Cook, *My Road to India,* pp. 48, 52, 328–30, 461–62. No record of such project was found at General Electric.

41 Letter to the author, January 5, 1975. I have not been able to locate a copy of the first program, said to have pictorial evidence.

Bibliography

I. Primary Sources

1. Plays

Barber, Mary Foster. "The Squealer." TS. Copyright Office, Library of Congress.

Barnes, Djuna. "An Irish Triangle." *Playboy* 7 (1921): 3–5.

————. "Kurzy of the Sea." TS. Copyright Office, Library of Congress.

————. "Three from the Earth." In Barnes, *A Book,* pp. 15–30. New York: Boni & Liveright, 1930.

Beach, Lewis. "Brothers." In *Fifty Contemporary One-Act Plays.* Edited by Frank Shay and Pierre Loving. New York: Appleton, 1920.

Bodenheim, Maxwell. "The Gentle Furniture Shop." *Drama Magazine* 10 (January 1920): 132–33.

————. "Knotholes." TS. Theatre Collection, New York Public Library, Lincoln Center.

Boyce, Neith. "The Faithful Lover." TS (several versions). Yale Collection of American Literature, Beinecke Library.

————. "The Two Sons." In *The Provincetown Plays, Third Series.* Edited by Frank Shay. New York: Frank Shay, 1916.

————. "Winter's Night." In *Fifty More Contemporary One-Act Plays.* Edited by Frank Shay. New York: Appleton, 1934.

Boyce, Neith, and Hutchins Hapgood. "Enemies." In *The Provincetown Plays.* Edited by George Cram Cook and Frank Shay. Cincinnati: Stewart Kidd, 1921.

Bryant, Louise. "The Game." In *The Provincetown Plays, First Series.* Edited by Frank Shay. New York: Frank Shay, 1916.

Chapin, Harold. *The Philosopher of Butterbiggins.* London, Glasgow: Gowans & Gray, Ltd; Boston: Leroy Phillips, 1921.

Cook, George Cram. *The Athenian Women.* Athens, Greece: "Estia," 1926.

———. "Change Your Style." TS. O'Neill Papers, Alderman Library, University of Virginia.

———. *The Spring.* New York: Frank Shay, 1921.

Cook, George Cram, and Susan Glaspell. "Suppressed Desires." In *The Provincetown Plays.* Edited by George Cram Cook and Frank Shay. Cincinnati: Stewart Kidd, 1921.

Crocker, Bosworth. "The Baby Carriage." In *Fifty Contemporary One-Act Plays.* Edited by Frank Shay and Pierre Loving. New York: Appleton & Co., 1920.

Davies, Mary Caroline. *The Slave With Two Faces.* In *Flying Stag Plays* no. 6. New York: E. Arens, 1918.

Dell, Floyd. "The Angel Intrudes"; "King Arthur's Socks"; "A Long Time Ago"; "Sweet and Twenty." In Dell, *"King Arthur's Socks" and Other Village Plays.* New York: Alfred A. Knopf, 1922.

Dreiser, Theodore. *The Hand of the Potter.* New York: Boni & Liveright, 1918.

Ferber, Edna. "The Eldest." In *The American Scene.* Edited by Barrett H. Clark and Kenyon Nicholson. New York: Appleton, 1930.

Frank, Florence Kiper. "Gee-Rusalem." TS. Copyright Office, Library of Congress.

Glaspell, Susan. "Bernice"; "Close the Book"; "The Outside"; "The People"; "Trifles"; "Woman's Honor." In Glaspell, *Plays.* Boston: Small, Maynard, 1920.

———. "Chains of Dew." TS. Copyright Office, Library of Congress.

———. *Inheritors.* Boston: Small, Maynard, 1921.

———. *The Verge.* Boston: Small, Maynard, 1922.

Glaspell, Susan, and George Cram Cook. "Tickless Time." In Glaspell, *Plays.* Boston: Small, Maynard, 1920.

Gold, Michael. "Money." In *The American Scene.* Edited by Barrett H. Clark and Kenyon Nicholson. New York: Appleton, 1930.

Head, Cloyd. "Grotesques." *Poetry* 9 (October 1916): 1–32.

Kemp, Harry. "The Prodigal Son." *Smart Set* 52 (1917): 83–93.

King, Pendleton. "Cocaine." In *The Provincetown Plays.* Edited by George Cram Cook and Frank Shay. Cincinnati: Stewart Kidd, 1921.

Kreymborg, Alfred. "Jack's House." In Kreymborg, *Puppet Plays.* New York: Samuel French, 1926.

———. "Lima Beans." In *Representative One-Act Plays by American Authors.* Edited by Margaret G. Mayorga. Boston: Little, Brown, 1922.

————. "Manikin and Minikin." In *A Treasury of Plays for Women*. Edited by Frank Shay. Boston: Little, Brown, 1922.

————. "Vote the New Moon." In Kreymborg, *Plays for Merry Andrews*. New York: The Sunwise Turn, 1920.

Kugelman, F. B. "The Hermit and His Messiah." TS. Yale University Library.

Langner, Lawrence. "Matinata"; "Pie." In Langner, *Five One-Act Comedies*. Cincinnati: Stewart Kidd, 1922.

Lindau, Norman C. "A Little Act of Justice." TS. Copyright Office, Library of Congress.

Loving, Pierre. "The Stick-up." In *A Treasury of Plays for Men*. Edited by Frank Shay. Boston: Little, Brown, 1928.

Millay, Edna St. Vincent. *Aria da Capo*. New York: Harper, 1920.

————. *The Princess Marries the Page*. New York: Harper, 1932.

————. "Two Slatterns and a King." In Millay, *Three Plays*. New York: Harper, 1926.

Mosher, John Chapin. "Sauce for the Emperor." *Smart Set* 51 (1917): 199–208.

O'Neill, Eugene. "Before Breakfast"; "Diff'rent"; "The Dreamy Kid"; "The Emperor Jones"; "The Hairy Ape." In O'Neill, *The Plays of Eugene O'Neill*. New York: Random House, 1955.

————. "Bound East for Cardiff"; " 'Ile"; "The Long Voyage Home"; "The Moon of the Caribbees"; "The Rope"; "Where the Cross is Made." In O'Neill, *"The Moon of the Caribbees" and Six Other Plays of the Sea*. New York: The Modern Library, 1923.

————. "Children of the Sea." In O'Neill, *"Children of the Sea" and Three Other Unpublished Plays by Eugene O'Neill*. Edited by Jennifer McCabe Atkinson. Washington, D.C.: NCR Microcard Edition, 1972.

————. "Fog"; "The Sniper." In O'Neill, *Ten Lost Plays*. New York: Random House, 1964.

————. "The Rope." TS with cuts and ground plan by Nina Moise. Yale Collection of American Literature, Beinecke Library.

————. "Thirst." In O'Neill, *"Thirst" and Other One-Act Plays*. Boston: Gorham, 1914.

Oppenheim, James. "Night." In *The Provincetown Plays*. Edited by George Cram Cook and Frank Shay. Cincinnati: Stewart Kidd, 1921.

Parker, Robert Allerton. "5050." TS. Bancroft Library, University of California, Berkeley.

Parkhurst, Winthrop. "Getting Unmarried." *Smart Set* 54 (April 1918): 91–99.

Pinski, David. "A Dollar." In *Contemporary One-Act Plays*. Edited by Benjamin Roland Lewis. New York, Chicago, Boston: Scribner's, 1922.

Reed, John S. "The Eternal Quadrangle." TS. Houghton Library, Harvard University.

———. "Freedom." In *The Provincetown Plays, Second Series*. Edited by Frank Shay. New York: Frank Shay, 1916.

———. "The Peace That Passeth Understanding." *Liberator* 2 (March 1919): 25–31.

Rostetter, Alice L. "The Widow's Veil." In *The Provincetown Plays*. Edited by George Cram Cook and Frank Shay. Cincinnati: Stewart Kidd, 1921.

Schnitzler, Arthur. "Last Masks." In Schnitzler, *Anatol, Living Hours, The Green Cockatoo*. Translated by Grace Isabel Colbron. New York: Boni & Liveright, 1917.

Scott, Evelyn. "Love." TS. Author's Collection.

Smith, Rita Creighton. "The Rescue." In *Plays of The Harvard Dramatic Club*. 1st ser. Edited by George P. Baker. New York: Brentano's, 1918.

Steele, Wilbur Daniel. "Contemporaries." TS. Steele Papers, Stanford University Libraries.

———. " 'Not Smart.' " In *The Provincetown Plays*. Edited by George Cram Cook and Frank Shay. Cincinnati: Stewart Kidd, 1921.

Stevens, Wallace. "Three Travelers Watch A Sunrise." In *Fifty Contemporary One-Act Plays*. Edited by Frank Shay and Pierre Loving. New York: Appleton, 1920.

Vail, Lawrence. "What D'You Want?" TS. Estate of the late Lawrence Vail.

Wellman, Rita. "Funiculi-Funicula." In *Representative One-Act Plays By American Authors*. Edited by Margaret G. Mayorga. Boston: Little, Brown, 1922.

———. "The Rib-Person." TS. Copyright Office, Library of Congress.

———. "The String of the Samisen." In *The Provincetown Plays*. Edited by George Cram Cook and Frank Shay. Cincinnati: Stewart Kidd, 1921.

Wied, Gustav. "Autumn Fires." In *Fifty Contemporary One-Act Plays*. Edited by Frank Shay and Pierre Loving. New York: Appleton, 1920.

2. Firsthand Accounts

The following have conveyed information by means of personal letters or interviews or both: Courtney Allen, Edward J. Ballantine, Sidney Bernard, Arthur Bickers, Susan Jenkins Brown, Kathleen Cannell, Nilla Cram Cook, Malcolm Cowley, Floyd Dell, Jasper Deeter, Max Eastman, Samuel A. Eliot, Jr., Charles Ellis, Reeves Euler, Jerry Farnsworth, Michael Gold (Irwin Granich), Harmon H. Goldstone, Alice Hall (Mrs. Henry Marion), Stella Bloch Hanau, Charles H. Hapgood, John F. Lenard, Tracy L'Engle, James K. Light, Geraldine Lust, Norma Millay,

Nina Moise, Zerka Moreno, Dr. Margaret Nordfeldt, Emily Abbot Nordfeldt, Ida Rauh, Lee Roberts, Dr. James M. Sacks, Louis Sheaffer, Jean Paul Slusser, Julia Ward Stickley, Cleon Throckmorton, Pauline Turkel, Lawrence Vail, Mary Heaton Vorse, Martha Ullman West, and Marguerite and William Zorach.

Anderson, Margaret C. *My 30 Years' War; The Autobiography: Beginnings and Battles to 1930.* New York: Horizon, 1970.

Boulton, Agnes. *Part of a Long Story.* Garden City, N.Y.: Doubleday, 1958.

Brown, Susan Jenkins. *Robber Rocks.* Middletown, Conn.: Wesleyan Press, 1969.

Browne, Maurice. *Too Late to Lament: An Autobiography.* Bloomington, Ind.: Indiana University Press, 1956.

Bryant, Louise. Letters to John Reed. June–December 1916. Houghton Library, Harvard University.

Cook, George Cram. *Greek Coins.* New York: H. Doran, 1925.

———. Letters to Susan Glaspell and unsent letters. Four folders, uncatalogued. Berg Collection, New York Public Library.

Cook, Nilla Cram. *My Road to India.* New York: Furman, 1939.

Copeau, Jacques. *Registres I: Appels.* Edited by Marie-Helene Dasté and Suzanne Maistre Saint-Denis. Paris: Gallimard, 1974.

Cowley, Malcolm. . . . *And I Worked at the Writer's Trade.* New York: Viking, 1978.

———. "A Weekend with Eugene O'Neill." *The Reporter,* September 5, 1957, pp. 33–36.

Dell, Floyd. *Homecoming, An Autobiography.* New York: Farrar & Rinehart, 1933.

———. *Intellectual Vagabondage.* New York: George H. Doran, 1926.

———. *Love in Greenwich Village.* New York: George H. Doran, 1926.

Deutsch, Helen, and Stella Hanau. *The Provincetown, A Story of the Theatre.* New York: Farrar & Rinehart, 1931.

Eastman, Max. *Enjoyment of Living.* New York, London: Harper, 1948.

Glaspell, Susan. *The Road to the Temple.* New York: Frederick A. Stokes, 1927.

Hapgood, Hutchins. "The Provincetown Players." TS. Yale Collection of American Literature, Beinecke Library.

———. *A Victorian in the Modern World.* New York: Harcourt, Brace, 1939.

Hartley, Marsden. "Farewell Charles." In *The New Caravan.* Edited by Alfred Kreymborg, Lewis Mumford, and Paul Rosenfeld. New York: The Macaulay Co., 1936.

———. "The Great Provincetown Summer." TS. Yale Collection of American Literature, Beinecke Library.

Huffaker, Lucy. Undated letters to Edward Goodman. Theatre Collection, New York Public Library, Lincoln Center.

Kemp, Harry. "A Few Words Beforehand." In Kemp, *Boccaccio's Untold Tale.* New York: Brentano's, 1924.

———. *More Miles.* New York: Boni & Liveright, 1926 .

———. "Out of Provincetown." *Theatre Magazine* 51 (April 1930): 22–23, 66.

———. *Tramping On Life.* Garden City, N.Y.: Garden City Publishing Co., 1922.

Kenton, Edna. Letters to George Cram Cook and to Susan Glaspell. 1921–1924. Includes two letters from Susan Glaspell and one from Eugene O'Neill. Harvard Theatre Collection.

———. "Provincetown and Macdougal Street." In George Cram Cook, *Greek Coins.* New York: George H. Doran, 1925.

———. "The Provincetown Players and the Playwright's Theater." *The Billboard,* August 5, 1922, pp. 6–7, 13–15.

———. "Unorganized, Amateur, Purely Experimental." *Boston Evening Transcript,* April 27, 1918, sec. 2, pp. 8, 9.

———. Untitled history of the Provincetown Players. TS. Fales Collection, New York University.

Kreymborg, Alfred. *Troubadour, An Autobiography.* New York: Boni & Liveright, 1925.

Langner, Lawrence. *The Magic Curtain.* New York: Dutton, 1951.

Millay, Edna St. Vincent. *Letters of Edna St. Vincent Millay.* Edited by Allan Ross Macdougal. New York: Harper, 1952.

O'Neill, Eugene. Letters to Nina Moise. 1918–1919. Yale Collection of American Literature, Beinecke Library.

Reed, John S. Letters to and from various persons. Houghton Library, Harvard University.

Tietjens, Eunice. *The World at My Shoulder.* New York: Macmillan, 1938.

Vorse, Mary Heaton. *A Footnote to Folly.* New York: Farrar & Rinehart, 1935.

———. Letters to Catharine S. Huntington. Provincetown Playhouse on the Wharf, Provincetown, Massachusetts.

———. *Time and the Town, A Provincetown Chronicle.* New York: Dial, 1942.

Zorach, William. *Art Is My Life.* Cleveland, Ohio: World Publishing, 1967.

3. Ephemera

In Memory of Fitzi, March 16, 1877-March 30, 1955. [Privately Printed]. Issued by Pauline H. Turkel, 333 West 57th Street, New York 18, N.Y. 16 pp. Author's collection.

Jasper Deeter and the Hedgerow Repertory. Publicity Packet. [post 1956]. Author's collection.

Kenton, Edna. Scrapbook. Fales Collection, New York University.

O'Neill, Eugene. Scrapbooks. Yale Collection of American Literature, Beinecke Library.

"Productions of the Provincetown Players for Eight Seasons, 1915–1922." 4 pp. Author's collection.

Provincetown Players, Etc. Announcements. One folder each for 1915–1917, 1918–1919, 1919–1920, uncatalogued. Berg Collection, New York Public Library.

The Provincetown Players. Inventory of Lighting Equipment, June 29, 1922. Kenneth Macgowan Papers, Special Collections, U.C.L.A.

The Provincetown Players. "Minutes." Hardbound notebook. Theatre Collection, New York Public Library, Lincoln Center.

Provincetown Players. Miscellaneous Material (one folder). Museum of the City of New York.

Provincetown Players. Poster for Opening Bill, 1918–19 Season. Theatre Collection, New York Public Library, Lincoln Center.

Provincetown Players. Programs and Announcements, 1916–1922. Large Box, Yale Collection of American Literature, Beinecke Library.

Provincetown Players' Scrapbook, 1916–1920. Harvard Theatre Collection.

"The Provincetown Playhouse in the Garrick Theatre." (A list of productions, 1915–1929, with Tributes to Achievement in alphabetical order.) New York, 1929. 8 pp. Author's collection.

The Provincetown Playhouse. Ground plan. Kenneth Macgowan Papers, Special Collections. U.C.L.A.

Provincetown Theatre. Federal Theatre Technical Survey. Production File, The Play Bureau, F.T.P., W.P.A. (May 1937), 13 unnumbered pages. Research Center for the Federal Theatre Project. George Mason University, Fairfax, Virginia.

4. Reviews

Block, Ralph. *New York Tribune,* Nov. 3, 1917, p. 13.

Broun, Heywood. "Looking Up, Down and Around, . . ." *New York Tribune,* March 18, 1917, sec. 4, p. 3.

————. *New York Tribune,* March 4, 1918, p. 9; April 29, 1918, p. 9; May 14, 1918, p. 9; May 26, 1918, sec. 4, p. 2; Nov. 25, 1918, p. 9; Dec. 23, 1918, p.

9; Jan. 23, 1919, p. 9; May 4, 1919, sec. 4, p. 2; Jan. 15, 1920, p. 11; Nov. 4, 1920, p. 8; Feb. 2, 1921, p. 6.

————. "Realism has Special Talent of Its Own." *New York Tribune,* March 30, 1919, sec. 4, p. 1.

————. "Satirist Should Select Rapier As Weapon." *New York Tribune,* Feb. 23, 1919, sec. 4, p. 1.

Castellun, Maida. *New York Call,* Nov. 10, 1920.

Corbin, John. *New York Times,* Nov. 1, 1917, p. 13; May 21, 1918, p. 13.

————. "Seraphim and Cats." *New York Times,* March 30, 1919, sec. 4, p. 2.

Drucker, Rebecca. *New York Tribune,* Nov. 16, 1919, sec. 4, p. 7.

————. "The Provincetown Players Show Their Best." *New York Tribune,* April 20, 1919, sec. 4, pp. 1–2.

Eaton, Walter Pritchard. *Freeman,* April 26, 1922, p. 161.

Fox, Beauvais. "Three One-Act Extraordinaries." *New York Tribune,* Jan. 11, 1922, p. 6.

"Funereal Drama and Childish Skit." *New York Herald,* March 24, 1919.

Hammond, Percy. *New York Tribune,* Nov. 15, 1921, p. 8; March 10, 1922, p. 8.

Hornblow, Arthur. *Theatre Magazine,* May 1921, p. 340; July 1921, p. 60.

Lewisohn, Ludwig. *Nation.* March 16, 1921, p. 411; April 6, 1921, p. 515; Dec. 14, 1921, pp. 708–9; Dec. 28, 1921, p. 762; March 22, 1922, pp. 349, 350; May 24, 1922, p. 627.

Macgowan, Kenneth. *New York Globe,* Nov. 3, 1919.

————. *Vogue,* March 15, 1921, p. 82.

Mantle, Burns. *New York Evening Mail,* April 4, 1917, p. 7; Feb. 14, 1920.

Morning Telegraph, Nov. 23, 1918; Jan. 20, 1919.

New York Herald. Dec. 21, 1918.

New York Tribune. Jan. 19, 1919, sec. 5, p. 2; Jan. 23, 1919, p. 9; Feb. 23, 1919, sec. 7, p. 1; April 26, 1919, p. 13; April 1, 1920, p. 13.

Provincetown Advocate. Aug. 31, 1916, p. 2.

Rathbun, Stephen. *New York Sun.* Nov. 6, 1920.

Woollcott, Alexander. "Second Thoughts on First Nights," *New York Times,* Nov. 6, 1919, sec. 8, p. 2.

————. "There Are War Plays and War Plays," *New York Times,* Dec. 14, 1919, sec. 8, p. 2.

————. *New York Times,* April 4, 1920, sec. 4, p. 6; Nov. 7, 1920, sec. 7, p. 1; Dec. 29, 1920, p. 8; Feb. 6, 1921, sec. 6, p. 1; March 27, 1921, sec. 7, p. 1; May 15, 1921, sec. 4, p. 1; March 10, 1922, p. 18; April 16, 1922, sec. 6, p. 1; April 28, 1922, p. 20.

5. Short Notices

New York Call. Feb. 14, 1920.

New York Clipper. March 24, 1920.

New York Sun. May 17, 1918, p. 9.

New York Times. Oct. 28, 1916, p. 11; Dec. 9, 1916, p. 9; Nov. 4, 1917, sec. 8, p. 7; May 26, 1918, sec. 4, p. 7; Oct. 27, 1918, sec. 4, p. 2; Dec. 6, 1919, p. 14; Jan. 22, 1920, p. 22; Feb. 10, 1920, p. 10; May 3, 1920, p. 18; May 25, 1920. p. 15; June 23, 1920, p. 14; June 29, 1920, p. 9; Dec. 10, 1920, p. 15; Dec. 11, 1920, p. 3; March 6, 1921, p. 20; Sept. 8, 1921, p. 14; Oct. 28, 1921, p. 15; Jan. 31, 1922, p. 11; March 23, 1922, p. 12; June 16, 1922, p. 20.

New York Tribune. March 31, 1918, sec. 4, p. 4; April 5, 1918, p. 11; Nov. 3, 1918, sec. 4, p. 2; Jan. 6, 1919; Feb. 2, 1919; Feb. 3, 1919; Nov. 11, 1920, p. 10; Nov. 18, 1920, p. 10; Dec. 3, 1920, p. 10; Dec. 13, 1920, p. 8; Dec. 17, 1920, p. 8; Feb. 6, 1921, sec. 3, p. 1; Feb. 10, 1921, p. 8; Feb. 17, 1921, p. 8; April 5, 1921, p. 8; April 12, 1921, p. 8; April 27, 1921, p. 10; April 28, 1921, p. 10; May 8, 1921, sec. 3, p. 2; May 17, 1921, p. 10; May 22, 1921, sec. 3, p. 5; Nov. 3, 1921, sec. 4, p. 1; Nov. 27, 1921, sec. 4, p. 4; Dec. 3, 1921, p. 8; Dec. 15, 1921, p. 10; Dec. 21, 1921, p. 8; Feb. 5, 1922, sec. 4, p. 1; Feb. 12, 1922, sec. 4, p. 1; Feb. 26, 1922, sec. 4, p. 1; March 25, 1922, p. 8; April 16, 1922, sec. 4, p. 1; June 16, 1922, p. 10.

New York World. Nov. 10, 1918.

Provincetown Advocate. June 8, 1916, p. 2; Aug. 24, 1916, p. 2.

II. Secondary Sources

Alexander, Doris. *The Tempering of Eugene O'Neill.* New York: Harcourt, 1962.

Anderson, Margaret. "Art and Anarchism." *Little Review,* March 1916, pp. 3–6.

Arens, Egmont. *The Little Book of Greenwich Village; A Handbook of Information Concerning New York's Bohemia.* 3d ed. New York: E. Arens, 1919.

Atlas of Barnstable County, Massachusetts. Boston, 1880.

Back, Kurt W. *Beyond Words: The Story of Sensitivity Training and the Encounter Movement.* New York: Russell Sage Foundation, 1972.

———. *Beyond Words: The Story of Sensitivity Training and the Encounter Movement,* 2d ed. Baltimore: Penguin, 1973.

Bentley, Eric. *The Life of the Drama.* New York: Atheneum, 1964.

———. *Theatre of War.* New York: Viking Press, 1972.

Berthold, Margarete. *Weltgeschichte des Theaters.* Stuttgart: A. Krone, 1968.

Blum, Daniel. *A Pictorial History of the American Theatre 1900–1956.* 4th rev. ed. New York: Greenberg, 1956.

Bogard, Travis. *Contour in Time: The Plays of Eugene O'Neill.* New York: Oxford University Press, 1972.

Boulton, Agnes. "An Experimental Theatre." *Theatre Arts* 8 (1924): 184–88.

Bowen, Croswell. *The Curse of the Misbegotten; A Tale of the House of O'Neill.* London: Hart-Davis, 1960.

Brewster, Mary K. "Newest Dramatic Venture." *Dramatic Mirror,* Nov. 27, 1953, p. 3.

Britten, Norma A. *Edna St. Vincent Millay.* New York: Twayne, 1967.

Brockett, O. G. *History of the Theatre,* 3d ed. Boston: Allyn & Bacon, 1977.

Brooks, Van Wyck. *The Confident Years: 1885–1915.* New York: Dutton, 1952.

Broun, Heywood. "All-American Dozen of Our Actresses." *New York Tribune,* April 13, 1919, sec. 4, p. 1.

———. "Diff'rent Comes to Broadway at the Selwyn." *New York Tribune,* Feb. 1, 1921.

———. "Down an Alley on Drama Trail." *New York Tribune,* Jan. 30, 1917, p. 9.

Bucco, Martin. *Wilbur Daniel Steele.* New York: Twayne, 1972.

Burns, Sister M. Vincentia. "The Function of Wagner's Theory of the Union of the Arts in the Dramaturgy of Eugene O'Neill." Dissertation, University of Pennsylvania, 1943.

Cargill, Oscar, N. Bryllion Fagin, and William J. Fisher, eds. *O'Neill and His Plays.* New York: New York University Press, 1961.

Chapin, Anna Alice. *Greenwich Village.* New York: Dodd, Mead & Co., 1917.

Cheney, Sheldon. *The Art Theatre.* New York: Knopf, 1925.

Churchill, Allen. *The Improper Bohemians.* New York: Dutton, 1958.

Clark, Barrett H. "End of the Provincetown Playhouse." *Drama* 20 (1930): 137.

———. *Eugene O'Neill; The Man and His Plays.* New York: Dover, 1947.

Coke, Van Deren. *Nordfeldt the Painter.* Albuquerque: University of New Mexico Press, 1972.

Corbin, John. "Little Theatre Plays." *New York Times,* Nov. 11, 1917, sec. 8, p. 6.

———. "The One-Act Play." *New York Times,* May 19, 1918, sec. 4, p. 8.

Cowan, Robert Arthur. "Off-Broadway, A History, 1915–1962" Dissertation, Purdue, 1963.

Cowley, Malcolm. *Exile's Return; A Literary Odyssey of the 1920s.* New York: Viking, 1951.

————. *The Literary Situation.* New York: Viking, 1954.

Craig, Edward Gordon. *On the Art of the Theatre.* London: T. N. Foulis, 1905.

Crowell, Joshua F., and Florence H. Crowell, eds. *Cape Cod in Poetry.* Boston: The Four Seas Co., 1924.

Dickinson, Thomas H. *The Insurgent Theatre.* New York: B. W. Huebsch, 1917.

Dijkstra, Bram. *The Hieroglyphics of a New Speech: Cubism, Stieglitz & The Poetry of William Carlos Williams.* Princeton, N.J. Princeton University Press, 1969.

Duffey, Bernard I. *The Chicago Renaissance in American Letters; A Critical History.* East Lansing, Mich. Michigan State College Press, 1954.

Dukore, Bernard Frank. "Maurice Browne and the Chicago Little Theatre." Dissertation, University of Illinois, 1957.

————. "The Noncommercial Theatre in New York." In *American Theatre Today,* edited by Alan S. Downer, pp. 155–67. New York: Basic Books, 1967.

Eaton, Walter P. *Plays and Players; Leaves from a Critic's Scrapbook.* Cincinnati: Stewart Kidd, 1916.

Else, Gerald F. *Aristotle's Poetics: The Argument.* Cambridge, Mass.: Harvard University Press, 1957.

Engle, Edwin A. *The Haunted Heroes of Eugene O'Neill.* Cambridge, Mass.: Harvard University Press, 1953.

"Famous American Theatres." *Theatre Arts* 41 (August 1957): 30.

Farnham, Emily. *Charles Demuth: Behind a Laughing Mask.* Lincoln, Okla.: University of Oklahoma Press, 1971.

Federal Writer's Project. *New York City Guide.* New York: Random House, 1939.

Findlay, Robert R. "The Emperor Jones: O'Neill as Scene Designer." *Players* 45 (October-November 1969): 21–24.

Gassner, John. "Pioneers of the New Theatre Movement." In *American Theatre Today,* edited by Alan S. Downer, pp. 15–24. New York: Basic Books, 1967.

Gebhard, David. *Lloyd Wright, Architect; 20th Century Architecture in An Organic Exhibition.* Exhibition organized by David Gebhard and Harriet Von Breton for Art Galleries, University of California, Santa Barbara, Nov. 23-Dec. 22, 1971. Calif. The Regents, University of California, 1971.

Gelb, Arthur. "Wharf-Theatre Era Takes Curtain Call." *New York Times,* July 24, 1963, p. 25.

Gelb, Arthur, and Barbara Gelb. *O'Neill.* 2d ed. New York: Harper, 1974.

Goldberg, Carl. *Encounter: Group Sensitivity Training Experience.* New York: Science House, 1970.

Goldberg, Isaac. *The Drama of Transition.* Cincinnati: Stewart Kidd, 1922.

Goldstein, Malcolm. *The Political Stage: American Drama and Theatre of the Great Depression.* New York: Oxford University Press, 1974.

Gould, Jean. *The Poet and Her Book: A Biography of Edna St. Vincent Millay.* New York: Dodd, Mead, 1969.

Hahn, Emily. *Romantic Rebels: An Informal History of Bohemianism in America.* Boston: Houghton Mifflin, 1967.

Hansen, Harry. *Midwest Portraits.* New York: Harcourt, 1923.

Hapgood, Hutchins. "The Instinct to Conform." *New Republic,* Nov. 29, 1933, p. 80.

Hart, John E. *Floyd Dell.* New York: Twayne, 1971.

Hartley, Marsden. *Adventures in the Arts; Informal Chapters on Painters, Vaudeville and Poets.* 1921. Reprint. New York: Hacker Art Books, 1972.

Heacock, Lee F. "Community or Little Theatre—Which?" *Drama* 17 (Dec. 1926): 79–88.

Helburn, Theresa. "Little Theatres." *Nation,* May 3, 1919, pp. 702–3.

Hicks, Granville. *John Reed; The Making of a Revolutionary.* New York: Macmillan, 1936.

Himelstein, Morgan Yale. *Drama Was a Weapon: The Left-Wing Theatre in New York, 1929–1941.* New Brunswick, N.J.: Rutgers University Press, 1963.

Hoffer, Eric. *The True Believer.* New York: Harper Bros., 1951.

Holden, Joan. "Collective Playmaking: The Why and the How." *Theatre Quarterly* 5 (June-August 1975).

"How Negro Actor Got His Chance." *New York Tribune,* Nov. 25, 1920, sec. 3, pp. 1, 2.

Hunt, Edward Eyre. "John Silas Reed." In *Harvard University Class of 1910. Twenty-fifth Anniversary Report,* Cambridge, Mass., 1935, pp. 640–644.

Ingersoll, Helen. "The Neighborhood Playhouse." *Theatre Arts* 13 (1929): 764–69.

Jaspers, Carl. *Tragedy is Not Enough.* London: V. Gollancz, 1953.

Johnson, Paul Emanuel. *Psychology of Religion.* New York: Abington, 1959.

Kagan, Norman. "The Return of the Emperor Jones." *Negro History Bulletin* 34 (November 1971): 160–62.

Kleb, William. *"Hotel Universe,* Playwriting and the San Francisco Mime Troupe." *Theatre* 9 (Spring 1978).

Kramer, Dale. *Chicago Renaissance; The Literary Life in the Midwest, 1900–1930.* New York: Appleton-Century, 1966.

Krueger, Paul P. "Theology and Literary Criticism: An Attempt at Common Categories." Master's thesis, Pacific Lutheran Theological Seminary, 1976.

Lewis, Emory. *Stages: The Fifty-Year Childhood of the American Theatre.* Englewood Cliffs, N.J.: Prentice Hall, 1969.

Lewisohn, Ludwig. "Harvest." *Nation,* May 17, 1922, p. 604.

Little, Stuart W. *Off Broadway, The Prophetic Theatre.* New York: Coward, McCann, & Geoghegan, 1972.

Macgowan, Kenneth. *Footlights Across America; Towards a National Theatre.* New York: Harcourt, 1929.

MacKay, Constance D'Arcy. *The Little Theatre in the United States.* New York: Holt, 1917.

Madison, Charles A. *Critics and Crusaders: A Century of American Protest.* New York: Holt, 1947.

Mantle, Robert Burns. *The Best Plays of 1921–22 and the Year Book of the Drama in America.* Boston: Mead, Dodd, 1922.

"Many Literary Lights Among Provincetown Players." *Boston* (Sunday) *Post,* Sept. 10, 1916, p. 44.

Matz, Mary Jane. *The Many Lives of Otto Kahn.* New York: Macmillan, 1963.

May, Henry F. *The Discontent of the Intellectuals: A Problem of the Twenties.* Chicago: Rand McNally, 1963.

———. *The End of American Innocence: A Study of the First Years of Our Own Time, 1912–1917.* New York: Knopf, 1959.

McNamara, Brooks. "Documents on the Pageant." *Drama Review* 15 (Summer 1971): 60–71.

Mike Gold: A Literary Anthology. Edited by Michael Folsom. New York: International, 1972.

Miller, Jordan Y. *Playwright's Progress: O'Neill and the Critics.* Chicago: Scott, Foresman, 1965.

Moderwell, Hiram Kelly. *The Theatre of To-Day.* New York: Dodd, Mead, 1927.

More, Jack B. *Maxwell Bodenheim.* New York: Twayne, 1970.

Morehouse, Ward. *Matinee Tomorrow: Fifty Years of Our Theatre.* New York: Whittlesey House, 1949.

Moreno, J. L. *Mental Catharsis and the Psychodrama.* New York: Beacon, 1944.

———. *Psychodrama: Third Volume, Action Therapy and Principles of Practise.* New York: Beacon, 1969.

———. *Das Stegreiftheater.* Potsdam: Verlag des Vaters, G. Kiepenheuer, 1924.

———. *Who Shall Survive? Foundations of Sociometry, Group Psychotherapy and Sociodrama.* 2d ed. New York: Beacon, 1953.

Munson, Gorham B. "Greenwich Village That Was—Seedbed of the Nineteen Twenties." *Literary Review* 5, no. 3 (Spring 1962): 313–35.

Nietzsche, Friedrich. *The Birth of Tragedy and The Case of Wagner.* Translation and commentary by Walter Kaufmann. New York: Vintage Books, 1967.

"No Mark of 'Sacred Cod' on Provincetown Players." *New York Herald,* Dec. 3, 1916, sec. 3, p. 10.

"On the Road from Cape Cod to Broadway." *Survey,* Oct. 28, 1916, p. 78.

"Original Director for O'Neil [*sic*] Tells of First Night." *New York Tribune,* Jan. 6, 1929, sec. 7, p. 5.

O'Rourke, Barry. "At the Sign of the Sock and Buskin." *Morning Telegraph* (New York), Feb. 16, 1919.

Parry, Albert. *Garrets and Pretenders: A History of Bohemianism in America.* 1933. Reprint. New York: Dover, 1960.

Paul, Norman H. "Copeau Looks at the American Stage." *Educational Theatre Journal,* March 1977, pp. 67–68.

Philpott, A. J. "Laboratory of the Drama on Cape Cod's Farthest Wharf." *Boston Globe,* Aug. 13, 1916.

Richter, Hans. *Dada: Art and Anti-Art.* New York: McGraw-Hill, 1966.

Robeson, Eslanda Goode. *Paul Robeson, Negro.* London: V. Gollancz, 1930.

Rogers, Irving. "Puffs and Pot Shots." *Provincetown Advocate,* Oct. 23, 1941, p. 2.

Sarlós, Robert K. "Dionysos in 1915: A Pioneer Theatre Collective." *Theatre Research International,* 3 (Oct. 1977): 33–53.

———. "Producing Principles and Practices of the Provincetown Players." *Theatre Research/Recherches Théâtrales* 10 (1970): 89–102.

———. "The Provincetown Players: Experiments in Style." Dissertation, Yale, 1965.

———. "Wharf and Dome: Materials for the History of the Provincetown Players." *Theatre Research/Recherches Théâtrales* 10 (1970): 163–78.

Sayler, Oliver M. *Our American Theatre.* New York: Brentano's 1923.

Seton, Marie. *Paul Robeson.* London: D. Dobson, 1958.

Shank, Theodore. "Collective Creation." *Drama Review* 16 (June 1972): 3–31.

Shaw, George Bernard. *Ruskin's Politics.* London: Christophers, 1921.

Sheaffer, Louis. *O'Neill: Son and Artist.* Boston: Little, Brown, 1973.

———. *O'Neill: Son and Playwright.* Boston: Little, Brown, 1968.

Silvestri, Vito N. "The Washington Square Players: Those Early Off-Broadway Years." *Quarterly Journal of Speech* 51 (1965): 35–44.

Sokel, Walter H. *The Writer in Extremis; Expressionism in Twentieth- Century German Literature.* 1959. Reprint. Stanford: Stanford University Press, 1968.

Solomon, Rakesh H. " 'Paradise Now Notebook I': Collective Creation of the Living Theatre." Seminar Paper, University of California, Davis, 1976.

Spolin, Viola. *Improvisation for the Theater.* Evanston: Northwestern University Press, 1963.

Sweeney, Charles P. "Back to the Source of Plays Written by Eugene O'Neill." *New York World,* Nov. 9, 1924.

Tashjian, Dickran. *Skyscraper Primitives; Dada and the American Avant-Garde. 1910–1925.* Middletown, Conn.: Wesleyan University Press, 1975.

Taylor, Karen Malpede. *People's Theatre in Amerika.* New York: Drama Books, 1973.

"A Theatrical Workshop for Acting Playwrights and Playwriting Actors." *Current Opinion* 61 (Nov. 1916): 323.

Tomkins, Calvin. "Time to Think." [A profile of Robert Wilson]. *New Yorker,* Jan. 13, 1975, pp. 43, 51.

Van Vechten, Carl. *Music After the Great War and Other Studies.* New York: Schirmer, 1915.

Vilhauer, William Warren. "A History and Evaluation of the Provincetown Players." Dissertation, University of Iowa, 1965.

Ware, Caroline F. *Greenwich Village 1920–1930: A Comment on American Civilization in the Post-War Years.* Boston: Houghton Mifflin, 1935.

Waterman, Arthur E. *Susan Glaspell.* New York: Twayne, 1966.

Wetzsteon, Ross. "Chaikin and O'Horgan Survive the 60's." *Village Voice,* Nov. 3, 1975, p. 81.

"When the Provincetown Group Began." *Theatre Arts* 8 (1924): 3–4, 5, 9–10.

Woollcott, Alexander. "There are War Plays and War Plays." *New York Times,* Dec. 14, 1919, sec. 8, p. 2.

Index

References to illustrations are italicized and follow other references.

Library of Congress Cataloging in Publication Data
Sarlós, Robert Károly, 1931–
Jig Cook and the Provincetown Players.
Bibliography: p.
Includes index.
1. Provincetown Players.   2. Cook, George Cram,
1873–1924.   3. Theater—Massachusetts—Province-
town—History—20th century.   4. Theater—New York
(N.Y.)—History—20th century.   5. American drama—
20th century—History and criticism.   I. Title.
PN2297.P7S27   792'.09744'92   81-16104
ISBN 0-87023-349-1   AACR2